ENERGY and
WORLD POLITICS

by **Mason Willrich**

with **Joel Darmstadter**
Robert M. Hallman
Lawrence Krause
Harry Perry
Rouhollah K. Ramazani

Published under the auspices of
The American Society of International Law

THE FREE PRESS
A Division of Macmillan Publishing Co., Inc.
NEW YORK

Collier Macmillan Publishers
LONDON

The Free Press
A Division of Macmillan Publishing Co., Inc.
866 Third Avenue, New York, N.Y. 10022

Collier Macmillan Canada, Ltd.
First Free Press Paperback Edition 1978
Library of Congress Catalog Card Number: 75–12058

Printed in the United States of America

printing number

SC 1 2 3 4 5 6 7 8 9 10
HC 4 5 6 7 8 9 10

Library of Congress Cataloging in Publication Data

Willrich, Mason.
    Energy and world politics.

    "Published under the auspices of the American Society
of International Law."
    Bibliography: p.
    Includes index.
    1. Energy policy. 2. Power resources. 3. Petro-
leum industry and trade. I. American Society of International Law. II. Title.
HD9502.A2W54   333.7   75-12058
ISBN 0-02-935520-6

ISBN 0-02-935800-0 pbk.
ISBN-13: 978-0-02-935800-9

To Patti, Chris, Stephen, Michael, and Kate

Contents

Preface   vii

Biographical Notes   ix

Introduction   xi

CHAPTER 1. Energy in the World Context   1

CHAPTER 2. The Energy Situation: Intrinsic Forces   27

CHAPTER 3. Energy and National Security   65

CHAPTER 4. Energy and the World Economy   103

CHAPTER 5. Energy and the Global Environment   141

CHAPTER 6. Energy and International Politics   180

Bibliography   213

Index   223

Preface

THIS BOOK HAS a complicated lineage. The work was begun and finished under the auspices of the American Society of International Law with support from the National Science Foundation (Project RANN).

In the fall of 1973 the society established a working group on international energy policy under my chairmanship and including Joel Darmstadter, Grenville Garside, Robert M. Hallman, Lawrence Krause, Martin Lobel, Arnold Packer, Harry Perry, Rouhollah K. Ramazani, Davis Robinson, Charles R. Ross, and Theodore B. Taylor. J. Lawrence Hargrove and Robert E. Stein of the Society's staff also participated fully in our work.

As a group we held a series of meetings during the spring and summer of 1974. An outline for a study was discussed, together with a preliminary overview paper which I authored. Thereafter we formed a small group of contributors composed of Darmstadter, Hallman, Krause, Perry, Ramazani, and myself. Each contributor set down in writing a succinct statement of his views in elaboration of various parts of the basic framework.

With these pieces in hand I set about the task of writing a first draft of the entire book during the fall of 1974. Time for this task was provided by a Guggenheim Memorial Fellowship. In the writing process I drew on the written work of the contributors and also the earlier working group discussions. However, the draft inevitably reflected largely my own analysis and views.

The draft was subject to comment and review by the contributors and the entire working group in early 1975. What is published is the original draft as I revised it extensively in light of criticism received from the contributors and the working group as a whole.

I am deeply grateful to all the persons and institutions that helped me in producing this book, although I am solely responsible for its contents.

Each contributor—Joel Darmstadter, Robert Hallman, Lawrence Krause, Harry Perry, Rouhollah Ramazani—was unstinting with his time, perceptive with his criticism, and patient in his explanations. During the course of our work together I think we learned a lot from each other.

Susan Smythe, my research assistant, merits special thanks and praise. She was always full of good suggestions and was, moreover, a constant source of encouragement.

Finally, this book could never have been published without the amazing typing talents of Diane Moss and all her helpers in the "pool" at the University of Virginia Law School. They must know every paragraph by heart.

Mason Willrich
Professor of Law
University of Virginia
Charlottesville, Virginia
February, 1975

Biographical Notes

The Author

Mason Willrich is professor of law at the University of Virginia. He was also Director of the Center for the Study of Science, Technology, and Public Policy at the university from 1968 to 1973. Mr. Willrich was Assistant General Counsel of the U.S. Arms Control and Disarmament Agency from 1962 to 1965. He has served as a consultant to the Ford Foundation, the RAND Corporation, and various government agencies and private corporations.

Mr. Willrich has published widely in the fields of energy and national security. His books include *Nuclear Theft: Risks and Safeguards* (coauthor with Theodore B. Taylor), 1974; *SALT: The Moscow Agreements and Beyond* (coauthor and coeditor), 1974; *International Safeguards and Nuclear Industry* (coauthor and editor), 1973; and *Global Politics of Nuclear Energy*, 1971.

Mr. Willrich graduated from Yale University in 1954 and received his law degree from the University of California, Berkeley, in 1960.

The Contributors

JOEL DARMSTADTER is an economist and senior research associate at Resources for the Future, Inc., in Washington, D.C.

ROBERT M. HALLMAN is a lawyer and member of the Center for Law and Social Policy, in Washington, D.C.

LAWRENCE KRAUSE is an economist and senior research fellow at The Brookings Institution, in Washington, D.C.

HARRY PERRY is a chemical engineer and energy consultant to National Economic Research Associates and to Resources for the Future, Inc., in Washington, D.C.

ROUHOLLAH K. RAMAZANI is a Middle East specialist and Edward R. Stettinius, Jr. Professor of Government and Foreign Affairs at the University of Virginia.

Introduction

THE ENERGY SITUATION rose to the top of the agenda of issues before the world community in 1973 and stayed there throughout 1974. In the years and decades ahead, energy is sure to remain a vital concern of government at all levels and of people in every nation.

Bookshelves are already loaded with energy studies—esoteric and basic, bland and sensational, read and mostly unread. News media are full of reportage and advertising about every new development from Kuwaiti investments in U.S. real estate as a means of recycling petrodollars to co-ed bathing in Great Britain as a recommended natural gas conservation measure. In such circumstances, the appearance of another book about energy should be explained.

This book's purpose is to provide a concise but comprehensive overview of the world energy situation from a political viewpoint. It was written for two reasons: because the most fundamental energy issues are political in nature and international in scope, and because these basic issues have received little critical analysis from a detached perspective. Most of what has been said so far about the issues at the core of the energy problem has been uttered by government officials, and they have spoken in often apocryphal and always vague generalities. This book is thus intended to help orient and clarify thinking about a vast and amorphous political challenge to the world community.

Many studies attack the energy problem from an economic viewpoint, emphasizing the impact of the recent oil price increases on various national economies, on incentives to develop additional or alternative energy supplies, and on international financial arrangements. There is also a profusion of studies that tackle the energy problem from a technological viewpoint, analyzing the costs and benefits of a variety of new technologies that are being, or might be, developed to produce, refine, convert, transport, distribute, and conserve energy. Optimists find a technological fix for every facet of the energy problem, while pessimists see in every proposed solution a plethora of unresolved risks.

It is, however, the political process operating within and among nations that will largely determine the extent to which economic efficiency and technological possibilities will control the future evolution of the world energy situation, and the extent to which other factors such as national security and prestige will come into play. Moreover, politics are the means for making key trade-offs, nationally and internationally, between, for instance, cheap energy and secure supplies or between self-sufficiency and environmental quality.

With a focus on international energy politics, this book attempts to achieve a perspective that is broadly global in outlook. Most studies so far have examined international energy issues from the viewpoint of a particular nation or region. Of course the United States is the world's largest producer and consumer of energy, and U.S. behavior will therefore have a major influence. But the oil crisis has taught us that the conduct of other nations will be important and in some respects decisive.

The time horizon dealt with is necessarily elastic. In economic analysis, appropriate discount rates are used in order to reduce all opportunities to their present worth. In technology assessment, what is ripe for commercial demonstration is distinguished from possibilities under engineering development and from efforts to establish the scientific feasibility of a new method. Demonstration may require three to five years, while development may require ten to twenty years. Scientific feasibility might with luck be established quickly or, more likely, only after several decades of painstaking and costly research, or never.

A political perspective, however, is at once immediate and long term, changeable and enduring. A nation's policy can be reversed or its government changed overnight. Yet a nation's foreign policy may be determined by perceptions of its basic interests and by cultural aspirations that remain fundamentally unchanged for centuries, despite wars and domestic revolutions.

The shock of the quadrupled price of crude oil in 1973–74 and the enormity of the flow of wealth that has since been under way to the countries belonging to the Organization of Petroleum Exporting Countries (OPEC) from Western Europe, Japan, and the United States have created immediate economic and political problems of baffling complexity. These problems must be dealt with promptly and effectively to avoid major threats to international stability and to enable economic development in oil-importing countries to resume, albeit more slowly than before. However, in seeking solutions to current problems, we must not lose sight of the enduring issues. For if we do, in solving immediate problems we may plant the seeds of much worse energy crises in the future.

At this writing, a number of major international conferences that will deal with various aspects of the world energy situation are under way or in the offing. Specifically, an intricate series of preparatory discussions is leading toward the convening of a conference of oil-exporting, industrial, and oil-importing developing countries to be held perhaps in the late summer or early fall of 1975. A conference to review the operation of the Treaty on the Nonproliferation of Nuclear

Weapons, a treaty that affects the worldwide development of nuclear power, is scheduled for May 1975. Moreover, the Third United Nations Conference on the Law of the Sea, which is dealing with a variety of issues pertaining to the energy resources of the outer continental shelves and the environmental implications of energy-related activities, is scheduled to conclude its work during 1975. In the background of all these large multilateral efforts is, of course, an endless round of economic and political talks and detailed negotiations concerned with international energy matters.

This book is not a guide to the formidable labyrinth through which the energy diplomats and their experts are presently groping their way. Rather, it probes beneath the labyrinth of current diplomacy in an attempt to illuminate the fundamental national and international interests that are deeply embedded in the evolving world energy situation.

Chapter 1 outlines the larger context in which the world energy situation has evolved in the three decades since the end of World War II. Chapter 2 analyzes the internal dynamics of the energy situation during the same period. Against this background, the major international political issues are discussed under three broad problem headings: national security in Chapter 3, the world economy in Chapter 4, and the global environment in Chapter 5. Finally, Chapter 6 explores whether a harmonious pattern of international energy relationships is possible and considers the development of international institutions to manage the world energy situation in the future.

ENERGY and
WORLD POLITICS

Chapter 1

Energy in the World Context

THROUGHOUT HUMAN HISTORY the foundations of civilizations have rested heavily on their energy supplies. Ancient Egypt under the Pharoahs, Athenian Greece under democracy, and the American South before the Civil War depended on human slaves as a primary energy resource. The nineteenth-century Industrial Revolution in Europe and North America was powered with coal, as is the process of industrialization now under way in the People's Republic of China. The dominant form of modern industrial societies, the sprawling metropolis, is based on transportation technologies requiring an abundance of petroleum. Moreover, the foundations of future postindustrial societies may well rest on electricity produced from nuclear, and possibly thermonuclear and solar, energy.

Many of the possibilities for groups of people to establish meaningful relationships in complex societies, and for nations to cooperate in larger international communities, depend on energy to power rapid and far-reaching systems for communication. Finally, adequate energy is an essential prerequisite for hope that billions of human beings in future generations will be able to live in reasonable material circumstances and with some dignity on this small planet.

Thus energy has been and will always be a vital factor in human affairs. Never before, however, has it played such a decisive role in international relations.

This chapter discusses how energy problems and issues relate to the world context as a whole. From the outset the reader should bear in mind that energy is a pervasive factor. Various trends and events which may seem unconnected are thus in fact related. The discussion in this chapter is, accordingly, far-reaching and not sharply focused.

We begin with the international political structure. Next we consider two historical currents running through the three decades since the end of World War II: the growth of economic interdependence and the development of nationalism. These currents can work at cross purposes. Conflict between them is, in fact, one of the main causes of the present energy crisis.

Political Structure

The world political system is decentralized, potentially unstable, and open to attack from many directions. The primary political units are nation–states, and the main actors are national governments. Governments are, of course, rarely of one mind. Their policies result from the interplay of contending political factions. Moreover, every government is more or less vulnerable to revolutionary political forces. International organizations play more or less important roles in the world political system, depending on the national policies and capabilities of their member states. Similarly, private multinational corporations enjoy more or less autonomy, depending on the capabilities and policies of the national governments of the territories in which they operate.

The vast bulk of the earth's land is now parceled out among well over 100 nations which are defined geographically in terms of land and people. Moreover, coastal states appear determined to expand their control over resources in and under vast ocean areas extending 200 miles seaward from their shores. The territorially based nation–state may be economically inefficient and environmentally unsound. It may even be militarily indefensible. Yet people will fight to the death to protect their homeland or to regain land others have taken from them. The ownership of land and natural resources is thus the most important and potentially explosive question in world politics. International peace and stability depend fundamentally on general acceptance and careful observance of the boundaries that describe the territories of the world's nations. And, largely as a result of political boundaries, all the basic ingredients of power—territory, population, resources, technology, wealth—are distributed unequally.

Disparities among countries are glaring and important in the case of energy. The United States has less than 6 percent of the world's population and uses more than 30 percent of its energy, while India contains 15 percent of the people and consumes less than 2 percent of the energy. On the one hand, Japan, an industrial country with a population of 107 million, ranks third in gross national product and yet is dependent on imports for 85 percent of its energy requirements. On the other hand, Abu Dhabi, a tribal society of 120,000, had a per capita income from government oil revenues alone of $17,500 in 1974. How, then, may we classify the nations of the world in order to discuss their energy relationships?

A simple division of the world into energy consumers and producers, or importers and exporters, is misleading. A few examples will illustrate the difficulties with this approach. The United States only recently became the world's largest oil importer. It remains one of the largest oil producers, though domestic production is likely to continue to decline slowly until oil begins to flow through the trans-Alaska pipeline from the North Slope reserves in the late 1970s. The U.S. is also a coal exporter, a natural gas importer, and by far the world's largest supplier of nuclear power reactors and uranium enrichment. Canada, considered as a whole, is self-sufficient in oil and gas. Since it lacks sufficient east–west pipeline capacity, however, oil and gas flow from fields in the western Canadian provinces south through pipelines to the United States. Canada's eastern provinces are almost totally dependent on oil imports from the Caribbean and the Middle East. Iran, the world's second largest oil exporter, plans to become a large importer of nuclear power technology and fuels. The Netherlands, which a few years ago was virtually without energy resources of its own, now exports increasing volumes of natural gas from the Groningen field. Similarly, Great Britain, which now depends largely on the Middle East producers for its oil, looks forward to becoming self-sufficient in the 1980s when its North Sea oil fields are fully developed. Finally, India, which was hit hard by the quadrupling of OPEC oil prices, has large undeveloped coal reserves, has made significant offshore oil discoveries, and has launched a nuclear power program that is approaching self-sufficiency.

When thinking worldwide about energy, as about other matters, we may try to divide countries into the free world and the communist bloc. Here again the real world is politically much more complex. Until recently, the Soviet Union and East European countries developed their energy resources, and their economies in general, on a largely self-contained basis. Substantial energy trade occurred among the socialist countries themselves, but not between the eastern and western halves of Europe. Now, the Soviet Union is exporting some oil, natural gas, and nuclear fuel to Western Europe, and is considering a number of massive arrangements to exchange oil, gas, and coal for Japanese, European, or American technology and capital. Meanwhile the socialist countries of Eastern Europe are importing increasing amounts of oil from the Middle East. The People's Republic of China has made energy self-sufficiency a matter of high principle, and thus far it has relied primarily on its immense coal reserves. In recent years, however, China has been rapidly expanding its oil production and is now exporting small amounts to Japan.

Finally, we may think of countries as rich and poor, or as belonging to the industrial world or the Third World. Indeed, the impulse for such a division has come from the poor countries in order to dramatize their plight and to increase moral and political pressure on the affluent countries to render aid. Regardless of the merits of such a polarization for other purposes, a division of the world into rich and poor as regards energy leads to confusion. On the one hand, some of the most industrially advanced and affluent countries, such as Japan and Denmark, are almost barren of energy resources. On the other, some very poor countries are rich in energy resources. Though most of their people live in poverty, Nigeria, Indonesia, and Iraq have large oil reserves, while Niger and Gabon have large uranium deposits. Moreover, as a consequence of the compound impact of high population growth rates, thin natural resource bases and worldwide inflation, a Fourth World of nations without hope may fall out from the Third World and into chaos. This may be happening already to Bangladesh.

The world energy situation is thus baffling. Although energy is a vital interest of almost every nation, energy politics may well create patterns that are inconsistent with other important patterns of international relations. Nation–states form the political bedrock of the world community. But it is difficult to find a general scheme for classifying the bedrock for purposes of defining international energy relationships.

Governments speak and act for nation–states in the world arena. However, we must see through the opaque front a national government tries to present to the rest of the world and take proper account of the dynamic balance of forces operating within each nation and the transnational links among them. No government is monolithic, whether it be a parliamentary democracy, a proletarian dictatorship, or a feudal monarchy. Government policy regarding an important matter such as energy results from a complex and endless process of domestic political bargaining, even within the most authoritarian regimes. Moreover, special interest groups in different countries are more or less continuously engaged in developing and dissolving transnational links to influence government policies.

For example, the economic fortunes of the U.S.-based multinational oil companies may depend in part on the personal political fortunes of those struggling for leadership of the major political parties in the United States. Saudi Arabia's oil prices and production rates may be influenced by the monarchy's hostility toward communism and fear of domestic insurgency, as well as by its doubts about the international economic outlook.

Domestic political factors condition not only production policies in exporting countries but also energy consumption policies in the importing countries. Fewer and fewer countries in the world have workable democratic political institutions. Most democracies are large energy importers. It remains to be seen whether democratic institutions and parliamentary procedures are luxuries to be enjoyed in times of economic growth and abundant energy supplies, or whether such institutions can also deal effectively with conditions of chronic resource scarcity that call for stringent conservation.

Since World War II private multinational firms, exemplified by the multinational oil corporations,* have operated with considerable freedom of action in the world arena. The formation in 1960 of the Organization of Petroleum Export-

---

* The eight multinational oil companies that are commonly known as "the majors" include five that are U.S. based and privately owned—Exxon, Gulf, Mobil, Standard Oil of California, and Texaco. The three others are Royal Dutch Shell, which is privately owned by British and Dutch interests, British Petroleum (BP), which is partly owned by the British government together with private British interests, and Compagnie Française des Petroles (CFP), which is partly owned by the French government.

ing Countries (OPEC)* as an intergovernmental oil producers' cartel and the subsequent widespread nationalization of oil reserves and production capacity by producer country governments have prompted the governments of consumer countries to respond in a variety of ways. Well before OPEC proved successful as a cartel, a few had launched their own petroleum corporations in order to bypass the private companies and bargain directly with producer governments for a share of their output and the right to develop additional reserves. In the early 1970s the number of consumer countries with national petroleum corporations increased, and the activities of such corporations now appear to be expanding.

The potential freedom of action of the private multinational oil companies is thus being restricted at both ends of their operations—production and marketing. Whether this result will be good or bad, and how far it should go, will be debated for years. The shrinkage in autonomy of the multinational oil companies that has so far occurred still leaves these corporate giants with substantial economic and political power to influence on a worldwide scale who gets how much oil at what price.

In the nuclear field, the role of the private sector and its relationship to government are not the same as with oil. First, government control is pervasive in view of the health and safety hazards and the security implications of nuclear power. Second, unlike research and development in the oil industry, nuclear power research and development required financing and direction on a scale that only government could provide. Third, diffusion of nuclear power technology is now occurring among the industrial countries mainly through licensing and other arrangements to transfer know-how, so that several are acquiring their own nuclear industry capabilities. These indus-

* The original members of OPEC were Iran, Iraq, Kuwait, Saudi Arabia, and Venezuela. It has been expanded in recent years to include Qatar, Libya, Indonesia, United Arab Emirates, Algeria, Nigeria, Equador, and Gabon.

trial countries, moreover, are competing with each other for power reactor sales to less developed countries which lack their own nuclear industrial capability. As nuclear power has taken off commercially, the role of private enterprise has rapidly expanded outside the communist countries. The resulting decentralization of decision making considerably complicates the task of governments seeking to control exports of nuclear materials and equipment as part of their broader policies intended to inhibit the uncontrolled spread of nuclear weapons.

Finally, our brief exploration of the political structure of the world community must consider international organizations. There is a plethora of international organizations with varying breadth of authority in the energy field, but there is a dearth of capacity in these institutions for independent action. Compared with the political power of nation–states, or with the power of private multinational energy companies, international organizations are weak indeed.

OPEC may appear to be a major exception. It controls 85 percent of oil moving in international commerce. However, OPEC's strength lies mainly in the weaknesses of the oil-importing countries. There are different views within OPEC on every issue, including oil prices and production rates. OPEC's members have radically different political outlooks, economic needs, security concerns, and even policies toward Israel. For example, oil supplies from Iran to Israel have so far been uninterrupted during Israel's hostilities with the Arabs.

OPEC's strength as a cartel demonstrates the weakness of other established international organizations in the energy field. The Organization for European Cooperation and Development (OECD),* composed of the industrial countries

* OECD member countries are Australia, Austria, Belgium, Canada, Denmark, the Federal Republic of Germany, Finland, France, Greece, Iceland, Ireland, Italy, Japan, Luxembourg, the Netherlands, New Zealand, Norway, Portugal, Spain, Sweden, Switzerland, Turkey, the United Kingdom, and the United States.

of Western Europe, North America, and Japan, the recently expanded European Common Market* and ad hoc arrangements such as the Oil Facility of the International Monetary Fund (IMF) have so far proved to be considerably weaker by comparison.

In the nuclear energy field, the International Atomic Energy Agency (IAEA) was established in 1957 as an outgrowth of the U.S. Atoms for Peace proposals in 1953. The IAEA is a framework for international cooperation in nuclear development. It provides technical assistance in civilian uses of nuclear energy to less developed countries, and it administers safeguards on civilian nuclear activities in a growing number of countries to ensure against diversion from civilian to military use. Several regions also have special international organizations to promote nuclear power development, and some of these also administer safeguards to ensure that nuclear fuel is not diverted. The European Atomic Energy Community (Euratom), established in 1957 in the wake of the Suez crisis, is the most important example of regional nuclear cooperation. But whether globally or regionally organized, the authority of these organizations to act independently or over the objection of any of their member states is severely circumscribed.

Finally, we should note the new International Energy Agency (IEA), developed largely as a result of a U.S. initiative in February 1974 in response to the Arab oil embargo. At this writing, it is unclear whether the Agreement on an International Energy Program,† which would establish the IEA, will become effective, as contemplated, on May 1, 1975.

---

* The European Common Market now includes the original six—Belgium, the Federal Republic of Germany, France, Italy, Luxembourg, and the Netherlands—and an additional three—Ireland, Denmark, and the United Kingdom.

† The signatories of the agreement include Austria, Belgium, Canada, Denmark, the Federal Republic of Germany, Ireland, Italy, Japan, Luxembourg, the Netherlands, Spain, Sweden, Switzerland, Turkey, the United Kingdom, and the United States.

The IEA membership would include most of the OECD countries, except France (which may become informally associated). The IEA's initial purpose would be to establish and implement, if necessary, a program for international sharing of oil supplies and demand restraint in an emergency. However, the Agency is also intended to serve as a mechanism for long-term energy cooperation, including conservation, development of alternative sources, research and development, and uranium enrichment. It is noteworthy that decisions by the Agency would be based on a voting system weighted to reflect oil consumption. It remains to be seen whether the IEA will function effectively either in another oil embargo or in overall energy cooperation.

Thus we return to nation–states as the basic political constituents of the world community and to national governments as the main actors. The national energy postures of the major energy consumers and producers merit analysis with the same care and attention to detail as the United States and the Soviet Union have applied over the years to the analysis of their own and each other's military postures.

In an energy assessment, a nation's posture with respect to each fuel cycle must be examined. Oil, natural gas, coal, nuclear, and hydroelectricity would be of primary interest at present, while thermonuclear fusion, solar, geothermal, and hydrogen might become major new sources in the future. For each primary fuel, a nation's energy system, including its resources, facilities (transport, processing, and conversion), know-how (technology and organization), financial capital, and industrial structure (including government–industry relationship) may be analyzed. A nation's energy consumption may be subject to similar scrutiny in terms of growth rate, factors influencing demand, and patterns and efficiency of energy use. A nation's particular relationships to other nations, to multinational corporations, and to international organizations active in energy matters may also be considered.

Analysis in depth of any nation's current energy posture and future potential would reveal a very complicated picture. But a searching inquiry seems essential as a basis for well-informed international energy policy.

Economic Interdependence

For three decades after World War II the economies of nations grew more and more interdependent. Interdependence led to, and resulted from, rapid recovery from the war's devastation and a long period of much-desired economic growth. But it also generated insecurity as nations lost control of their particular economic destinies. Oil played a leading role both in promoting economic growth and in creating economic insecurity.

The trend toward interdependence in the post-World War II era was initiated by political decision. The United States emerged from the war with unparalleled political and economic power. It used that power initially to determine and thereafter to influence international economic policy outside the communist countries. Having learned the lessons of the 1930s, the United States government espoused freer trade and economic cooperation in the belief that the American people could prosper over the long run only if "free world" countries in general experienced economic advance. The underlying assumptions were that private enterprise operating in free markets would best promote economic development, and that harmony among nations would flow from widespread economic prosperity. Such a structure for economic growth would also prevent the spread of communism.

Building on the experience of the U.S. Marshall Plan in the late 1940s, economic interdependence developed regionally in Europe through the Common Market in the 1950s and 1960s. In the same period, interdependence among industrial

countries increased globally through the larger and looser
OECD framework, which included the United States, Canada, and Japan in addition to the West European countries.
Moreover, less developed countries, as well as industrial countries participated in the General Agreement on Tariffs and
Trade (GATT) and the complicated set of World Bank
financial institutions.

Meanwhile the economies of the communist countries of
Eastern Europe became closely tied to the Soviet Union and
to each other through state trading mechanisms. They remained largely disconnected from the Western-oriented cooperative arrangements, however. Government policies on
both sides prevented capitalist and socialist economies from
becoming deeply intertwined.

Evidence of increasing economic interdependence was
everywhere. The international trade of most countries expanded faster than their national economies. The principal
capital markets around the world were joined by the spread
of commercial bank operations from one country to another
and the development of such devices as the Eurocurrency
market. Labor migration grew in response to shortages in
some industrial countries. The jobs and living standards of
more and more workers in every country came to depend on
foreign development.

Perhaps the most important and controversial aspect of
growing interdependence was the development of multinational business enterprise. Soon after the end of World War
II large private corporations renewed their worldwide search
for raw materials and markets. In the early postwar years the
more powerful multinational enterprises were controlled by
U.S. shareholders. As the economies of the West European
countries and Japan recovered, however, their private business
interests also penetrated foreign markets and took on multinational attributes. Multinational corporations were able to
transfer large amounts of capital from one country to another,
and to transplant the other essential ingredients for business

activity. They succeeded in integrating all phases of economic activity from resource extraction to retail distribution of manufactured products. In short, private business developed the capacity to operate on a global scale.

Changes in technology gave a strong impetus to the trend toward economic interdependence. Advances in transportation enabled rapid movement of goods between countries, often at less cost than within countries. The development of jet passenger aircraft not only unleashed a burgeoning tourist industry but also permitted scarce managerial talent to manage worldwide business enterprises. Electronic communications enabled the many subsidiaries of multinational firms to stay in constant contact with their parent companies and also revolutionized the international banking business. In many fields the evolution of manufacturing technology continually increased the minimum size of industry required to conduct commercially competitive operations. Economic self-sufficiency thus became more and more impractical for all but the largest countries. Gains in the smaller countries could be achieved only by specializing in certain products for export, while importing a range of other products for domestic use. The economic principles of specialization and comparative advantage were thus applied on a global scale.

The energy sector exemplified the post-World War II growth of economic interdependence. Petroleum was the most important commodity in international trade. Moreover, privately owned oil companies were the most powerful multinational enterprises. For almost three decades they supplied the noncommunist world with oil produced very cheaply from a few vast reservoirs located far from the large markets. Countries like Great Britain, France, and Germany, which were once largely self-sufficient in energy because of their domestic coal production, became increasingly dependent on imported oil, which was cheaper, cleaner, and more convenient to use. Other industrial countries like Italy and Japan, which were previously dependent on energy imports, greatly increased the magnitude of that dependence as their economies advanced and their energy demands grew. Even the United States, which had been largely self-sufficient, became one of the world's largest oil importers in the 1970s. In general, many nations developed energy-intensive economies, spurred on by abundant low-priced energy supplies.

The quadrupling of OPEC oil prices during 1973–74 reinforced the overall importance of energy in international trade. Trade in petroleum exceeded $100 billion in 1974, accounting for more than 15 percent of the total value of world trade.

Overall, the trend toward an interdependent world economy produced the desired results—economic growth with private enterprise as the main driving force. The three decades after World War II constituted the most rapid and prolonged period of worldwide economic expansion in recorded history. The products of the entire world became available to consumers in the wealthier countries, and many new products were developed because of the profit potential foreseen in a global market.

The same factors working toward interdependence, however, created tensions where particular national interests diverged from the general interests of a world economy. Moreover, growth primarily through private enterprise tended to limit the power of governments to shape economic development in ways they believed appropriate in their particular national circumstances. With freer international trade in goods, countries became less able to determine their own industrial structures and consumption patterns. With labor markets joined, some countries suffered a "brain drain" of their trained professionals and skilled workmen.

The integrating of world financial markets eroded the effectiveness of government monetary policy as a means of controlling national economies. Business firms could undercut government monetary measures by private borrowing or lending activities in the Eurocurrency markets. Furthermore, integrated multinational enterprises could circumvent capital restrictions and profit limitations by the prices they charged for sales between their different corporate subsidiaries. Multinational corporations could even affect overall economic growth rates and employment levels in various countries through their investment and production choices.

Viewed from the perspective of the poor, nonindustrial countries—which included most of the world's people—economic interdependence may well have appeared to be a revival and extension of their enforced dependence under colonialism. Multinational corporations replaced colonial administrations, but the results were largely the same: low prices for raw material exports, and high prices for manufactured imports. The fragile governments of the new and the less developed nations were, during the late 1940s and 1950s, no match for the corporate giants of the industrial countries. The multinational corporations appeared to their poor host governments to be the agents of Western economic imperialism, even as these same entities seemed increasingly autonomous to the governments where most of their products were marketed and their stockholders lived. The multinational corporations were becoming actors in the world arena beyond the reach of any national government.

Diminishing economic self-sufficiency thus created feelings of insecurity in many countries, and led to government reactions in some. In an interdependent world, however, protectionist actions by importing countries can undermine the economic security of countries heavily dependent on foreign markets to sell their products. Furthermore, the interruption of deliveries by exporting countries can threaten the economic security of countries dependent on imported raw materials, foods, or critical manufactured products. A memorable example was the U.S. suspension of soybean exports to Japan in 1973.

The oil crisis in 1973–74 posed by far the most traumatic challenge to economic interdependence in the post-World War II period. In all countries substantially dependent on foreign oil, not merely in nations on the Arab's unfriendly list, the Arab oil embargo drove home the point that the lifeblood of their national economies was under foreign control. Interdependence in oil thus led to profound economic insecurity throughout much of the noncommunist world.

While the Arab oil embargo caused widespread feelings of insecurity in an evolving world economy, the quadrupled OPEC oil price placed severe stresses on the international financial institutions that were designed to make economic interdependence workable. The oil price increases produced large imbalances in international trade, amounting to over $50 billion in 1974 alone.

Thus far, petroleum-exporting governments have invested their surplus revenues primarily in short-term claims in private financial markets and in government securities. Importing countries have borrowed these funds for a much longer period in order to pay their oil bills. Private and central banks alike have thus been forced into a precarious position. Even when the OPEC countries recycle their surplus petrodollars into long-term investments, serious imbalances are likely to remain. The exporting countries may concentrate their investments in countries with relatively strong economies, thereby compounding the damage to those that are weak.

Finally, the rising oil price has been a factor, though not the largest, contributing to inflation, which is currently a worldwide phenomenon. Most noncommunist countries face, simultaneously, inflation and recession. If these contradictory trends remain unchecked, they are likely to lead to social tensions which governments in the past have had extreme difficulty dealing with.

The world energy situation thus makes it necessary to rethink international economic policy. On the one hand, is it desirable to continue an economic strategy that promotes growth and efficiency but results in less national self-sufficiency? On the other hand, has economic interdependence within the noncommunist world already advanced so far that it cannot be reversed without catastrophe? On balance, is it possible to design new international policies and institutions that will enhance economic security without sacrificing economic efficiency?

The need for decisive action seems urgent. Yet in a dynamic situation, doing nothing may be the most decisive action of all. This much seems clear: mismanagement of the energy crisis could rip apart the complex web of international institutions that have facilitated economic growth through interdependence since World War II.

Nationalism

For two decades after World War II the adversary relationship between the United States and the Soviet Union dominated world politics. Then, as the Cold War appeared to approach stalemate in the 1960s, resurgent nationalism in Europe loosened military alliances. New nations also claimed more freedom of action in their international relations and began to use their political power more effectively. Throughout the period, oil played a vital role in East–West politics and in the politics of the Middle East region.

The United States emerged from World War II as the one truly global power. Other participants in the war—victors and vanquished alike—were prostrate. The West European countries were incapable of reasserting hegemony over most of their former far-flung colonial possessions. The Soviet Union consolidated its position in Eastern Europe, and despite its own weakened condition, it soon tested the resolve of its wartime allies to resist communist expansion. The Soviets probed in Greece, Iran, and Berlin and then backed large-scale military action in Korea.

The Cold War polarized much of the world into two hostile blocs. The central issue was control of Europe. NATO and the Warsaw Pact were formed to contest this issue along the Iron Curtain. However, the United States and its NATO allies recognized a vital interest in containing the spread of communism elsewhere in the world. Therefore alliances and mutual defense arrangements were forged by the U.S. with many of the countries on the periphery of Asia. Neutralism, or nonalignment, was a difficult stance for any country. It was a posture the United States scorned and the Soviet Union tried to manipulate for its own purposes. Soviet–American rivalry permeated every major issue.

Middle East oil, perceived through Cold War lenses, was part of the East–West political and economic struggle. Oil was essential to the industrial economies which undergirded NATO and the other U.S.–sponsored alliances. Consequently, from the Western perspective, continued access to the Middle East oil resources, controlled under concessions by private American and British companies, was vital to Western security. From the Soviet perspective, one way effectively to undermine the Western "encirclement" of the Soviet Union would be to eliminate the British and American oil interests in the Middle East. This might be done by exploiting national aspirations.

Iran is a striking example of the linkage between the Cold War and the problem of control of oil resources. In 1951 the Musaddiq regime carried out the earliest oil nationalization in the Middle East. The paramount consideration underlying Anglo-American cooperation in the overthrow of the Musaddiq government in 1953 was fear that the Soviet Union and the Iranian communist party (Tudeh) were, in concert, about to destroy the government and create a people's republic of Iran that would be subservient to Moscow. The same strategic–political consideration motivated the United States in the formation of a new international consortium to replace the former Anglo–Iranian Oil Company in 1954 and the negotiation of a new oil agreement between the consortium and National Iranian Oil Company under the government of the Shah.

Over the years the contours of stalemate and possible détente between the United States and the Soviet Union gradually surfaced. The new superpower relationship was based on NATO–Warsaw Pact recognition of the political status quo in Europe and Soviet–American acceptance of mutual nuclear deterrence and strategic arms parity, or "equivalence." In early 1975, however, superpower détente was by no means irreversible.

Throughout most of the Cold War, undercurrents of nationalism eroded the hegemony of each superpower within its sphere. Great Britain's early acquisition of nuclear weapons was motivated largely by its desire for a place at the superpower conference table, as well as a "special relationship" with the United States. France took up the search for national grandeur through development of a nuclear *force de frappe* and an independent role in world affairs. In the French case, it was an independence that often nettled not only the United States but also West European neighbors.

The development of the European Common Market, with its often conceived but aborted roles in the energy field, illustrates the persistent conflict between regional cooperation and nationalism among the industrial countries of Western Europe. Some Europeans saw the Common Market as a major step toward the political ideal of a United Europe—a "third force" in the world. Others saw it as a defense against domination of European national economies by the American corporate giants. Still others feared the Common Market as a threat to their national economic interests—concrete interests which should not be sacrificed for the ephemeral advantages of integration into a much larger whole. Over the years, the United States was ambivalent: it supported the Common Market as an essential part of a strong Atlantic Community, but it resisted efforts to make Western Europe into a potent economic rival of America in the industrial world. In any event, the performance of the Common Market was disappointing for those who wished it to become the basis for developing strong supranational institutions in Europe.

As to energy specifically, on paper the European Atomic Energy Community (Euratom) was ambitious as well as idealistic. As a force for regional cooperation in the accelerated development of nuclear power, however, Euratom's impact over the years has been small. It has conducted a few multinational scientific research projects and is responsible for assuring that nuclear fuels are not diverted to nuclear weapons by the governments of Euratom members which do not already possess them. However, nuclear power development, including large-scale industrial research, has been conducted primarily on a competitive basis within the various national programs in Western Europe.

The Common Market did not reach agreement on a common energy policy. Despite the Arab–Israeli wars in 1956 and 1967, and the resulting oil supply insecurities in Europe, European reliance on oil imports from the Middle East continued to grow. Faced with the 1973–74 Arab oil embargo and urgent U.S. pleas for consumer country cooperation, the West European countries found in the Common Market a useful device for launching an independent initiative with the OPEC countries. But there was ambivalence. Some West European countries wanted to use the Common Market to negotiate with OPEC, while others were mainly interested in making bilateral deals of their own. It may be doubted whether those Common Market members with access to North Sea oil and gas resources—principally Great Britain, Norway, and the Netherlands—will share their resources with other members on terms that are much more favorable than those obtainable in the world market.

As nationalism disrupted Atlantic cooperation and blocked the emergence of supranational institutions in Western Europe, the same force erupted much more violently within the Soviet bloc. In Eastern Europe, Yugoslavia struck off on its own shortly after World War II ended. The Soviet army then crushed a series of attempts to break away from the strictures of the Warsaw Pact—East Germany in 1953, Hungary in 1956, and Czechoslovakia in 1968. China, however, was successful not only in leaving the Soviet bloc in 1960 but in establishing itself subsequently as the nuclear-armed champion of the poor countries in their struggle against the rich. Meanwhile, Romania cautiously managed to achieve a degree of independence from the Soviet Union that has thus far eluded its neighbors.

In terms of energy, the East European countries until recently had no political alternative but to import Soviet oil and natural gas in exchange for other raw materials and manufactured goods. Moreover, it was understood that the Soviet Union would be the sole supplier of nuclear power reactors and fuel within Eastern Europe. With increased oil and gas prices, however, the Soviet Union now seems willing to have East European countries increase their oil imports from the Middle East. This may well be due to interest on the part of the Soviet Union in making its own deals with the OECD industrial countries, exchanging energy raw materials (pegged at the new high prices) for Western technology and capital for large internal development projects. Moreover, the door now may be ajar for Western countries to make nuclear power deals in Eastern Europe.

The growth of nationalism in the new nations, and especially in the Middle East, was perhaps the most important political factor influencing the world energy situation. Immediately after World War II, the decolonization process engulfed many regions of the world. Prewar struggles for independence gained momentum when the British, French, and Dutch colonies won their formal independence at the war's end. India, Pakistan, Sri Lanka (Ceylon), Burma, Indonesia, and many African nations sprang up from the wreckage of Western empires. Indeed, well over half the world's present population of nation–states were born after World War II.

Arab nationalism brought independence to Syria, Lebanon, and Jordan in the Middle East, and to Morocco, Tunisia, Algeria, and Libya in North Africa. It also gave rise to the emergence of revolutionary regimes in Egypt, Iraq, and Yemen. Independence from the West, however, came belatedly to some of the states bordering the Persian Gulf. The historic British withdrawal in 1971 from "east of Suez," and specifically from the Persian Gulf, terminated special treaty relations and resulted in the independence of Qatar and Bahrain and the formation of the Union of Arab Emirates out of the Trucial states.

Arabs and Jews continued after World War II to make irreconcilable claims to Palestine, then under British rule. A war-weary Britain dumped the problem into the lap of the newly organized United Nations. The creation of the new state of Israel, the outbreak of the first Arab–Israeli war in 1948, and the unsettled problems of the Palestinian refugees and Israel's territorial boundaries sowed the seeds of periodic warfare in the Middle East.

The long-standing Arab nationalist struggle, which prior to World War II had aimed at independence from Britain and France, was now directed primarily against the United States because of its support for the Israeli cause. Arabs viewed the creation of the state of Israel as the convergence of Western imperialism and Zionism, while Israelis saw it as the fulfillment of an ancient and sacred promise through a modern nationalistic struggle of their own.

Following legal independence, the new nations began in the 1960s to seek ways to maximize their freedom of action in world affairs. Freedom from external political constraints would not only serve to enhance security and prestige abroad but also help to build a sense of national identity at home. Nationalism was necessary for the centralization of government authority and the development of a political infrastructure for economic development.

Many of the new nations pursued policies of nonalignment, independently and also collectively through a variety of international conferences. There gradually surfaced a new alignment of "have nots" against "haves," of less developed against industrial nations. The movement received forceful expression through agreement on common proposals for restructuring trade and development assistance. These proposals were put forward by the group of seventy-seven less developed countries at the UN Conference on Trade and Development in 1964, and stronger versions have since been developed and presented on numerous occasions within and outside the United Nations framework.

Soviet–American determination to avoid nuclear confrontation and interest in détente can tend to enlarge the freedom of action of other nations, including the oil-exporting countries. Relaxation of East–West tensions may mean that nonalignment and dealings with both superpowers can be pursued without raising the suspicions and risking the disapproval of either one. Superpower détente may mean that nations can quarrel and even fight with their neighbors with less risk of involvement of outside powers. However, as China has been quick to point out, détente may threaten the freedom of action of the new nations by creating an overriding mutual interest of the United States and the Soviet Union in preservation of the status quo. Thus the Arab states went to war in 1973, perhaps feeling compelled to do so before the superpowers' overriding interest in developing détente led to permanent Israeli occupation of Arab territories taken in the 1967 war.

For a new nation carved out of a colonial empire or for an old nation riddled with foreign concessions, freedom of action meant, first and foremost, regaining unfettered sovereignty over its natural resources. Expropriation of foreign interests in natural resources was, of course, easier in an era when military intervention to reverse the process was no longer considered a permissible option.

Under the old concessionary system foreign corporations were granted, in exchange for royalty payments, more or less complete ownership over the mineral rights on vast tracts of land. Foreign corporations determined the rate of development and amount of production from their concessions, and they set the price.

The governments of new nations found nationalization of foreign concessions to be good politics. At home, such moves were generally highly popular. Indeed, governments which resisted domestic political pressures to take over foreign investments were sometimes overthrown by more nationalistic groups. Abroad, the nationalizing government would gain stature in the Third World, and losses in its relations with the United States could be offset by gains with the Soviet Union. More often than not the expropriated American or European business interests would adjust to nationalization in order to continue as contractor rather than concessionaire. The potential for profits still existed further downstream in the operations of their enterprises.

So it was with oil. The 1973-74 oil price explosion came in the wake of the October war in the Middle East, but was not produced by it. The OPEC countries unilaterally determined oil prices for the first time in 1973, marking the end of a long struggle between the oil producers and the major multinational oil companies. The struggle could be traced back to 1960, when OPEC was formed as the result of a unilateral oil price cut by the major companies. But long before the formation of OPEC the relationship between the majors and the oil-exporting countries had been studded with differences. Usually the disputes were couched in terms of prices and production levels. Permeating the conflict, however, was the post-World War II quest of the new nations for freedom of action and participation in the international system on a more equal footing. A vital commodity such as oil could not be insulated from the upsurge of nationalism, and indeed oil became a major instrument in the diplomatic revolution instigated by the Third World nations.

As mentioned previously, the oil concessionary system, which originated at the turn of the twentieth century, was first attacked by nationalist elements in Iran during the late

1940s and early 1950s. From the nationalist viewpoint, the system was inseparable from Western political control and influence. Even in countries like Saudi Arabia, where it had not been imposed by a colonial power, the oil concessionary system was increasingly viewed as an unpalatable contradiction to sovereign control over natural resources.

Algeria, Libya, and Iraq chose the path of complete nationalization of foreign oil operations. Iran, the second largest oil exporter, did the same in 1973, though legal sovereignty over its resources had been regained much earlier. Meanwhile Saudi Arabia, the largest exporter, and Kuwait, Qatar, and Abu Dhabi subscribed to the "participation" principle. Kuwait then escalated its demand from 25 percent to 60 percent, and Saudi Arabia followed suit. Most recently, Saudi Arabia has been insisting on 100 percent control. Before 1971 the multinational oil companies set prices unilaterally. Between 1971 and 1973 oil prices were determined bilaterally in negotiations between the oil companies and OPEC. Since 1973 the OPEC governments have established oil prices in negotiations among themselves.

The collapse of the concessionary system means, therefore, that the private multinational oil companies no longer determine world crude oil prices, production levels, or production capacity development. These decisions are now made primarily by the governments of the exporting nations. The shift in control does not mean, though, that the multinational companies no longer have a role to play in the world petroleum market—indeed, they have a vital and lucrative role. The exporting countries still need and want their know-how as service contractors. The role of the major companies in refining and marketing, and in exploration and development outside OPEC, is the subject of intense scrutiny by consumer country governments. However, that role remained largely intact in early 1975.

In any event, the movement to gain government control over the production end of the worldwide petroleum industry is now on firm political ground and would appear irreversible.

In large measure, the success of the movement was due to the strength of nationalism as a driving force in world politics.

* * *

The world energy situation is embedded in a larger political and economic context. Within that context, we now appear to have entered a period of profound transition. The dominant trends since World War II seem to have slackened. The Cold War has ended in stalemate, and a bipolar world has dissolved. Economic interdependence has deepened worldwide, and nationalism has grown among the nonindustrial countries. Nationalism has stalled the further development of a world economy, but economic interdependence has gone so far that the major countries are unable to extricate themselves. In a world of politically independent nation–states, too much economic interdependence may lead to insecurity in particular nations and thus to instability in the international system as a whole.

In the postwar era, the evolving patterns of energy production and use have been shaped by, and also exemplify, the dominant forces that have been at work in the world as a whole. A new set of trends that will shape world politics on the other side of the transition period has not yet emerged. We would do well, however, to search for clues within the world energy situation. The energy factor may indicate the direction and pace of larger forces that will determine the problems and choices before the world community in the future.

Chapter 2

The Energy Situation:
Intrinsic Forces

WITH THE BROAD THEMES of Chapter 1 in mind, we turn to
the forces at work within the world energy situation as it
evolved in the three decades after World War II. The interplay of these intrinsic forces has determined the options
which are now practical for dealing with energy problems;
and the momentum behind these same forces is a major
constraint and source of potential difficulty. Hindsight re-
veals a complex and dynamic world energy picture. However,
it is a picture with certain dominant features: exploitation
of the world's low-cost fossil energy resources; development of
nuclear power; growth of energy interdependence on a global
scale; and emergence of environmental constraints on energy
resource development and use.

Each of these basic features will be discussed in turn. The
question of resource exhaustion is dealt with at the end.
Whereas in Chapter 1 we viewed the world energy situation
from the outside, our perspective here is from the inside out.

Cheap Fossil Energy

The period from the end of World War II until the 1970s was an era of cheap energy derived from fossil fuels. The era was based primarily on the development and production of vast low-cost oil deposits. These were concentrated in the Middle East. The United States had large oil reserves, but they cost substantially more to produce than the Persian Gulf reservoirs. However, in the United States extensive natural gas fields were discovered within pipeline distance of large potential markets. From the end of the Korean war until the 1970s, oil prices declined worldwide compared to the prices of other basic commodities and goods and services generally. In the United States, natural gas prices showed a similar decline.

Energy became not only cheaper but also cleaner and more convenient to use. Oil supplanted coal in transportation and residential uses, and it also made substantial inroads in industry and electric power generation. In the United States, natural gas was used extensively as boiler fuel in industry. Thus a major shift from coal to oil and gas occurred.

Though the timing and pace varied from country to country, the basic transition to oil and natural gas was worldwide. The use of gas depended, however, on the overland proximity of reservoirs to markets. For the industrial countries of Western Europe and Japan, the transition to oil and subsequent prolonged period of rapid growth in consumption was especially significant because it meant much heavier reliance on energy imports than in the past. In the United States, import quotas imposed in 1959 and lasting until 1973 served to protect the high-priced domestic oil industry from foreign competition, while government regulation kept the wellhead price of natural gas very low in relation to other fuels.

Oil imports also fueled the incipient processes of industrialization in many less developed countries that lacked indigenous energy resources. These countries were scattered throughout Asia, Africa, and Latin America. Oil bill payments were always difficult for the poorer countries, however, even when the price was cheap. The transition from coal to oil and gas occurred later in the Soviet Union and later still in China, both of which were careful to maintain their energy self-sufficiency. But the shift is now advanced in the Soviet Union and under way in China.

During the cheap energy era the principal actors in the world arena, politically and economically, were the eight "major" multinational oil companies—Exxon, Gulf, Mobil, Standard Oil of California and Texaco, which are American owned, and British Petroleum (BP), Royal Dutch Shell, and Compagnie Française des Petroles (CFP). The largest and most powerful were privately owned. Their task was to find, produce, refine, and market the world's low-cost deposits of petroleum.

In their work the private oil companies were relatively unhindered by national governments. Indeed, they were often helped. Two restraints were the United States oil import controls and substantial taxes levied on petroleum products by the West European countries in order, among other things, to protect domestic coal industries. The foreign tax credit was a major incentive for U.S. oil companies to operate outside the United States. Oil concessions in resource-rich areas were easy to obtain, and revenues to the host government were low. The communist countries were the only major area from which the private oil companies were excluded in their global search for low-cost oil.

Throughout most of this period it was a buyer's market. The main problem was to avoid a glut. Through a system of production rationing, the Texas Railroad Commission played a leading role in controlling the excess of production capacity that existed in the United States until the early 1970s. Outside the U.S., the multinational oil companies themselves, acting through a series of overlapping joint ventures, were able for the most part to manage production rates so as to avoid chronic oversupply.

The large, vertically integrated majors were also keenly interested in maintaining their power in the world petroleum market. By regulating production rates of their low-cost crude oil reserves in the Middle East, the few integrated companies were able to maintain substantial control over growing markets for petroleum products in non-communist countries throughout the world. They rivaled each other for shares of expanding markets, but it was advantageous for all of them to avoid strong price competition in promoting sales of their products. The major companies concentrated profits in their jointly owned producing affiliates through the transfer pricing mechanism, and conducted their downstream refining and distributing operations with low profit margins. This made it difficult for independent companies to enter the market, and, at the same time, maximized the tax advantages for the integrated companies and enhanced their ability to finance worldwide expansion largely from retained earnings.

Abundant oil at low prices facilitated the rapid recovery of Western Europe and Japan from the devastation of World War II, and their later achievement of very high standards of living. Consumers generally responded to the low prices by adopting energy-intensive technologies. The flow of energy replaced control switches and insulation in the designs of factory buildings, offices, and signs of commercial and private vehicles. The private automobile largely replaced public transportation. Energy-intensiveness was rational economic behavior, given the price incentive and failure of the price mechanism to take into account the related environmental and social costs. The price of energy was declining relative to the prices of other factors of production—labor, capital, and most raw materials. In short, energy conservation measures were uneconomical.

Cheap oil and gas had two major effects worldwide. First, declining energy prices created high exponential growth rates in demand throughout the world. Growth rates in European countries exceeded the growth rate in the United States, because the U.S. began the postwar era from a much higher level of per capita consumption. In recent years, the growth rates in energy consumption of the less developed countries have outstripped even the European industrial countries. Prior to the 1973–74 oil crisis, therefore, the large gaps between countries in per capita energy consumption were narrowing, although slowly.

High growth rates resulted in a very high total energy demand. Rapid growth continued because prices remained quite stable. To sustain the trend, there was a need for discovery and development of enormous and continually growing additional supplies of energy resources.

The second result of declining real prices for oil and gas, however, was a slowdown in development of petroleum reserves outside the Middle East. The development of alternative sources of energy was also discouraged. Many existing coal mines were abandoned, and new ones were slow to be started; instead, low-cost strip-mining methods, which were especially destructive of the environment, were widely used. There was little incentive to develop advanced coal technology, whether for production or for conversion of coal into gaseous or liquid form. Even nuclear power development, which did proceed, could not have been justified on commercial grounds.

A declining price is socially desirable if it reflects an abundance of a natural resource. But such a price trend can be very costly in the long run if it fails to anticipate resource scarcity or reflect environmental and social costs. In a properly functioning market, therefore, the economic rent on a nonrenewable natural resource tends to rise rather steadily so that higher-cost alternatives will be available when the cheaper resource is exhausted.

Well over half the world's low-cost oil reserves are in the countries of the Middle East which surround the Persian Gulf. If declining energy prices, led by low-cost oil, had persisted, even the immense Persian Gulf reserves could have been drained in a very few decades.

Several factors prevented or at least postponed this. First, a large enough fraction of the world's producible oil was concentrated in few enough places to make the monopolization of crude oil production a distinct possibility. Second, the governments of producing countries, strengthened by nationalism, became able to reclaim sovereignty over their natural resources. Third, the continuing Arab–Israeli conflict eventually galvanized those Arab nations which were oil rich and sparsely populated to bring the oil weapon to bear in the conflict. And fourth, military adventures by American or European forces aimed at recapturing cheap energy were effectively deterred, perhaps more by the risk of war with the Soviet Union than by the capabilities of the indigenous national governments to resist.

It is ironic that the power of the Middle East monarchs, who view communism as their archenemy, may in fact be substantially enhanced by the constraints which Soviet military power now places on possible coercive actions by the Western countries that might be aimed at recapturing the cheap oil era. It is also noteworthy that a substantial fraction of the oil revenues now flowing from the industrial countries to the Middle East are being used to purchase large quantities of the most modern armaments. The resulting increase in the military capability of Iran, especially, is thus a strong deterrent to either Soviet or Western intervention in the Persian Gulf region. Moreover, if there is another Arab–Israeli war, the Israelis will face Arabs armed with sophisticated Western weapons as well as Soviet equipment.

After a difficult period of gestation during the 1960s, OPEC entered the world arena in the 1970s as a major political and economic actor. The cartel rapidly closed the post-World War II era of cheap fossil energy. The political consensus on which those actions rest is narrow and tenuous, however. It remains to be seen whether the high prices OPEC is currently charging for its low-cost crude oil can be maintained in the face of multiple tensions within the cartel and growing pressures from outside. If oil prices were previously artificially low, they now are artificially high.

Nuclear Power Development

The second major feature of the world energy situation in the post-World War II period was the development of nuclear power. The U.S. proposals in 1946 for nuclear weapon disarmament and for developing civilian nuclear power on a supranational basis failed. Crash programs to develop nuclear technology for military purposes followed. These military programs provided the technological foundations for the main alternative to fossil energy that is presently practical. While the worldwide oil industry was politicized only quite recently, the nuclear power industry was politicized from the start.

The uranium fuel cycle used to generate electricity employs the same fissionable materials and processing and conversion facilities as the fuel cycle used to produce materials for nuclear weapons. Technologically, civilian nuclear power was initially developed as an "add-on" to, or "spin-off" from, military weapons programs. U.S. power reactor technology is partly an adaptation of the technology used in submarine propulsion reactors. A power reactor produces large amounts of plutonium, which may be recycled as fuel in power reactors, or the same material may be diverted and used in nuclear explosives. All of the industrial-scale uranium enrichment plants that are now in operation and producing low-enriched fuel for reactors were constructed in order to produce high-enriched uranium for nuclear weapons. Without effective safeguards, therefore, the widespread use of nuclear fuel to generate electricity would greatly increase the risk of nuclear weapon proliferation to governments and also to criminal or terrorist groups.

The U.S. Atoms for Peace proposals in 1953 provided the political foundation for the enormous effort in money and technical manpower devoted to the development of nuclear power technology over the past two decades. The U.S. proposals were motivated by a complicated set of factors: recognition of, and frustration with, the approaching U.S.–U.S.S.R. strategic nuclear stalemate; realization that any chance for the development of civilian nuclear power under pervasive international control, such as contemplated in 1946, was lost; and belief that failure to share nuclear power technology would be likely to accelerate nuclear development on a nationalistic basis and thereby to enhance the risk of nuclear weapon proliferation.

From 1953 onward, international cooperation in civilian nuclear research of a scientific character was freely expanded worldwide. But Atoms for Peace, though couched in terms of broad cooperation, fostered a political atmosphere that helped to sustain competitive power reactor development programs in the United States, the United Kingdom, France, Canada, and the Soviet Union. International competition was much more effective than cooperation could have been in bringing about commercial nuclear power. Nevertheless, development of economical power reactors took over a decade to achieve, and it required the investment of several billions of dollars by the various countries involved.

Nuclear power development not only was carried out on an internationally competitive basis but was essentially government controlled in all countries. Public funds were spent for research and development, and government agencies determined how these funds were to be used, although much of the actual work was done by private enterprise under government contracts. In the U.S., two giant electric equipment manufacturers—General Electric and Westinghouse—both vertically integrated and selling everything from turbine generators to clock–radios, were among the major government contractors. Both firms operate on a global scale through a complex network of foreign affiliates and licensees.

The drive for nuclear power was thus politically motivated, in contrast to the primarily economic character of the drive for low-cost fossil energy that was occurring at the same time. The pace of nuclear power development was not determined by a clearly perceived need for the energy at a particular time due to fossil fuel exhaustion. Indeed, any such perception would have been erroneous, since world oil reserves which can be produced at low costs are still very large. More important, while governments were preoccupied with the international nuclear power competition, the development of other energy technology was almost entirely overlooked. The private sector was investing moderate sums in coal mine mechanization and offshore oil and gas technology, but nothing like the billions governments were devoting to the race for a nuclear power reactor.

The United States won the first heat with the light water reactor which uses low-enriched uranium fuel. Which country will win the second heat for a commercial breeder reactor remains to be seen.

The race is being run by the Soviet Union and the United States on a primarily national basis. It has involved massive infusions of money into the development of a single technological type—the liquid metal fast breeder reactor, which uses the uranium–plutonium fuel cycle. Recently there have been doubts about the U.S. breeder program, which is lagging behind its foreign competitors. The main questions concern costs, fast reactor safety, and safeguards against plutonium diversion.

The upshot is that nuclear fuel is now economically very attractive relative to fossil fuel as a means of generating electric power. In fact, this situation began to take shape in many regions of the world in the late 1960s, well before the recent fossil fuel price increases.

In general, the advent of nuclear power reinforces a major worldwide trend toward electrification. The consumer preference for energy in the form of electricity seems pervasive and strong, except in the transportation sector. Even there, most modern mass transit systems are electrified. Where prices are competitive, electricity is often preferred over fossil energy, since it is clean and instantly available at the point of consumption. Thus over the period since World War II electric power consumption grew in most countries at roughly twice the rate of energy consumption as a whole. The fact that an increasing fraction of the energy used was consumed as electricity means that an increasing fraction of the world's energy raw materials were being consumed in generating electric power.

The trend toward electrification may not abate in the near future. Indeed, the increased physical scarcity of oil and gas (apart from the politically created scarcity), the costs of converting solid hydrocarbons into liquids or gases for consumption, and the availability of coal and nuclear fuel for power production may accelerate the electrification trend, even though overall energy growth rates may slow.

Energy Interdependence

The petroleum-importing countries responded in a variety of ways to the Arab oil embargo in 1973–74. Some governments which had previously supported Israel adopted an "even handed" policy toward the Arab–Israeli conflict, while others reversed themselves and tilted toward the Arabs. The United States government's initial reaction was to announce Project Independence. At first, this was widely interpreted to mean a determination to achieve energy self-sufficiency by 1980. It did not take long to determine, however, that such an objective was unattainable in such a short time. The original Project Independence goal has since been watered down to the achievement of a reduced level of oil imports and substantial invulnerability to Arab supply interruptions by 1985.

The idea of U.S. self-sufficiency in energy struck some people as withdrawal into a Fortress America, despite the fact that the United States had only recently become a large oil importer. For foreign policy purposes, therefore, Project Independence was quickly recast by the government as a step toward interdependence. The irony is that deep interdependence was already the basic and intractable fact in the world energy situation.

In Chapter 1 we discussed the growth of economic interdependence generally. Here we focus on interdependence in the energy sector specifically. Each type of fuel—petroleum, natural gas, coal, and nuclear—involves interdependence in varying degrees.

Petroleum

As to the petroleum fuel cycle, we noted previously that the bulk of the world's known oil reserves are located in regions far away from markets where the largest demands exist for petroleum products. Western Europe consumes 26 percent of all petroleum products, but the region accounts for only about 3 percent of the world crude oil reserves. Further development and additional discoveries of North Sea reserves may alter this in the future, however. The United States consumes 31 percent and has only 6 percent of the reserves. The Middle East, on the other hand, consumes only 2 percent of the petroleum products and has 58 percent of the reserves. (See Figures 2.1 and 2.2.)

Long-distance transport of crude oil is largely controlled by the major importing nations. For economic reasons, most tankers fly the Liberian or Panamanian flag. Some OPEC countries are now, however, buying their own tanker fleets.

Crude oil is refined into a variety of petroleum products which are then distributed and sold for different uses. The refinery is thus the strategic processing facility in the petroleum fuel cycle. Additions to refinery capacity, control of the

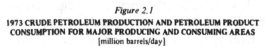

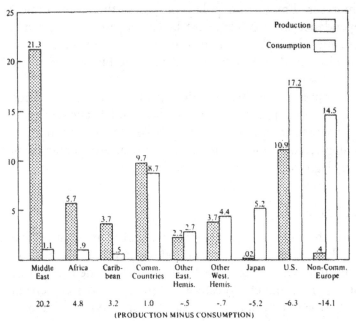

Figure 2.1
1973 CRUDE PETROLEUM PRODUCTION AND PETROLEUM PRODUCT
CONSUMPTION FOR MAJOR PRODUCING AND CONSUMING AREAS
[million barrels/day]

Source: Federal Energy Administration. *Project Independence Report.* Washington: Government Printing
Office, 1974, p. 352.

output mix, and refinery location are therefore decisions with important political, as well as economic, implications.

Gasoline for automobiles is one of the lighter distillates, while fuel oil for electric power generation and industrial boilers is among the heavier. The output of a refinery can be adjusted, within limits, to produce more or less of certain petroleum products. In the past, U.S. refineries have usually been run to maximize gasoline output, whereas refineries in Europe have been run to obtain a larger proportion of fuel oil.

Refineries may be located either close to markets, in which case tankers or pipelines are used to transport crude oil from producing fields, or close to the producing region. Oil refineries

Figure 2.2
1973 CRUDE PETROLEUM RESERVES FOR MAJOR PRODUCING AREAS

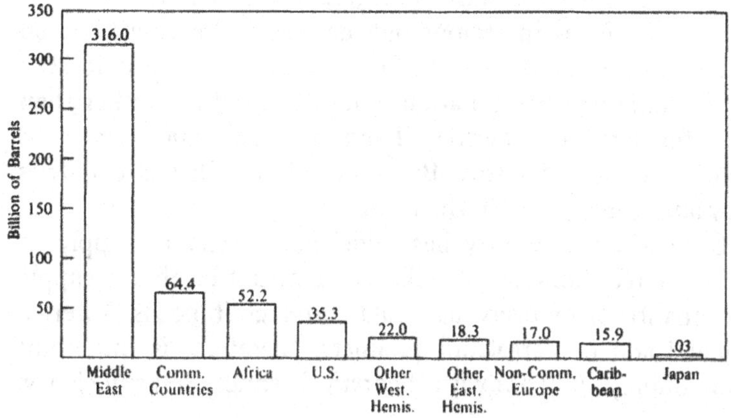

Source: Federal Energy Administration. *Project Independence Report.* Washington: Government Printing Office, 1974, p. 351.

are more widely distributed geographically and have a greater diversity of ownership than either oil reserves or transport facilities.

Many small or less developed countries have refineries that supply part or all of their domestic needs. However, there are only a few exporting centers for refined petroleum products, and each one has a much larger capacity than the total capacity of all the smaller countries together.

The largest refining centers from which petroleum products are exported are located in Rotterdam, the Caribbean–Bahamas area, and the Middle East. Another export center is being developed in eastern Canada. The capacities of these centers range from 1 million to 4 million barrels per day. In the Middle East, of course, the refineries are processing crude oil produced from indigenous reservoirs, whereas the other principal exporters of refined products must import their crude.

Countries or regions that are oil importers have even greater refining capacity than the large exporting centers noted above. For example, refinery capacity in the United States is about 13 million barrels per day, and in Western Europe it is about 18 million.

For the noncommunist countries, therefore, nearly all refining capacity is in regions outside where the very large oil reserves are located, and the bulk of the capacity is located in the large importing nations, close to markets, rather than near the large oil reserves. There are economic as well as political reasons for this. But some of the OPEC countries may alter this pattern in the future.

Even when a country has sufficient capacity to supply its domestic requirements, its refineries may not be able to supply the quantities of every particular product it needs. International trade in petroleum products, therefore, is important even among countries with theoretical refinery self-sufficiency.

NATURAL GAS

The situation for natural gas is markedly different than that for crude oil, since very little gas is marketed in world trade. Gas is used widely only where large markets exist nearby or where extensive overland pipeline systems for transmission and distribution have been created.

The United States, with a well-developed gas pipeline system, consumes more than 50 percent of the natural gas used worldwide. Nearly all of it comes from domestic resources. However, the U.S. has only about 15 percent of the world's known natural gas reserves. The other large natural gas producer and consumer is the Soviet Union, which accounts for about 20 percent of total world production and consumption. The largest natural gas reserves are in Asia, including the Soviet Union. These represent 55 percent of total proven reserves.

Natural gas is beginning to be liquefied and transported overseas in special tankers. If the world natural gas trade develops as expected, the transport control will probably remain in the hands of the importing nations, as with oil. The largest tonnage of liquefied natural gas (LNG) ships is owned by Japan; the balance of the noncommunist tonnage flies the Liberian or Panamanian flag. As with oil, most of this tonnage is owned by U.S. and West European interests. The Soviet Union also has an LNG tanker fleet.

Most facilities to convert natural gas into a liquid so that it can be exported by ship are generally under construction or are in the final testing stages. Only a few are in operation on a small scale. The largest operating facilities are in Algeria and Libya. If suitable financial and marketing arrangements can be made, large liquefaction facilities will probably be built in the Middle East to utilize the associated gas being produced with the exported oil. In the Middle East, large quantities of this type of natural gas are still being flared. For example, the equivalent of one-sixth to one-quarter of present U.S. natural gas consumption is being flared in Saudi Arabia alone.

The LNG importers are Japan, the United Kingdom, and the United States, but other European countries will probably start such imports if the Middle East natural gas export plans materialize, as well as plans for expansion in Algeria and Libya. Future plans to export LNG from the Soviet Union to the United States and Japan, which have been widely reported, still appear to be in the preliminary stages.

In addition to exports of natural gas across oceans, overland pipelines exist which carry gas from the Soviet Union to Eastern Europe and, in smaller quantities, to Western Europe, and from Canada to the United States. These pipeline networks may well be expanded to carry larger volumes and to collect gas that is produced in more remote fields (for example, the McKenzie Delta region in arctic Canada). Moreover, overland gas pipelines may be built to carry gas from the Middle East across Eastern Europe into Western Europe.

Substantial interdependence between countries would be an inevitable result of major expansion in world trade in natural gas. Whether internationally transported overland or overseas, the necessary infrastructure would be very capital intensive, and the prices for imported gas would be much higher than for gas produced domestically.

COAL

World coal resources not only are very large, but they are widely distributed geographically. This is in marked contrast to oil and gas. Large coal deposits are found in nearly all the industrialized, large, energy-consuming countries. The United States accounts for 19 percent, Western Europe 19 percent, and Asia and the Soviet Union 26 percent of total world coal consumption. The corresponding percentages of proven coal reserves for these regions are 17 percent, 7 percent, and 74 percent. These figures indicate an imbalance between areas of consumption and location of reserves. However, the known reserves are so large in comparison with current consumption levels—at least 300 years in the case of the United States— that the imbalance is relatively unimportant. The United States exports the largest amount of coal, followed by Australia, Poland, Canada, and the Soviet Union.

The coal situation is thus a counterpoint to oil and gas. Coal represents 76 percent of the world's proven fossil fuel reserves, oil 13 percent, and natural gas 6 percent. Expanded use of the world's vast coal reserves could substantially reduce reliance on oil and gas and ease the severe strains placed on the world community's political and economic institutions resulting from that dependence. For example, India, which has been hurt as much as any country by the 1973–74 oil price increase, has relatively large, hitherto undeveloped coal reserves.

Yet coal production currently continues to decline, even in some countries that are desperate for energy. The reasons are not hard to find. The use of coal involves more serious environmental and health and safety risks than the use of an equivalent amount of oil or natural gas. Moreover, underground coal mining is a dangerous and distasteful occupation. As between energy security, on the one hand, and environmental and social costs, on the other, most countries have so far chosen a better environment.

New technologies are being developed for converting coal into either gaseous or liquid form for more convenient consumption. In the future, therefore, use of coal need not be confined to electric power generation, industrial boiler fuel, coking for metal productions and the like. Moreover, conversion technologies may ease many of the environmental problems associated with increased use of coal. But it is likely to be a decade or more before new technology for "clean" energy from coal can begin to have much of an impact.

NUCLEAR POWER

The use of nuclear fission to generate electric power involves a fuel cycle composed of a series of interrelated steps. Because the nuclear fuel cycle is less familiar than the various steps involved in using oil, natural gas, or coal, and because of the important and controversial role nuclear power will play in the immediate future, the discussion that follows is somewhat more extensive than for the fossil fuels.

Unlike the fossil fuels, which can be used as a fuel directly if necessary in some important applications, nuclear resources must first be intensively processed. Certain steps are very expensive, and the technologies involved are extremely complex compared to those required for fossil fuels. Moreover, the use of large nuclear power plants may require transmission grids that are interconnected, thereby increasing the interdependence of electric generating supply systems in countries that are geographically close.

The power reactors currently in commercial use are based on the uranium–plutonium fuel cycle. One type of reactor, known as the light water reactor (LWR), uses low-enriched uranium as fuel and ordinary water as moderator. This type was developed initially in the United States. Another type, the heavy water reactor (HWR), uses natural uranium as fuel and heavy water (D_2O) as moderator. This reactor was developed initially in Canada.

The high-temperature gas-cooled reactor (HTGR), based on the thorium–uranium-233 fuel cycle and using high-enriched uranium fuel, is now being commercially demonstrated in the U.S. and is likely to receive widespread use in the future. A variety of types of breeder reactors that convert more fissionable fuel than they consume as they generate electric power are being investigated in a number of countries. As noted previously, the liquid metal fast breeder reactor (LMFBR) is receiving top priority in each of these research and development programs.

The uranium-plutonium fuel cycle for the LWR involves uranium exploration, mining and milling, enrichment, fuel fabrication, irradiation in a power reactor, chemical reprocessing of irradiated fuel, recycling produced plutonium and depleted uranium, and disposal of radioactive waste. For the HWR, the enrichment step is omitted, but a heavy water manufacturing plant is required. For the HTGR, the uranium is highly enriched (to over 90 percent uranium-235) and uranium-233 (instead of plutonium) is the fissionable byproduct of thorium conversion. Like plutonium, the uranium-233 may be recycled as fuel.

Fissionable materials are extremely valuable as nuclear fuel. For example, plutonium is worth about $10,000 per kilogram, or substantially more than gold.

World nuclear power capacity was more than 60,000 megawatts in early 1975, and is expected to increase to more than 360,000 megawatts by 1985. The United States accounts for about half the existing and projected totals. (See Table 2.1.)

More than fifteen nations now have operable nuclear power reactors, and that number is expected to increase to about

TABLE 2.1   Nuclear Electric Generating Capacity, in megawatts, December 31, 1974*

	In Commercial Operation	Under Construction or Ordered	Total
U.S.A.	31,000	190,000	221,000
OECD (excluding U.S.A.)	24,100	86,100	110,200
Austria		692	692
Belgium	390	3,190	3,580
Canada	2,512	6,236	8,748
Finland		2,160	2,160
France	2,888	18,478	21,366
Fed. Rep. of Germany	3,908	16,198	20,106
Italy	547	2,814	3,361
Japan	4,537	11,016	15,553
Netherlands	532		532
Spain	1,073	7,262	8,335
Sweden	1,020	6,329	7,349
Switzerland	1,006	4,847	5,853
United Kingdom	5,332	6,450	11,782
Communist Countries	4,009	7,825	11,834
Bulgaria	440	1,320	1,760
Czechoslovakia	110	1,320	1,430
Hungary		880	880
Romania		440	440
U.S.S.R.	3,459	3,250	6,709
Yugoslavia		615	615
Developing Countries	1,044	15,200	16,244
Argentina	319	600	919
India	600	1,140	1,740
Iran		4,200	4,200
Korea		1,764	1,764
Mexico		1,320	1,320
Pakistan	125		125
Philippines		1,252	1,252
Taiwan		4,924	4,924
WORLD	60,253	299,125	359,278

* Source: *Nuclear News,* Mid-February, 1975.

thirty by 1980. In addition to the United States, countries which have launched large nuclear power programs include the Federal Republic of Germany, Japan, France, the United Kingdom, the Soviet Union, Spain, Sweden, Canada, and Italy. However, most nations with power reactors are dependent on other countries for raw materials or for fuel cycle services such as enrichment, fuel fabrication, and reprocessing, and for some years at least will continue to be.

Economies of scale and considerations of reliability tend to limit nuclear power plants to geographic areas where a relatively large electric power grid exists and a rapid increase in demand is expected. Although nuclear power plants with capacities less than 200 megawatts have been built in a number of countries, 600 megawatts is generally considered a minimum efficient size, and 1,000 to 1,200 megawatts is the normal size range of nuclear plants built in industrially advanced areas. A typical 1,000-megawatt nuclear power plant costs about $600 million to $750 million, considerably more than a comparable fossil fuel plant. Fuel costs for a nuclear power plant, however, are substantially less than for a fossil plant.

The vast bulk of the world's proven reserves of low-cost uranium are concentrated in a relatively few countries—the United States, the Soviet Union, Canada, France, South Africa, Australia, Gabon, and Niger. Hence the most economical deposits of uranium so far discovered are concentrated in fewer countries than in the case of oil. Several countries have small reserves of low-cost uranium, and a few, such as Sweden, have very large reserves of higher-cost uranium.

Up to now, however, uranium and thorium resources have not been nearly as well explored as fossil fuel resources in most areas of the world. Even in the United States the exploration effort has been at a relatively low level because uranium has been in excess supply and there is as yet little demand for thorium. The world's reserves are therefore probably understated. Because of differences in past exploration efforts in the various regions, an attempt to draw conclusions about the relationship between where uranium and thorium reserves are located and where they will be extensively used could be misleading. Nevertheless, a number of industrial countries with large nuclear power programs, such as Great Britain, the Federal Republic of Germany, Italy, and Japan, lack indigenous uranium. These countries will have to depend on foreign countries for nuclear raw materials, as they do now for oil.

With respect to uranium enrichment the U.S., with its very large gaseous diffusion capacity, enjoyed until quite recently a monopoly position in the commercial sector. Smaller diffusion plants in Great Britain and France could not compete with the U.S. enrichment price. Now, however, the U.S. position of dominance is eroding, and the number of sources of enrichment is growing. The Soviet Union is offering enrichment services at prices reportedly 5 percent lower than U.S. prices and on more flexible commercial terms. Moreover, under a tripartite agreement, Great Britain, the Federal Republic of Germany, and the Netherlands are aggressively pursuing the development and commercial demonstration of the gas centrifuge process as an alternative to diffusion. France is playing the leading role in a project to construct a large diffusion plant in Europe under multinational ownership. South Africa is reportedly developing its own enrichment capability, based on a secret process. Finally, Canada and Australia have recently adopted policies to encourage the export of uranium as enriched product, thereby bargaining for enrichment technology.

It is noteworthy that gaseous diffusion involves very complicated technology and requires a very large plant capacity to be economical, and that the enrichment operation by this method requires a large amount of electric power. A typical commercial diffusion plant would have a capacity large enough to provide enrichment services for perhaps 80,000 megawatts of nuclear power capacity. This is a much larger nuclear capacity than any single country except the U.S. will have until well into the 1980s. On the other hand, centrifugation, though also very complex, can be used in smaller plants, and the process requires substantially less electricity per unit of output. The use of lasers to separate uranium isotopes is under intensive scientific investigation in a number of countries. If successfully developed, a laser method could probably be used efficiently on a very small scale.

Large commercial fuel fabrication facilities and chemical-reprocessing facilities are presently concentrated in a very few countries. The technology for both of these steps in the nuclear fuel cycle is complicated, especially chemical reprocessing. Unlike enrichment technology, however, the relevant information has not been kept secret within the various national programs. An economically efficient size for a fuel fabrication or reprocessing plant is one that serves a relatively large operable nuclear power capacity of 10,000 to 20,000 megawatts. Consequently, there is a strong commercial argument against the construction of nuclear fuel cycle facilities—enrichment, fuel fabrication, or chemical reprocessing—in any country until it has a large nuclear power capacity. Pilot or demonstration facilities have already been constructed, however, in several countries in the early stages of nuclear power development, and this trend will probably be difficult to curb in the future.

Given the present realities of the international context, there are various motives for national governments to establish nuclear power programs. These include low-cost electric power, increased energy security, creation of a nuclear weapon option, and prestige. The extent to which commercial arguments will prevail over other considerations remains to be seen in the future development of the worldwide nuclear power industry.

The economic case for nuclear power was strengthened by the 1973–74 increases in world oil prices. Subsequently, inflation and recession caused substantial reductions in nuclear expansion plans in a number of countries, and hence in their expected growth in installed nuclear plant capacity in the early 1980s. As long as fossil fuel prices remain at or near 1975 levels, however, nuclear power will be very competitive.

Nuclear power can offer increased security of energy supply in two different ways. First, nuclear fuel can be substituted for oil for electric power generation in new plants to be constructed, thereby diminishing a country's future dependence on a world oil market that OPEC has, for the near term at least, effectively cartelized. Second, nuclear power can be exploited in ways that will lead to the eventual development of a maximum degree of national nuclear self-sufficiency. It is difficult to stockpile more than a few months of current oil requirements, but a handful of nuclear fuel pellets are equivalent to 85 tons of coal or 15,000 gallons of fuel oil. In most national circumstances, however, nuclear self-sufficiency could be achieved only if the domestic industry were able to acquire and operate sophisticated fuel cycle technologies and if the government were willing to pay an economic penalty.

Nuclear power as a long-run energy option depends on the successful development of breeder reactors. Otherwise, low-cost uranium resources would be exhausted in a few decades, and higher-cost uranium and thorium resources would be depleted in the twenty-first century. Breeder reactors, which produce more fissionable material than they consume, would substantially reduce the amount of raw materials—uranium or thorium—needed to sustain a growing nuclear power capacity. This type of advanced reactor could stretch the viability of the nuclear fission option to hundreds of years at least. But a commercial breeder reactor has not yet been developed.

Nuclear power can result in a nuclear weapon option in a large number of ways. The basic requirement for such an option is the availability of plutonium or high-enriched uranium. The use of nuclear power inevitably involves the processing, production, and use as fuel of very large amounts of weapon-grade materials. Very small amounts of these materials are sufficient to make nuclear explosives. If high-enriched uranium or plutonium is available, the manufacture of fission explosives is no longer considered a technically difficult or economically costly task.

Considerable governmentally authorized diversion of nuclear fuel to weapon uses has occurred already. Nuclear reactors have been operated for the dual purpose of producing electricity and plutonium for military uses in Great Britain, France, and, quite likely, the Soviet Union. India produced the plutonium used so far in its nuclear explosives program in a small reactor given to it by Canada for peaceful research purposes.

The widespread use of nuclear power will bring a nuclear weapons capability within reach of many governments or political factions within governments. The Treaty on the Nonproliferation of Nuclear Weapons together with the international safeguards administered by the IAEA may not serve as a completely effective general restraint. Nuclear weapon proliferation among governments may thus continue.

Nuclear weapon acquisition by particular nations could be extremely destabilizing in the short run. The cumulative effect of many nuclear weapon powers in a politically unstable world may in the long run pose a deadly threat to the security of all mankind.

In addition, criminals or terrorists might make crude fission explosives if they were able to steal the requisite nuclear materials. No thefts of weapon-grade nuclear materials are known to have occurred to date. However, plutonium and high-enriched uranium have not been generally available in large quantities in nuclear power industries, because commercial recycling of plutonium has not yet begun and power reactor types that use high-enriched uranium are only now being commercially demonstrated.

Beyond 1980, the annual plutonium output from nuclear power programs throughout the world will increase rapidly to hundreds of thousands of kilograms, and toward the end of the twentieth century, millions of kilograms of plutonium will be produced annually if nuclear power forecasts are fulfilled. Yet only a few kilograms are enough for a bomb.

In the long run, whether the risk of nuclear theft can be kept at a very low level will depend in part on whether the governments of nations with nuclear power programs make the political commitments necessary to develop effective safeguard systems and provide adequate resources to support those systems. But the risk of nuclear violence will depend largely on general trends in violent behavior. No system of nuclear safeguards can work in a world in which terrorism and violent revolution are acceptable means toward political ends. And no solution can be found to the growing problems of politically inspired violence unless we deal with the root causes, rather than try merely to contain the effects.

ECONOMIES OF SCALE

A salient trend in the world energy situation in the post-World War II years has been the realization of economies of scale. This trend has prevailed throughout most sectors of the energy industry, in each of the fossil and nuclear fuel cycles. A brief general discussion of economies of scale will provide a useful summary and conclusion to our consideration of the growth of energy interdependence.

In the three post-World War II decades, the capacity of crude oil tankers increased from tens of thousands to hundreds of thousands of tons; the capacity of oil refineries increased from hundreds to thousands of barrels per day; the diameter of natural gas pipelines increased severalfold; and the capacity of electric power generators, whether nuclear or fossil fueled, increased from 100 to over 1,000 megawatts. Technology development made possible economies of scale which resulted in lower unit costs for the energy output. These lower costs in turn spurred growth in demand. High growth rates on top of large demands made possible even larger-scale facilities that incorporated further technological improvements. The progressive realization of economies of scale was in large measure responsible for diminishing the significance of distance between producing and consuming regions and for the prolonged worldwide decline in real energy prices during the cheap energy era.

Economies of scale in the energy industry have profound political implications. Supertankers largely nullify the strategic importance of the Suez Canal for oil transport, though not for military deployments. One large oil refinery is adequate to serve the needs of several small countries, as is one efficient nuclear fuel enrichment or reprocessing facility. The most economical electric power plant size means that relatively few plants are needed, and interconnections of power grids across national borders may be necessary.

The efficient use of energy technology thus requires a multinational scale in many regions of the world. The result of economic efficiency is deep interdependence as a physical fact.

Furthermore, centralized management is needed to control the geographically dispersed yet intimately related facilities involved in a large-scale fuel cycle. With political power decentralized among a large number of independent and diverse nation–states, a large role for private corporations would seem necessary for efficient management of interdependent energy operations on a worldwide scale.

In contradiction of these efficiency requirements, however, political intervention in the energy industry seems inevitable. Inequalities in the distribution of energy resources among nations and the vital role of energy in all societies are two obvious reasons for political involvement. In addition, large-scale energy technology, implying a relatively few very large facilities, makes location decisions a highly political matter with strategic consequences. Despite the possibility of multinational ownership and the distribution of output in several countries, the essential energy production or processing facility will be located in only one of the countries involved, and the government of the country where the strategic facility is located will have a potential for control that other governments will not.

Finally, highly centralized, large-scale operations in the transportation, refining, and conversion steps of the various fuel cycles tend to create possibilities for accidental and intentional interruptions of energy supplies. Such interruptions could occur as a result of a political act by the host government on whose national territory the strategic facility was located, but they might also result from an act of war against the host government or a terrorist attack. Or interruptions might be caused simply by a labor strike or domestic turmoil.

Of course vulnerability to interruptions and the extent of damage if they occur may be reduced by using energy technology on a smaller and less efficient scale, by stockpiling in advance of needs, and by decentralized management. However, the economic and environmental costs of these approaches may be large.

Environmental Risks and Constraints

Energy is essential to sustain life. The supply and use of energy, however, have a wide range of adverse environmental and social effects: air, water, and thermal pollution; degradation of land; destruction of wildlife; and health and safety hazards for workers and the public generally. As energy use grows, adverse environmental effects also tend to increase and spread, and new environmental risks may be created. The extraordinary growth in energy use over the last three decades has focused attention on the environmental impacts of energy supply and use, especially in industrial countries.

The world was rudely awakened to the impacts of energy on the environment in the late 1960s by the break-up of the

oil tanker *Torrey Canyon* off the coast of England and by the
blow-outs at oil rigs drilling in the Santa Barbara Channel off
the California coast. The problems of air pollution were also
demonstrated a few summers ago when ugly clouds of gases
led to emergency alerts in several cities throughout the world,
including New York, Washington, Los Angeles, Tokyo, and
Sydney.

Men have created many nations, but the earth has only
one biosphere. Air and water pollution know no political
boundaries. The energy pattern in one country can thus have
adverse effects in other countries or areas beyond national
jurisdiction, such as the oceans.

The character and extent of environmental problems posed
by energy depend on the level of energy consumption, the
effectiveness of pollution control measures, and the particular
energy supply systems used. Given the energy-intensive nature
of the economies of the industrial countries and the strong aspirations in the rest of the world to industrialize, it appears certain that energy consumption will continue to increase. Therefore the environmental, health, and safety risks are likely
to multiply, given the energy systems we must use for the
next quarter century at least.

The largest cause of air pollution throughout the world is
the combustion of fossil fuels in automobiles and other forms
of transport, power plants, industrial processes, commercial
buildings, and homes. Major pollutants include hydrocarbons,
sulphur and nitrogen oxides, and particulate matter. In various
ways each of these pollutants may adversely affect the health
of humans, plants, and animals and cause damage to buildings and materials. It is estimated that air pollution could
cause approximately $15 billion of damage in the United
States alone in 1977. (This estimate was made before the
1973–74 OPEC actions and the ensuing pressures to switch
from oil to coal burning in electric power plants and industrial
boilers and to relax air quality standards.)

Examples of energy-related water pollution are discharges
of waste heat from electric power plants, acid drainage from

coal mines, and oil spills in the oceans. It is important to note that many steps in energy fuel cycles require large amounts of water for cooling or processing. In many areas, such as the Rocky Mountain region in the United States, water supplies may prove to be the factor that limits development of a variety of energy supplies, such as shale oil and coal for gasification or mine-mouth electric power generation.

Much of the environmental impact of growing fossil energy use will be concentrated in the oceans—two-thirds of the earth's surface which the world community shares in common. Of course a great deal of marine pollution is caused by activities on land. However, use of the oceans for energy-related activities is also expanding rapidly.

Increasing volumes of oil are being transported overseas in very large crude carriers (VLCCs). Over 400 tankers of 200,000 tons or more were in operation, under construction, or on order in 1973. Exploration and development of oil and natural gas reserves on the continental shelves are increasing dramatically. Offshore oil may account for over half of world production by 2000. Offshore siting of increasing numbers of energy facilities, such as deepwater ports and nuclear power plants, is contemplated. If the past provides any indication of the future, we can expect more large oil spills caused by accidents involving tankers and offshore drilling, and thousands of small oil spills during normal tanker operations.

Use of nuclear fuel to generate electric power eliminates the air pollution problem associated with fossil fuel combustion. Moreover, the disruption of the landscape involved in the nuclear fuel cycle is considerably less than that resulting from use of coal. Other nonradiological effects of nuclear power appear comparable to the use of fossil fuels, with the exception of thermal pollution. The types of power reactors now in use are less efficient in thermal conversion, and they discharge up to 50 percent more waste heat than modern fossil plants. Technological improvements in advanced reactor types, however, could narrow or eliminate this nuclear disadvantage.

The unique environmental problems created by nuclear power are radiological. As to these risks, the main areas of concern are the operational safety of nuclear power reactors and other facilities where highly radioactive materials are present and the long-term safety of radioactive waste disposal methods. Sharp controversy is likely to continue about safety, the consequences of possible accidents, and acceptable levels of risk. All sides in the debate, however, seem to agree that keeping the radiological risks associated with nuclear power at acceptably low levels requires us (and commits future generations) to maintain extraordinarily high levels of technical competence and managerial vigilance in the industry.

So far in human history, the debris of civilizations which perished long ago has been innocuous when encountered by later civilizations. Indeed, without the debris of earlier civilizations mankind would be largely without its history. When a civilization based on fission power perishes, it will leave behind wastes that will be deadly for hundreds of thousands of years to any living matter that might touch them. Radioactive waste is indeed a problem that transcends all national and cultural differences and spans the centuries ahead. Any solution involves much more than technology.

The ultimate environmental constraint on energy consumption may be neither resource exhaustion nor the specific pollution effects previously mentioned. Rather, the ultimate constraint may prove to be the impact of man's energy use on the earth's climate. Of course the climate has undergone profound changes in the past. Ice ages have come and gone, and fertile lands have turned into parched deserts. Undoubtedly, natural forces beyond human control will cause equally profound climatic changes in the future.

Now, however, human activity—in particular energy use—is approaching a level where the possibility of irreversible effects on the earth's climate is an increasing concern. Climatic change might in the long run be either beneficial or detrimental to the evolution of life on earth, but most people tend to believe that such change would be for the worse.

Regardless of long-term consequences, however, any major alteration of the earth's climate over a relatively short period of time would raise catastrophic political problems. Climatic change could well render obsolete our geographically anchored political institutions. For example, a melting of the polar ice caps could inundate some of the world's most important urban areas. A new ice age, on the other hand, might cover Canada, Scandinavia, and much of the Soviet Union with glaciers.

The expanded use of fossil fuels might substantially affect the earth's climate in various ways. Particulates emitted into the atmosphere as a result of coal combustion might block out enough incoming solar energy to decrease the earth's temperature. Carbon dioxide, another by-product of fossil fuel combustion, might trap enough solar energy in the earth's atmosphere to cause an increase in temperature. This is the so-called "greenhouse" effect.

According to the second law of thermodynamics, heat is the end product of practically all energy consumption, regardless of the technology or fuel employed. The implication of this physical law for man's insatiable appetite for energy is that as energy consumption continues to grow, the heat released will eventually become significant in relation to the amount of solar energy received by the earth. When this threshold is reached, further increases in man's energy use would alter the earth's heat balance, thereby causing grave climatic disturbances. According to some meteorologists, the maximum quantity of heat energy that could be added to the biosphere by human activity without exceeding the thermal limit would be about 1 percent of the solar energy reaching the earth's surface.

The heat produced by man was equivalent to 0.01 percent of the incident solar energy in the early 1970s. If world energy consumption continues to increase at historical growth rates of 5 percent per year, which now appears doubtful, the quantity of heat released by human activity will amount to 0.1 percent of the incoming solar energy toward 2010, 1 percent in 2050, and 10 percent in 2100. It is noteworthy that efforts to preserve the quality of the natural environment through technological means will involve energy use, thereby reinforcing the trend.

Energy use and consequent heat injection into the biosphere are much more concentrated in some geographic regions than in others. Thus "heat islands" resulting from concentrated energy use in urban regions are already having an impact on local and regional weather. It is also possible that large quantities of heat injected into the atmosphere in one location could alter the climate in another region. For example, some scientists have speculated that a causal connection might exist between waste heat rejection in Europe and drought in Sub-Saharan Africa. Long before the thermal limit on worldwide energy consumption is reached, therefore, it is quite possible that substantial local or regional effects will occur.

In summary, man's increasing energy use may inject a powerful destabilizing factor into the interplay of the natural forces that determine the earth's climate. Any alterations in climate could have profound effects upon man's environment, including habitable lands and food and water supplies.

Energy Resource Exhaustion

A voracious, perhaps insatiable appetite for energy is built into industrial society. Industrialization is generally believed to be an essential step in economic development and social modernization.

At present industrial societies depend mainly on fossil fuels, which are depletable, although hydroelectric power has been intensively developed in suitable locations. As a result of the development of nuclear power technology, it is now practical to use uranium and thorium, in addition to fossil fuels, to produce steam-electric power. However, the reactor types currently available for use in power generation release only about 1 percent of the energy potentially available in the fission fuels. Should energy resource exhaustion be a major concern in these circumstances?

As previously discussed, our immediate difficulties are not due to physical scarcity of energy resources or to economic scarcity of low-cost resources; rather, they have arisen because of monopolization by a relatively few governments of the world's known low-cost oil resources.

Nevertheless, the question remains: Should exhaustion of the earth's finite energy resource base be viewed as a major concern in the long run? Fortunately, a "no" answer appears to be more reasonable than a "yes."

The following paragraphs briefly outline the reasoning that leads toward an optimistic conclusion about the future availability of energy. In so doing, we put aside momentarily the political and institutional factors which, as they operate in the international arena, are our primary concern. This will enable us to face the question of resource exhaustion directly. It will also help us to see more clearly the central role of international politics in the world energy situation.

Without the oil price revolution, the earth's low-cost fossil energy resources would have probably been depleted more rapidly than will occur if 1975 oil prices are maintained. One effect of the oil price revolution has been to reduce significantly consumption of all energy resources. To the extent higher prices dampen demand, any potential problem of resource exhaustion is postponed. In short, there was more reason to be concerned about energy resource depletion in 1972 than there is in 1975.

A second and perhaps more important effect of the oil price revolution has been to catapult the world a decade at least into the future with respect to energy options that appear economically attractive. The earth's vast resources of solid hydrocarbons—coal and oil shale—can be converted into liquids or gases for consumption, and coal can of course be burned directly. Moreover, low- and intermediate-cost reserves of uranium and thorium can be used to expand electric power production. Of course, real energy prices will gradually rise further unless enormous additional low-cost fossil or fission energy resources are discovered, or unless dramatic breakthroughs in technical efficiencies of energy conversion or transmission are achieved.

We may thus conclude that with reasonable efforts devoted to the discovery of additional fossil and fission energy resources and to the improvement of technology that is already demonstrated to be practical, the earth's energy resource base appears adequate for another half century at least. Our conclusion assumes that during this period a high level of per capita energy consumption is achieved by a growing world population.

Optimism about energy resources does not turn to pessimism if we extend the time horizon beyond the first half of the twenty-first century and indefinitely into the future. In the long run, breeder reactors might multiply the estimated lifetime of the earth's fission energy resources by a factor of 50 to 75. Controlled fusion reactors might make available a virtually inexhaustible source of energy in heavy hydrogen (deuterium). Geothermal energy might be tapped in favorable locations in order to meet a significant fraction of future energy needs. And the sun supplies a continuous flow of enormous quantities of energy to the earth. Solar energy might be captured and used in a variety of ways to meet some, eventually perhaps most, of man's energy needs until the sun exhausts its own supply of thermonuclear fuel, bringing life in this solar system to its end.

The technologies to exploit these energy resources are in various stages of development. Over more than a decade, several billions of dollars have already been spent by the large industrial countries in efforts to develop the liquid metal fast breeder reactor (LMFBR). Demonstration reactors are already operating in Europe and more are under construction and planned, but additional billions may be required before a breeder reactor is available for commercial use. Commercial breeder reactors may go into operation in Europe in the late 1980s and in the United States in the 1990s. Alternatively, the technological problems may prove to be too difficult or costly to solve; or large additional discoveries of low-cost uranium may make the breeder less urgent; or concerns about the operational safety of fast fission reactors and the security implications of enormous plutonium flows may slow the pace of breeder reactor development programs. Indeed, the breeder may be bypassed entirely in favor of less costly or safer energy supply alternatives.

Billions of dollars have already been invested worldwide in scientific research aimed at establishing the feasibility of controlled fusion. One basic concept being investigated intensively would use electromagnetic confinement of thermonuclear fuel which would be heated in the form of an ionized gas, or plasma, to the extremely hot temperatures required to initiate fusion reactions. A variety of such confinement techniques are being explored. Another basic concept would use lasers to implode small pellets of thermonuclear fuel, thereby creating a series of tiny explosions.

Despite almost two decades of well-supported research effort, the problems have proved to be so intrinsically difficult that the feasibility of controlled fusion has not yet been experimentally demonstrated. The worldwide scientific community has not yet reached the milestone in the development of a controlled fusion reactor that was passed in 1942 when a fission chain reaction was first achieved experimentally in an atomic pile. When and if the scientific feasibility of controlled fusion is established, which some expect to occur within the next five years, the costly and time-consuming stage of technology development will begin.

The primary fuel for fusion power will be deuterium, a heavy isotope of hydrogen which occurs in a concentration of one atom per six thousand in hydrogen. Relative to the energy it contains, deuterium is abundant, and it can be extracted cheaply from water. The successful development of fusion power would thus make available a virtually inexhaustible energy resource.

Fusion power is also likely to be safer than fission power, since there is no possibility of the thermonuclear reaction continuing after an accident in the operation of a reactor. Like fission, however, the fusion reaction releases neutrons. These may be used to convert fertile uranium-238 or thorium into fissionable plutonium or uranium-233. Indeed, the most practical use of fusion reactors initially may prove to be for the production of fission fuels rather than for the production of electricity directly. Therefore controlled fusion will not necessarily avoid the security risks of fission fuels.

The sun has always been and will continue to be the ultimate source of energy that sustains all life and powers the natural environment. Indeed, fossil fuel combustion releases solar energy that was captured by living matter in previous geological eras. Solar radiation could provide more than 500 times the world's total energy consumption in 1974.

Energy from the sun may be captured in a variety of ways. Plants and trees can be grown on land or in water and then burned directly as fuel or converted into more convenient fuel forms. Solar energy can be used to heat and cool buildings. Moreover, it can be converted into electricity directly by using photovoltaic devices or indirectly by focusing the incoming diffuse energy in order to produce steam for use in conventional electric power generators. Whether large-scale applications of solar energy would escape the possible heat limit, discussed in the previous section, would depend on the technique used and the effect of the technique on the earth's reflectivity, or albedo. Moreover, it may be possible to use satellites in space to capture and convert solar energy into electricity and, thereafter, to transmit the electricity to earth stations by means of microwaves. Spaced-based techniques are likely to be much more costly than earth-based methods.

Development of the technology required for most industrial applications of solar energy is still in the early stages. The oil price revolution has led to substantial increases in the efforts devoted to solar energy research and development.

The central point about solar energy is that it solves the energy resource exhaustion problem. The sun supplies the earth with an enormous and continuous quantity of energy that is more than enough to sustain a high-energy worldwide civilization. When the earth's supplies of solar energy are interrupted, all questions of resource exhaustion will become irrelevant.

In depleting the earth's stocks of nonrenewable fossil, fission, and even fusion fuels, successive generations will not be depriving some future generation of energy resources that will be essential to human survival. Instead, each generation may feel quite free to develop and use energy resources—nonrenewable and renewable—in ways that will make the maximum contribution to its own welfare. Political and security factors, economic costs, and environmental and safety constraints will loom large in considerations of how best to develop and use various energy resources in order to enhance current welfare. However, energy resource exhaustion need not be a primary concern.

Nevertheless, apart from fossil energy, the main long-run energy supply options discussed above—fission fuels based on breeder reactors, controlled fusion, and solar radiation—will require substantial research and development prior to introduction for large-scale use. Thereafter, the adoption of new energy technologies and substitution of new sources and forms of energy for old will proceed incrementally, requiring several decades to be fully felt. Barring a world war or other major catastrophe, therefore, world energy supply and demand patterns are likely to shift rather slowly, although the cumulative effects of continuous incremental changes will be dramatic.

In the chapters that follow, we are concerned primarily with international energy politics in the last quarter of the twentieth century. Therefore we focus mainly on fossil energy and nuclear energy using technology that is already developed or in the advanced stages of development.

* * *

Intrinsic in the world energy situation is the struggle between rich and poor countries and their peoples for shares of the world's resources and material wealth. Inherent in the widespread use of nuclear power is the worldwide diffusion of a means for awful violence. But in the long run the environmental effects of ever-increasing energy use may pose the gravest challenges of all. These fundamental challenges should be borne in mind as we take up, in the following chapters, specific problems in the overall energy situation and consider how they might be managed on an international basis.

Chapter 3

Energy and National Security

SECURITY IS A PARAMOUNT concern in international energy politics. This is due to the vital role energy plays in both industrial and developing societies; the large inequalities among nations in the distribution of energy resources, technology, and capital; and the world political structure, which lacks a central governmental authority capable of allocating resources.

Security is a particularized and largely subjective problem. Each national government must perceive its country as reasonably secure in the world community. The more powerful the country is, the more important its security is to international order in general. In a country with a strong national government, personal security requires a clearly defined set of citizen rights and duties. But in a world community without any supranational government, national security requires freedom of action and bargaining power.

It is important, therefore, to view energy security initially from the perspective of the individual country. For purposes of analysis, it is useful to classify countries as energy importers or exporters. We should recall, however, that several countries import one fuel and export another, and that some import a particular fuel into one region and export the same fuel from another. Moreover, the ideal energy security posture may be self-sufficiency in fossil energy, but one country's self-sufficient nuclear power program may be another's security threat. Nevertheless, the basic classification provides a point of departure.

Importing Country Security

An importing country is primarily concerned with the security of its energy supplies. Each importing country may view foreign energy supplies as more or less vulnerable to interruption.

The most obvious security risk is an embargo instituted by a foreign supplier or suppliers' group for political reasons. The Arab oil embargo of "unfriendly" countries in the 1973–74 winter is the classic example. Also, countries relying on the United States for uranium enrichment may be fearful of politically motivated nuclear fuel supply interruptions.

In addition to an exporter-imposed embargo, fuel supply interruptions may result from actions by a third party, hostile to either the exporter or the importer. A hostile government or terrorist organization may seize or destroy a key production facility or block a transport link.

With respect to worldwide energy security, it is difficult to imagine a more strategic link than the Strait of Hormuz joining the Persian Gulf and the Indian Ocean. Twenty million barrels of oil per day, or more than 40 percent of current oil consumption in the noncommunist importing countries, pass through this narrow waterway in tankers destined for ports all over the world. The security of the Strait has been a vital concern to Iran and the Arab states bordering the Gulf, as well as to the world's oil-importing countries.

With secure supplies in mind, the problem each importer faces revolves around three issues: What is "energy security?" What basic strategies will enhance security? What specific measures will implement various strategies? As we shall see, a consensus among energy-importing countries on answers to these questions seems unlikely, though not impossible.

CONCEPTS

From an importing-country viewpoint, at least three different concepts of "energy security" are possible. Each concept may be more or less important in the formation of a particular country's foreign policy.

First, energy security may be viewed narrowly as the guarantee of sufficient energy supplies to permit a country to function during war. In World War II Germany showed that drastic cutbacks in civilian energy consumption are possible without substantially impairing a nation's capability to wage war. In the same conflict, most Americans accepted gasoline rationing with little hesitation and some patriotism.

Second, energy security may be viewed very broadly as the assurance of adequate energy supplies to maintain the national economy at "normal" levels. If growth is considered normal, then security is likely to require some growth in guaranteed energy supplies over time. Such a concept of energy security allows for no gap between what a society wants and what it is willing to accept or tolerate. While the first concept appears too restrictive, the second seems too permissive and expansive. For most purposes, some concept of energy security between the two extremes seems desirable.

It is easier to point out the limitations of extreme views of energy security, however, than to state clearly the meaning of an intermediate, more balanced, concept. Perhaps the best we can do is to view energy security as the assurance of sufficient energy supplies to permit the national economy to function in a politically acceptable manner. Such a concept makes all-important the question of what is "politically acceptable."

Although this may appear to be begging the question, it does point in a useful direction. As to political acceptability, international and domestic perspectives may be distinguished.

From the viewpoint of other countries and international order in general, there would seem to be a common interest in assuring sufficient energy to an importing country to prevent its sinking into political chaos. This common interest of the world community would be strong in the case of large importing countries such as Great Britain, France, West Germany, or Japan. Domestic chaos in any large industrial country could send dangerous shock waves throughout the international system. In the case of a small or less developed country, however, the common international security interest would be weak, since it could sink without seriously endangering other nations. (On the other hand, such a country might be rescued by other countries with comparatively little effort.)

From the viewpoint of the particular importing country, where it will draw the line between energy security and insecurity depends on its economic and political organization and on its stage of industrial development. In an affluent, industrial country with strong democratic institutions, there may be little room for maneuver between enough energy to sustain a growing economy and the politically acceptable minimum. In many importing countries, sufficient energy to assure political stability may be equated with the minimum energy required to sustain a tolerable level of economic activity. Energy security is thus closely and directly linked to general economic security.

STRATEGIES

The strategic options available to an importing country wishing to increase its energy security depend substantially on that country's energy assets, in the form of natural resources, technology, capital, and management skills, and on its overall industrial base.

An energy importer that is industrialized and that possesses a large domestic resource base may enhance its energy security in basically two ways: by strengthening its guarantees of foreign supplies and by increasing its self-sufficiency. An importer lacking a large domestic energy resource base has only one way to enhance its energy security: that of strengthening its guarantees of foreign supplies. Whether rich or poor in domestic energy resources, an industrial importer has things of value to offer energy exporters in exchange for strong assurances of continued supply. However, most nonindustrial importers have nothing, or very little, to use in bargaining for more energy security.

In other words, a resource-rich, industrialized energy importer such as the United States, Australia, or South Africa can seek to enhance its energy security through increasing either its interdependence or its autonomy, or by a complex policy composed of measures drawn from both approaches. A resource-poor, industrialized energy importer such as West Germany, France, Italy, or Japan can attempt to enhance its energy security only through interdependence. But a resource-poor, less developed country, such as Bangladesh or Ethiopia, is doomed to energy insecurity or dependence (as well as insecurity in most other aspects of national economic life).

These propositions go a long way toward explaining the very different and often conflicting approaches which various importing countries have adopted so far in attempting to solve their energy security problems. In particular, the United States is in a fundamentally stronger position as to energy security than most of the countries of Western Europe and Japan.

MEASURES

An energy-importing country may consider a variety of specific measures in seeking to enhance its energy security. These may be grouped into three categories according to their effect.

First are measures to decrease damage from possible supply interruptions. These include stand-by rationing plans and stockpiling. By rationing we mean demand restraints and allocation devices aside from prices. Rationing is possible for every energy importer. However, the creation of energy stock-piles that are large enough to be meaningful may not be practical in some circumstances and may cost more than many countries can afford. In any event, damage-limiting measures are an important part of energy security unless a country is completely self-sufficient.

Second are measures to enhance energy security through strengthened guarantees of foreign supply. Such measures in-clude not only diversification of supply sources but also in-creased interdependence through exporter investments and industrial development assistance. In general, these measures are available mainly to importing countries that are already industrialized.

Third are measures to enhance energy security through in-creasing self-sufficiency. As a practical matter, these measures are limited to industrial countries that, nevertheless, possess relatively large undeveloped domestic energy resources. Once again, the prospects for many less developed countries to in-crease their energy self-sufficiency appear limited. Even if they possess undeveloped resources, they must import tech-nology, capital, and management.

Our discussion of specific measures to enhance energy security includes the total fuel picture. The comparisons and contrasts among the various fuels are striking, the most im-portant being between oil and nuclear fuel. Although most energy security measures are relatively simple in concept, none appear easy to apply in practice.

Rationing. Prices, long queues, and government rationing are devices to allocate available supplies and limit consump-tion. In general, reductions in consumption will diminish the magnitude of many energy supply problems and extend the time for solving them. Thus reduction in energy demand reduces the need for imports, extends the lifetime of domestic energy resources, and reduces domestic environmental effects of energy consumption and production.

Specifically, government rationing plans may enhance a country's energy security in several ways. In normal times such plans would not be operative in countries with market economies. However, their existence—and political acceptance in advance—may provide a useful signal. An exporter contemplating supply interruptions would know that the importer is reasonably prepared and therefore determined to resist such coercion. In the event of a serious supply interruption, a well-designed rationing scheme will minimize damage to the economy.

Political acceptance in advance of a specific threat or an imminent supply interruption is a critical factor in energy rationing. A scheme that is merely discussed or proposed may lack credibility abroad. Moreover, in an actual emergency a rationing plan that was merely proposed might well be pushed aside in a mad scramble for priorities and special deals within the importing country. The effectiveness of rationing depends on people knowing in advance what they are supposed to do. Each person may then take precautions and will be more likely to cooperate with the government in an emergency.

To enhance energy security, rationing measures must result more or less immediately in actual energy savings. Energy conservation measures such as a miles per gallon performance standard for automobiles or insulation requirements for buildings may result in very large savings in the long run, but they can do little to limit damage from an immediate supply interruption. (Conservation measures are discussed in Chapter 5 in the context of environmental issues.)

Raising thermostats in summer or lowering them in winter and reductions in automobile speed limits may immediately yield large energy savings if compliance is widespread. However, such measures are very difficult to enforce, and savings are thus not assured. Gas station closings are relatively easy to enforce. Here again the energy savings are uncertain, since people may either drive less or drive the same distance as before the emergency but at different times. Moreover, station closings are clearly an inefficient and inequitable rationing method, favoring those who can afford the time to wait in line.

A basic question is whether rationing plans will be credible unless the core of the plan is mandatory—for example, gas coupons in the case of automobile drivers, and fixed allocations in the case of industrial and business consumers. The major issues in developing a mandatory rationing plan are the trigger events, the basic approach—a system of priorities or percentage cutbacks in use—and responsibility for administration.

In general, the stronger an importing country's energy posture to begin with, the more effective rationing will be as a security-enhancing measure. In a resource-rich and affluent importing country such as the United States, an emergency rationing plan may have a major security impact. Implementation of a well-designed plan could yield substantial savings with minimal damage to essential economic activity. In a resource-poor industrial country, contingency planning to restrict energy consumption may be even more necessary to undertake than in a country with a large fraction of its energy requirements covered by domestic supply sources. In a less developed country without energy resources, some sort of cutbacks in consumption will be immediately necessary to the full extent of the supply interruption, since probably there will be no stockpile to cushion the effect. Moreover, the impact of the enforced cutbacks is likely to be especially damaging in a poor country. Proportionately less energy is consumed in a less developed country for personal comfort and amenities, and more for essential agricultural and industrial uses, than in a country that is already fully industrialized.

In any importing country there are practical limits on the ability of government to cut back energy consumption if the result would be large reductions in employment and economic activity. Especially in a market economy, there is always danger of a downward spiral destroying the economy or bringing about the downfall of the government or both.

Nevertheless, the security gains to be derived from careful planning and preparation for rationing in the event of an energy supply emergency far outweigh the costs. Indeed, the costs of contingency planning are negligible, whereas the costs of failure to plan effectively can be very high. The difficulties lie in overcoming the tendency to procrastinate and in obtaining advance public acceptance for a plan. Both these difficulties seem inherent especially in a political democracy.

Stockpiles. A fuel stockpile for use in emergency may reduce an importing country's vulnerability to a supply interruption by providing a cushion against its effect. The existence of an adequate stockpile may serve as a deterrent to an embargo and may also strengthen the bargaining position of the importing country in diplomatic efforts to lift it.

An emergency fuel reserve may also serve as a hedge against abnormal price fluctuations. In countries with market economies, this would involve the government in a very sensitive matter. If stockpiles of fuels were conceived with a multipurpose objective in mind, it would be important to find means to ensure that use to smooth out market prices did not erode the effectiveness of the stockpile for energy security.

The circumstances in which an emergency stockpile may be desirable depend on judgments about a number of factors: the significance of the particular fuel within the nation's energy economy; the degree of reliance on imports; the number of sources of foreign supply and the political reliability of each; the world market outlook and the likelihood of cartelization; and the substitutability of another form of fuel. In short, the desirability of a stockpile depends on the importing country's assessment of the overall security of its position with respect to the particular fuel involved.

If a stockpile is desirable, is it practical in a technical sense? The practicality of a stockpile will vary substantially depending on the fuel, the form in which it is set aside, and the geography of the importing country.

Among the fossil fuels, oil stockpiling has received the most attention because of oil's importance in total energy consumption and the heavy reliance in many industrial countries on imports from the Middle East. The West European members of OECD are already committed to a sixty-day emergency reserve, and the International Energy Program contemplates a ninety-day reserve goal. Studies indicate that the United States could establish an oil stockpile sufficient to supply 2 million barrels per day for one year (against imports in 1974 of about 7 million barrels per day) at a cost of about $1 billion per year.

Oil stockpiles may be established by setting aside installed domestic production capacity or by storing crude oil in surface tanks or underground in geological formations or by stockpiling refined products. Storage is likely to be cheaper than production capacity that is set aside. Moreover, only a country with a large domestic production capacity, such as the United States, has the latter option. Geography may limit the feasible size of an oil stockpile in a country such as the Netherlands or Japan. A stockpile of refined petroleum products seems indicated if the importing country lacks domestic refining capacity.

Because of the relatively small volumes involved so far in international trade, natural gas stockpiling for security purposes has received little attention. Some gas utilities now use large underground cavities to store natural gas for use during periods of peak demand. Natural gas storage for national energy security purposes may prove to be impractical, however, because of the difficulty of developing a large enough storage capacity. Gas storage in liquefied form would involve safety risks and very high maintenance costs.

Coal is practical to stockpile, but the security incentives for doing so are small in view of the large world coal reserves and the diversity of sources of supply. In any event, large coal users, such as electric utilities and certain industries, have traditionally maintained relatively large inventories to protect themselves against miners' strikes and railroad supply interruptions.

Nuclear fuel stockpiling seems quite practical. Whereas development and maintenance of a ninety-day emergency oil reserve would be a major task, a five-year strategic stockpile of fuel for a large nuclear power program would be relatively easy to accomplish. The striking difference is, of course, due to the compactness of refined uranium. Nuclear fuel may be stockpiled either as uranium oxide—"yellow cake"—or as enriched product ready for fabrication into reactor fuel. Of course if an importing country lacks its own enrichment capacity, it will seek to stockpile enriched uranium—low-enriched for LWRs or high-enriched for HTGRs. Plutonium for recycling in LWRs or use in breeder reactors may also be stockpiled. As discussed in Chapter 2, if breeder reactors can be successfully developed for commercial use, they will eventually reduce to a minimal level the amount of uranium or thorium input required to sustain a growing nuclear power capacity.

From the viewpoint of strengthening the energy security of an importing country, stockpiling oil is a tactical device to reduce vulnerability to short-term supply interruptions. Nuclear fuel stockpiling, however, may alter an importing country's basic strategic energy relations. Even though it lacked uranium reserves or enrichment capacity, an importing country might use stockpiles of nuclear fuel to make its electric power program quite impregnable against foreign embargo risks.

In implementing an emergency fuel reserve scheme, the government of an importing country faces a number of difficult domestic issues. Other strategic stockpiles, whether of grains or of metals, have often become political footballs, and they sometimes have chilling effects on normal market operations.

The threshold issue is ownership. The government may own the stockpile, or, in countries with market economies, the responsibility may be imposed on the private sector of the energy industry. A second issue is defining the circumstances in which the stockpile will be used. Concrete criteria are desirable to ensure that the government will neither act precipitously nor procrastinate too long in an actual emergency. In this respect, the International Energy Program provides for allocations from emergency oil reserves to begin when a participating country sustains a reduction in its oil supplies that is greater than 7 percent of its consumption during the base period. A third issue is how a stockpile will be used over time. It is desirable to coordinate stockpile use with energy rationing. Timely rationing can considerably stretch the useful life of a stockpile. In any event, a stockpile allocation and use scheme needs to be worked out carefully in advance. This involves making a series of hard political choices on a basis that is firm, though hypothetical.

Do the energy security gains from a fuel stockpile outweigh the costs? Answers to this question will be largely subjective. They will depend on an importing country's assessment of the probabilities and magnitudes of foreign supply interruptions, its overall economic strength, and other available means for strengthening its energy security.

In assessing stockpiling costs, the first issue is whether the same or greater energy security gains may be achieved for less cost by investing an equivalent amount of money in some other measure, such as developing additional domestic energy resources or establishing new foreign energy relationships. Such alternative investments may yield important economic benefits in addition to increasing energy security, whereas stockpiling is primarily useful as a security measure.

The second issue is whether the security gains outweigh the welfare gains of investing an equivalent sum in any area not related directly to energy security. One energy-importing country may conclude that expanding domestic food production is more important than oil stockpiling, while another may reach the same conclusion about developing national parks.

Nuclear fuel stockpiling also has a unique aspect that

merits attention. What is a security gain for the importing country may be a substantial security loss for any country in an adversary relationship to the importing country. The problem is that a small fraction of a fuel stockpile for a nuclear power program is enough material to produce a substantial stockpile of nuclear weapons. This is especially true of plutonium or high-enriched uranium. However, low-enriched uranium may be diverted and highly enriched for weapons use if the country involved has a small enrichment facility. Unlike fossil fuel stockpiles, nuclear fuel stockpiles may thus appear threatening to other countries. Perhaps the security costs to other countries of nuclear fuel stockpiles can be offset by international inspection arrangements and multinational forms of ownership.

It is interesting to note in passing that Iran, which is presently a large oil exporter, will eventually be a large nuclear fuel importer. Iran may use a stockpile to immunize its nuclear power program from the threat of supply interruptions, thereby creating apprehensions in the Middle East about its nuclear intentions. Alternatively, Iran may choose to rely for nuclear fuel supply security on the obvious interdependence resulting from its oil export position.

On balance, an emergency oil reserve, such as contemplated in the International Energy Program, seems worthwhile. In Western Europe and Japan, which are also heavily dependent on nuclear fuel imports, strategic nuclear stockpiles may also result in substantial gains in energy security.

Finally, it seems doubtful that resource-poor, less developed countries will be able to develop stockpiles of essential fuels, whether fossil or nuclear. Only the wealthy can afford such insulation from the storms of world politics.

Diversification. We turn now from measures that are designed primarily to limit damage from energy supply interruptions (recognizing that the existence of such measures may deter cut-offs) to measures that are intended to strengthen assurances of foreign supply. In the first place, an energy-importing country may enhance its security by diversifying its foreign sources of supply.

If there is idle world production capacity, an importer may quickly achieve considerable diversification. For example, until recently the excess U.S. oil production capacity offered Western Europe the possibility of offsetting cutbacks in supplies of cheap Middle East oil with more expensive imports from the United States. However, the present excess production capacity within the OPEC cartel might do little to increase an importing country's security if the cartel were to operate as a unit in a future embargo.

An importing country may also achieve rapid diversification if it has sufficient market power to preempt supplies originally committed to other countries. Thus when interruptions occur, the United States may be in a position to obtain favorable treatment in the world petroleum market due to the combination of its ability to pay and the fact that the U.S. government has greater potential leverage on most of the private multinational oil companies, which are U.S. based, than other importing countries have. Of course use of such leverage in a tight or partially embargoed market would have very serious political repercussions on relations with other importing countries. Although the U.S. government avoided such action in the 1973–74 Arab embargo and may not contemplate it in the future, other importing countries are nevertheless aware of the leverage and may fear the possibility.

The more interesting diversification options are long term. Presently, two main bottlenecks are motivating importers to diversify their foreign energy supply sources. One is the OPEC cartel; the other is the U.S. uranium enrichment monopoly.

As for diversification of oil supplies, there is already substantial diversity within OPEC itself. There is little likelihood that all cartel members will agree on an embargo aimed at any particular importing country. The main risk is an embargo by Arab OPEC members, and this risk is solely, though firmly, linked to the Arab–Israeli conflict. Even here, however, there is no unanimity among the Arab producers. Neither Iraq nor Libya agreed to the embargo after the October 1973 war.

Therefore an oil-importing country may attempt to assure itself of continued supplies from OPEC in one of two ways: it may make special arrangements with non-Arab OPEC members, or it may support the Arabs in their conflict with Israel. It is noteworthy in this regard that U.S. oil imports from Nigeria increased dramatically after the 1973 Arab embargo. The other industrial oil importers, which have no real alternative to continued reliance on Arab oil for perhaps the next decade, have tilted noticeably toward the Arab side in the conflict. Consequently, the U.S. now finds itself almost alone in its strong support for Israel.

If the Arab nations reimpose an oil embargo, the United States may be the only target. However, the Arabs may impose the embargo on all industrial importing countries regardless of their policies toward Israel, on the theory that the West European countries and Japan would then pressure the United States to force Israel into a Middle East settlement on terms favorable to the Arabs.

The preceding discussion assumes that during a selective embargo the oil-exporting countries will trace their exports through the world market to the final destinations. This is not now easy to do, since the private multinational oil companies act as middlemen in the world market. Oil en route in tankers is often bought and sold many times, and its destination may be changed several times.

Private operations in the world oil market thus offer an importing country two security advantages. The existence of a market with many buyers and sellers creates more possibilities for supply diversification than a series of country-to-country arrangements. Under normal conditions, moreover, countries selling in the market do not know where much of the oil they export is ultimately to be delivered.

Thus during the 1973 Arab embargo the U.S.-based multinational oil companies were able to mitigate the damage by juggling supply sources. The private companies were able to substitute non-Arab for Arab oil in the case of embargoed countries, and Arab for non-Arab oil in the case of non-embargoed countries. The result was to spread the shortage among importing countries in a way that their governments apparently accepted as fair—a noteworthy achievement. Despite these advantages, a privately controlled world oil market could well be a casualty of the energy crisis and the resulting attempts by importing countries to gain more secure oil supplies through government-to-government deals.

In addition to diversification of oil supply sources within OPEC itself, there may be opportunities for the development of additional energy supplies outside OPEC. Such diversification may occur either by the addition of countries to the list of large oil exporters or through the substitution of different fuels for oil by the importers. But the time scale for either type of development is quite long.

Will the development of additional sources of non-OPEC oil increase the energy security of an importing country? The answer depends on the domestic oil needs of the potential exporting country and the amount of productive capacity and reserves added. It also depends on the political relations between the new oil exporter and OPEC, on the one hand, and the exporter and importing countries, on the other.

Any producer of new oil, whether it be Norway, Greece, South Vietnam, China, or Mexico, is likely to give its own domestic needs top priority. Quantities may be exported in exchange for assistance in oil exploration and drilling. But if domestic demand is growing, the security of any long-term export contracts seems questionable. Moreover, it seems likely that a new exporter will add fairly small increments to the world market. If demand is strong, it will not be likely to shave the OPEC price.

Political relations will also affect supply security with a new exporter, as with existing OPEC members. This, of course, would be a major consideration in deals between the OECD industrial countries and the Soviet Union or China. Indeed, energy imports from the communist countries may be interrupted not only because of worsening bilateral relations between the exporter and the importer but also because of support the communist exporter may wish to give to general political movements, such as Arab nationalism in the Middle East, black nationalism in southern Africa, or socialist revolution anywhere.

In addition to seeking additional sources of oil supply outside OPEC, a country may import natural gas or coal in lieu of oil. If the sources of foreign supply for the substituted fuels are more secure than present oil supplies, this will enhance an importer's energy security. In Western Europe, natural gas imports from the Netherlands, the Soviet Union, or the Middle East would each have a different security calculus. Moreover, natural gas imports via overland pipeline may be vulnerable to interruption not only by the exporting country but also by every country the pipeline crosses en route. Oil pipelines have been blown up in Iraq and Syria, and this makes the West European countries understandably wary of building pipelines across Eastern Europe to tap gas fields in Iran or the Arab countries.

Coal may appear to be a much more secure source of imported energy than oil or natural gas. Oil-importing countries may therefore seek to substitute coal for oil in electric power generation and industrial boilers. In many cases it is possible to adapt installed oil-burning equipment to burn coal, so that substitution can occur in existing as well as future industrial capacity. Of course switching from oil to coal is doubly advantageous if domestic coal resources are exploited.

But the world coal market may also expand. The Soviet Union, China, and to a lesser extent the United States have sufficient reserves to supply a very large world market. Since coal mining is much more labor intensive than oil or gas production, coal imports may be more vulnerable to supply interruption due to strikes. This potential vulnerability would be slight in the case of imports from communist countries, however.

Substitution of coal for oil implies a willingness to absorb somewhat more environmental pollution and health hazards than in the case of oil. The less developed countries especially may be quite willing to absorb these added external costs in exchange for the increased energy security resulting from a switch to coal. Moreover, the less developed countries may view either the Soviet Union or China, or both, as a relatively secure source of coal supply.

Increased use of nuclear fuel will not rapidly result in an oil import reduction. Nuclear fuel is used only for electricity production. In view of the long lead times required for new power plant construction, the main effect of nuclear substitution will be felt gradually.

The less developed countries face special difficulties in substituting nuclear fuel for part of their future growth in energy imports, since most of these countries have no domestic reactor-manufacturing capability. There is no shortage of foreign reactor vendors, but there is a shortage of vendors willing to manufacture and sell reactors that are small enough to be suitable for use in small electric power grids. Moreover, the less developed countries face a perennial shortage of easy credit terms necessary to finance such capital-intensive imports.

Thus far we have focused on oil supply diversification as a means of avoiding the security threat posed by an OPEC-type cartel. An importing country may also wish to enhance its energy security by diversifying its sources of nuclear fuel.

As described in Chapter 2, the most efficient types of commercial power reactors presently available require low-enriched uranium fuel. Until recently the United States enjoyed a monopoly position in the supply of enrichment services to noncommunist countries, whereas the Soviet Union monopolized nuclear fuel supplies to Eastern Europe. Even though the Soviet Union is now competing quite successfully for enrichment contracts in noncommunist countries, many nations are likely to find distasteful the prospect of long-term reliance on such a potential duopoly for nuclear fuel supplies.

A nuclear fuel–importing country seeking further diversification may either participate directly in the enrichment stage or adopt power reactors that use natural uranium fuel. In view of the expense and complexity of the technology involved, direct participation in enrichment is likely to be confined mainly to industrial countries. Moreover, ventures in this field are likely to be multinational, such as the tripartite British–German–Dutch effort and the French-led Eurodif venture which are moving ahead in Western Europe. The U.S. government is also becoming more willing to share its advanced enrichment technology with others, and the development of cooperative uranium enrichment programs is now a task of the new International Energy Agency.

If all goes well with the new multinational enrichment ventures, sources of enrichment services will be substantially diversified by the early 1980s. Nevertheless, the U.S. will continue to play a preponderant role in this critical area both as the largest supplier of services and as the developer of much of the advanced technology. Fears of dependence on primarily the U.S. for enrichment have led many of the less developed countries that have launched nuclear power programs to put political independence above economics. These countries have opted for natural uranium–fueled power reactors. A country using this type of reactor, which bypasses the enrichment step, can either use domestic uranium supplies, if available, or buy uranium on the world market.

Whether they are industrial or less developed, countries that lack sufficient domestic uranium reserves may be concerned about the risk of a cartel emerging among the uranium-exporting countries. Though uranium has been abundant and the price depressed until recently, the low-cost reserves presently available for the world market are highly concentrated in Canada, South Africa, Australia, Gabon, and Niger. World uranium demand is increasing rapidly in order to fuel nuclear power reactors that are already operable, under construction, and planned.

The security risk of a uranium cartel seems small. The few countries in a position to export uranium in large quantities are unlikely to embargo all exports on political grounds. However, the possibilities seem strong that uranium exporters, either in concert or alone, will adopt strategies to make their operations in the world uranium market highly profitable after many lean years of oversupply.

First, the exporters may simply peg the price of uranium high. Nuclear fuel costs are a small part of the costs of nuclear-electric power, unlike fossil fuel costs. Moreover, the ultimate purchasers are electric utilities, which are generally able to pass through fuel cost increases automatically to their customers. Thus uranium sellers may be able to bargain successfully for a high price despite plentiful supplies. Second, the exporters may insist on supplying uranium in the highest possible form, namely, enriched uranium for reactors using that type of fuel. This would enable the uranium exporters to greatly increase their foreign exchange earnings.

Interdependence. From an importing-country viewpoint, energy insecurity is created not merely by the necessity of reliance on foreign supply sources but also by the fact that the particular foreign sources relied on enjoy a substantial measure of independence or autonomy. The oil importer's energy insecurity may thus be largely a function of OPEC's actual or perceived freedom of action. Similarly, countries depending on the U.S. for uranium enrichment services may feel insecure because the U.S. government unilaterally dictates the price and main contract conditions for nuclear fuel enrichment.

Faced with such insecurity, an importing country may attempt to diversify its foreign sources of supply, as discussed in the previous section. Alternatively, it may seek to strengthen its security through interdependence with its present supply sources. The latter alternative would involve a willingness on both sides to negotiate deeper forms of mutually dependent relations. Neither the importer nor the exporter would dominate the relationship.

Interdependent relations of this sort may be very difficult to reverse, and hence they are not likely to be created quickly or easily. Moreover, in terms of international security generally, much depends on perceptions of ambiguous circumstances and ambivalent situations. Whether an energy-importing country will view deeper interdependence with certain foreign fuel suppliers as strengthening or threatening its position will depend largely on how the problem is perceived.

An importing country may seek to achieve greater interdependence in two different ways: long-term investments by the exporter in the importing country and industrial development assistance by the importer to the exporter. The fact that such economic measures have an important security aspect to them simply reflects the interweaving of energy security and economic issues. Interdependence through a foreign investment policy aimed generally or selectively at energy-exporting countries would be most relevant to exporters with large surplus revenues, while interdependence through development assistance would apply mainly to the more populous, less developed energy exporters with large capacities to absorb domestic investment.

Exporter investments in the importing country may take a variety of forms with different impacts on the importer's economy and the importer–exporter relationship. The exporter may invest downstream in the energy industry, in manufacturing concerns whose output the exporter would like to purchase or in a diversified portfolio of holdings designed to yield a maximum rate of return commensurate with the risks taken. In any event, exporter investments in an importing country may be distinguished as to whether the exporter has control over the enterprise, whether control is shared, or whether the exporter has a small minority interest.

From an importing country's viewpoint, an exporter's investments may be viewed as strengthening the importer's security in a number of ways. The investments may give the importer leverage on the exporter through the threat of nationalization or the ability to freeze the exporter's assets. Less directly, the investments may also give the exporter a stake in the importer's economy, so that a supply interruption would amount to a self-inflicted wound.

For the purpose of enhancing the importer's security of supply, what foreign investment policy is preferable? First, short-term investments may appear threatening. In the absence of central banking institutions or cooperative action, quick withdrawal of liquid assets could cause financial institutions to collapse. Arab use of the money weapon might thus be more devastating in the future than the oil weapon has been in the past.

Second, minority positions in various companies seem to have little security-enhancing effect for the importing country, although the economic benefits may be substantial. Such investments are subject to liquidation. A quick sale may threaten the financial security of the enterprise, but large-scale economic impacts might be quite small unless an entire portfolio were abruptly liquidated. The defect from a security viewpoint is that the exporter would not be locked in and, therefore, committed to the energy importer.

Third, either shared control, such as 50-50 ownership, or majority control by the exporting country of long-term investments in the importing country may offer the importing country substantial security advantages. The exporter would be visibly and obviously locked into investments that would be easily identified. These investments could not be quickly liquidated, and they could be seized by the importing country in the event of a fuel supply interruption.

From the standpoint of the importer's energy security, the most effective form of investment may be downstream in the energy industry. Thus an oil exporter would be encouraged to invest in refining and marketing operations in the importing country, or a uranium exporter would invest in offshore enrichment operations. Such an investment would give the exporter a direct economic stake in keeping the fuel supply line open. In general, it seems that the largest security gains are to be realized from highly visible, long-term forms of investment. This reasoning runs counter to the current trend of thinking regarding petrodollar-recycling policy. American political and financial leaders have voiced alarm about proposed investments of some Middle East countries in basic U.S. industries. West European governments, on the other hand, have permitted petrodollar investments in such basic industries as uranium enrichment, steel, and automobile manufacturing. American reluctance may well be only temporary, due in part to lack of experience with foreign investment in the United States—unlike Western Europe, which has long experience with large American investments.

An importing country may also enhance its energy security through its own development assistance to an exporting country or countries. Here the importing country would seek to create interdependence between the flow of energy from the exporter to the importer and the flow of development assistance from the importer to the exporter. Since the importer would have a vital need for a secure foreign supply of oil, for example, it would be important that the reciprocal flow be equally vital to the exporter and that substitute sources of supply not be readily available. The United States may view the exchange of food for energy as a useful way to strengthen its security with certain exporters.

In this context, it may be noted that the major flow from the U.S. and West European countries into the Middle East so far has been composed of armaments. It seems natural for the Middle East countries to want more arms and for the

Western countries to supply them at the highest possible prices in exchange for oil. However, in doing so, both the United States and Western Europe are running substantial military security risks without improving their energy security.

The Middle East arms race is a cause, as well as an effect, of political tensions that could erupt into war. War in the Middle East, whether between the Arabs and Israelis or among some of the Persian Gulf states, would threaten the continued flow of oil from the region. Moreover, the credibility of any potential threat of Western military intervention in order to restore access to Middle East oil supplies is being negated by the build-up of large, well-equipped armies in the Gulf states. Despite the financial attractions of paying off oil import bills with sophisticated arms, such deals may not only increase the destruction in future wars in the world's most explosive region but also diminish the energy security of all oil importers.

Self-sufficiency. Of the various ways for an importer to enhance its energy security, self-sufficiency has received by far the most attention in the United States. This is understandable because the U.S. only recently became a large oil importer. In view of its domestic resource base, the U.S. has the capability of substantially reducing its level of reliance on foreign oil sources, which in 1974 accounted for more than one-third of total American oil consumption. This will, however, require strong and continued action both to restrain demand and to expand domestic supplies.

Self-sufficiency as an objective has several possible meanings. Energy self-sufficiency may mean actual and exclusive reliance on domestic energy resources, the potential to rely indefinitely on domestic resources after some transition period, or the capability to rely exclusively on domestic resources for only a limited period of time.

Complete self-sufficiency would amount to a self-imposed embargo on energy imports in order to assure that an embargo would not be externally imposed. In some national circumstances, an extreme view of self-sufficiency may be derived from a strong political desire to develop self-reliance and autonomy. This would seem to be the case with China, for example. In other cases, however, such an extreme would appear close to national masochism.

The capability for energy self-sufficiency after a period of time may be useful in slowly deteriorating circumstances but of little value in a world where political action can result in rapid changes in world energy flows. The capability to be self-sufficient for a period of time in the event of supply interruptions seems a reasonable national energy posture, as our previous discussion of stockpiles showed. It may be noted here, however, that as energy consumption grows, stockpiles would have to grow proportionately for such a policy stance to maintain its effectiveness.

In any event, energy self-sufficiency would involve substantial economic penalties for most countries which are theoretically capable of achieving that solution to their energy security dilemma. Expansion of domestic energy production for security reasons implies the development of a production capacity that may not be competitive economically. If domestic supplies were lower cost than world prices, economic reasons alone would justify their development. Self-sufficiency may also cause serious environmental consequences for the country concerned, as will be seen in Chapter 5.

Of course self-sufficiency to an important degree depends on a country's energy consumption requirements and its resource base. Industrialization creates enormous energy demands. Thereafter a consumer-oriented society may pile large additional energy demands on top of the industrial base load. Thus many countries in Western Europe lost their energy self-sufficiency through industrialization, general affluence, and decline in coal production. Nevertheless, there are a variety of ways whereby many countries can expand their domestic energy production and thereby become substantially more self-reliant than they are at present.

A country may fully exploit its present domestic energy resource base regardless of cost. Many governments of industrial countries are likely to find this politically unfeasible. They will probably settle for something less than substantial self-sufficiency in the interests of economic development or environmental protection or both. But countries such as Canada and Australia, which are industrially advanced and yet possess large undeveloped resource bases, may find their long-term prospects quite secure this way.

A country may also expand its current domestic supply base by adding new resources. A political way to accomplish this would be to extend its claims of jurisdiction over off-shore energy resources, perhaps at the expense of others. Thus China, Taiwan, and Japan have asserted conflicting claims to the continental shelf in the China Sea, and Greece and Turkey have been on the verge of war over the offshore oil resources of the Aegean Sea.

The scientific way of expanding the domestic resource base is to develop the technology required to tap new energy sources, such as thermonuclear fusion and solar radiation. The scientific approach to self-sufficiency may avoid the substantial costs associated with other approaches—slower economic growth or greater environmental pollution or increased international tension. However, the pay-offs of science often seem elusive and remote, especially when immediate political interests are at stake.

For any option to expand domestic energy supplies to actually increase a country's security, a variety of conditions must exist. Adequate undeveloped reserves of a particular energy resource must be under national control. If, for example, a country currently imports 50 percent of its energy and has sufficient (though higher-cost) domestic resources to develop and sustain a productive capacity that would reduce its imports to 10 to 20 percent of requirements, then expansion of domestic energy production could substantially enhance energy security. If, on the other hand, a country imports 85 percent of its energy supplies and has sufficient domestic resources to cut imports to 60 percent, the security gains from expanding domestic production would seem to be much smaller.

Beyond resources, in order for domestic supply expansion to increase security, a country would have to possess or develop the other assets required for energy independence—the requisite fuel cycle facilities, managerial capabilities, and finance. Otherwise, in developing its domestic energy resources, the country would be trading one form of dependence for another. The security-enhancing effects of expanding domestic energy production may therefore be limited to industrial countries with adequate untapped energy sources. Many less developed countries, even those with domestic resources that are potentially adequate, may not be able to enhance their security in this way, since they lack the know-how and capital.

Qualifications should be added to this analysis, however. First, a less developed country may opt for the long hard row of self-reliance, emulating the People's Republic of China. This seems to imply a stable authoritarian form of government in order to have the domestic political will to resist the temptation to trade a bit of security in order to gain more rapid economic development. Second, a less developed country may concentrate its efforts and advance rapidly in a particular sector of the energy economy. India has done this with nuclear power, achieving in two decades a posture of substantial nuclear power self-sufficiency, albeit on a small scale.

Increased domestic production is thus likely to enhance the energy security of a nation such as the United States, Canada, Australia, Argentina, or India. But such efforts are likely to contribute much less to the security of heavily industrialized, large energy importers, such as Japan and most of the West European countries. In this connection, the North Sea oil reserves being developed by Britain and Norway may dramatically improve the energy security of these two countries in the 1980s but have relatively little impact on the supply security of Western Europe as a whole unless the reserves prove to be very large indeed.

In any event, the expansion of domestic energy production will take a long time, while foreign supplies remain interruptible on very short notice with potentially massive economic damage. New productive capacity takes years to bring on stream. Then, once it is on stream, the country that has it is stuck with it. The government cannot turn it off in order to increase imports in order to take advantage of a lower world market price. Therefore substantial subsidies and marketing guarantees may be required if private enterprise is expected to play the leading role in expanding high-cost domestic energy production as a way of increasing national security.

In concluding this discussion from the energy-importing country's viewpoint, two indirect effects of the pursuit of self-sufficiency should be noted. One is a benefit and the other a detriment to the security of the world community as a whole.

The benefit is that one country will, by reducing its level of energy imports, reduce competition among other importers and increase it among exporters in the world market. Thus if the U.S. enhances its security through reducing its oil imports, the energy security of the rest of the OECD countries will also be improved. The reverse is also true. The rapid shift of the U.S. from self-sufficiency to being the largest oil importer during the early 1970s diminished the energy security not only of the U.S. but of all other oil-importing countries.

Nuclear power, however, is a specific case where the pursuit of national self-sufficiency may destabilize international security. This case, mentioned previously, deserves further discussion. The civilian nuclear power program of a country which already possesses nuclear weapons may or may not be self-sufficient, but this is largely irrelevant to the security threat its weapons capability may pose to other countries. However, nuclear power self-sufficiency for a country without nuclear weapons means that it would be impossible to deter or prevent diversion of nuclear fuels from civilian to military purposes by foreign interruption of nuclear fuel supplies or critical services. Consequently, a non-nuclear-weapon nation which, at great cost, develops a self-contained nuclear power program may appear thereby to threaten the security of neighboring countries.

A variety of offsetting responses may be considered by a country that feels itself threatened by another country's nuclear power program. The country perceiving a threat may seek to develop its own nuclear self-sufficiency. Civilian nuclear power development in the two countries involved would then take on some of the attributes of an arms race. Alternatively, a small country faced by a hostile neighbor with a large self-sufficient nuclear power capacity may decide to acquire nuclear weapons preemptively. The government may conclude that a plutonium stockpile in the neighboring country, coupled with the possibly short time between a decision to develop nuclear weapons and actual deployment of nuclear warheads, creates an untenable security situation unless it arms itself with its own nuclear deterrent.

A final issue in this regard is whether coercive measures may be justified in order to prevent a country from diverting nuclear fuel to weapons. An importing country may have agreed in advance to the interruption of its fuel supplies if it engages in nuclear diversion. Such a condition is part of the sanctions for violations under the IAEA safeguards system and the Nonproliferation Treaty. In such circumstances, nuclear fuel supply interruptions would be not only warranted but a necessary response to diversion.

More intense coercion, such as armed intervention to prevent diversion of nuclear fuels to weapon use, does not seem justified. The Kremlin has reportedly considered a surgical strike to take out China's nascent nuclear arms capability, and Soviet leaders have hinted at forcible intervention in West Germany if necessary to prevent nuclear weapon acquisition. However, it now seems widely recognized that the decision whether or not to acquire nuclear weapons is a sovereign prerogative. Thus interruptible nuclear fuel supplies and strong interdependence among nuclear power programs may be an important feature of energy security and international security broadly considered.

Exporting Country Security

Exporting country views of energy security are in several respects the reciprocal of importing country perspectives on the same problem. While an importing country is concerned primarily with access to resources and supply security, an energy exporter is preoccupied with access to markets and security of demand. However, the exporter's security problem also contains distinctive features such as the basic concern about national sovereignty over its natural resources. Moreover, an exporter's particular viewpoint, and hence its security requirements, will depend on the extent of its energy resource base and the stage of its industrialization.

CONCEPTS

An exporting country may view energy security solely as national sovereignty over its energy resources, or it may view security more broadly as sovereignty over resources plus guaranteed access to foreign markets. Even more expansively, an exporter may view security as sovereignty plus market access plus financial security for the assets it receives in exchange for energy raw materials.

Sovereignty over natural resources is perhaps the minimum energy security concept for the exporter. This very concept was only belatedly and grudgingly accepted by the oil-importing countries in the 1970s. Sovereignty in this respect has a double aspect: security against military intervention to deprive a nation of control over its energy resources, and freedom from external interference in national decision making regarding exploitation of those resources. This does not preclude a variety of more or less important roles for foreign enterprise, either private or government owned. It does require, however, that the appropriate role be a matter of national decision, not foreign dictation.

Recognition and observance of national sovereignty over natural resources seem to be necessary security conditions for every country. They may not, however, be sufficient as a security concept for many energy exporters. Since World War II the world oil market has suffered decades of glut and only a few years of artificial scarcity; coal has been abundant except when there were labor difficulties; the excess production capacity has overhung the world uranium market. Therefore an exporter may adopt, as a corollary to sovereignty over its basic raw materials, a concept of energy security that includes guaranteed access to foreign markets. Demand security may be as important to energy exporters as supply security is to importers. This raises possibilities for mutually beneficial negotiations between exporters and importers, based on overlapping areas of interest in stability and equilibrium.

Beyond sovereignty and market access, an exporter may stretch the concept of energy security to cover financial security for the investments made with its export earnings. This seems to be overreaching. Nevertheless, energy resources below ground are a precious national heritage. Once extracted, that heritage can easily be lost by an improvident government or eroded by inflation. Thus exporting countries may be seriously concerned about preserving the value of investments made with oil earnings.

Here again exporters and importers seem drawn toward each other in their reciprocal concerns for energy security. The importer that conceives energy security as guaranteed supplies sufficient to fuel a growing national economy seems to be asking too much. So also, the exporter that seeks a guaranteed market and investment security seems to be over-reaching. Here, however, may be a basis for bargaining between equals.

STRATEGIES

In its search for energy security, an exporting country may attempt to make an importer or importers fundamentally dependent, or it may attempt to forge more balanced inter-dependent export–import relationships.

Countries with raw materials have traditionally been dependent on, and subservient to, the countries with large markets and manufacturing capabilities. The communist countries are a noteworthy exception, however. The Soviet Union —the dominant country—exports raw materials to, and imports mainly manufactured products from, the East European countries. It remains to be seen whether a fundamental shift in political power is now occurring in the noncommunist world away from the country with a market for raw materials and toward the natural resource owner.

A particular resource owner may seek to test the extent of the shift, being satisfied with nothing short of reverse imperialism. A few OPEC members may indeed have visions of such grandeur. But most oil-exporting countries seem fully aware that their cartel rests on a wasting asset and a narrow area of agreement.

Nevertheless, the basic requirement for making the importer fundamentally dependent on the exporter is for the exporter to be in a position of unusual strength. Saudi Arabia may be in such a strong position in oil, while the United States has been in a dominant position in regard to uranium enrichment. Technological development makes the U.S. monopoly of uranium enrichment a temporary situation.

Though economists may consider Saudi Arabia's vast low-cost oil reserves to be technically a wasting asset, if carefully conserved they may be a very durable source of political strength for several generations.

Most energy exporters will be in a posture where they, like most importers, have no alternative to interdependence. In this category are such diverse oil-exporting countries as Venezuela, Nigeria, Indonesia, and Iran. The change created by the new energy situation is that now such exporters need not settle for less than real equality in their interdependent relations.

Measures

Measures to enhance the energy security of an exporting country may be grouped for discussion under the three basic security concepts outlined above.

Security against military intervention. We considered in Chapter 1 the post-World War II drive in new or less developed nations to gain sovereign control over their natural resources. Aimed at ousting foreign private enterprises from their strategic resource control positions, the movement has been largely successful. The process of supplanting the old oil concessions with new service contracts is nearing completion. In the future evolution of the world energy situation, this political aspect of national sovereignty is likely to be relatively unimportant as an international issue. Therefore our discussion here is limited to the military aspect of national sovereignty, namely, freedom from foreign armed intervention in order to secure access to a country's natural resources.

The possibility of Western military intervention in the Persian Gulf in the event of another Arab–Israeli war or Arab oil embargo has been mentioned often. In dealing with this possibility from the exporter's viewpoint, the first issue is whether there is a credible risk. Apart from the effectiveness of possible defensive action by the Gulf states themselves, there are several factors working against military intervention by the United States or one or more West European countries to gain control over some of the Persian Gulf oil fields.

Western intervention would raise a serious risk of Soviet counteraction in a region where the Soviet Union enjoys substantial geographic and logistic advantages. If the U.S. militarily intervened alone, it might find itself in a direct confrontation with Soviet armed forces in a location where escalation would be a serious possibility and would work in favor of the Soviets. Moreover, the NATO allies and Japan might be suspicious of unilateral action by the United States, since U.S. interests both in regard to Israel and Middle East oil are not the same as the interests of the other OECD countries.

If certain West European countries intervened without the United States, again the lack of a congruent set of trans-Atlantic interests in the Middle East might prompt the U.S. to object strongly. The U.S. reaction would be especially strong if, as is likely, the Soviet Union threatened counteraction that would generally involve NATO security interests.

Finally, the likelihood of the U.S. and a group of West European countries launching a coordinated military intervention in the Middle East seems more remote now than in 1956. Then, Great Britain and France took over the Suez Canal ostensibly to protect Western Europe's oil lifeline, the Soviet Union rattled its rockets, and the United States declared itself opposed to the action of its NATO allies.

In addition to the risks of intra-NATO and East–West conflicts, military intervention in the Persian Gulf would have repercussions throughout the Third World. The precedent that such action would establish is likely to be perceived widely as a threat to all raw material suppliers. Though powerless to react militarily, the Third World countries would be likely to develop a very hostile diplomatic response.

Beyond these adverse consequences of intervention it is difficult to see how Western seizure of the Persian Gulf oil fields could accomplish anything positive. If a more secure flow of oil to the OECD countries were the objective, armed intervention would be a short-term expedient that would be self-defeating in the long run. The oil could stop flowing after the military force was withdrawn. Military intervention might thus entrap the intervenor.

Moreover, it is difficult to imagine a basically more pro-Western group of rulers than the present Shah of Iran and the Arab gulf state sheiks. Any intervention to overthrow one or more of this group would be likely to unleash the very revolutionary forces that the present rulers of most Middle East countries have long feared and sought to avoid.

It is also difficult to see how military intervention in the Gulf could help Israel. The immediate provocation for intervention might be an Arab embargo instituted because of lack of progress toward an Arab-Israeli political settlement and an Arab desire to pressure the U.S. into pressuring Israel. If so, U.S. intervention would be likely to make both sides in the Arab–Israeli conflict more intransigent. With U.S. forces occupying the rear areas behind the frontline Arab countries, the prospects for any negotiated settlement of the conflict would be bleak.

The immediate provocation for intervention might, however, be renewed warfare between the Arabs and Israel. If so, U.S. military intervention in the Gulf states would be likely to make both sides fight that much harder. If the survival of Israel were seriously threatened, a direct approach via a landing in Israel itself would seem more politically relevant, less risky in terms of a U.S.–Soviet confrontation, and more likely to be militarily effective than any direct action against the oil producers.

Given the risks involved and the probable lack of positive results, Western military intervention in the Persian Gulf thus seems quite implausible as a course of action, even without considering specific measures the Gulf states may take to protect themselves. There are, however, three steps that these states could take that would greatly raise the cost of Western armed intervention.

One is to ensure that oil production capacity would be rendered inoperable for a long period of time following intervention and military takeover. This may be accomplished by last-minute destruction of certain key facilities, such as pipelines from producing fields to ports or the port facilities themselves. These facilities could be rebuilt, though presumably imported labor and materials would be required. This would take at least a few months, and in the meantime oil supplies from the Gulf would be more or less completely stopped.

Emergency oil stockpiles in the OECD countries may or may not be sufficient to offset the stoppage that would occur following intervention. The size of an emergency reserve would be an important factor, of course. In addition, unless the intervention were fully authorized in advance, any OECD emergency sharing agreement might not be put into effect to assist an intervenor.

A second, additional step against intervention is to build up armed forces capable of resisting. As mentioned earlier, this is under way as a result of massive Western arms sales to the Gulf states in exchange for oil. If the Western countries have ever seriously contemplated military intervention in the Gulf states, they have acted in a self-defeating manner.

A third possibility would be to add a collective security arrangement to OPEC or the Gulf state component of OPEC. This might take the form of a pledge on the part of all participating countries to interrupt immediately all oil supplies to any country that intervenes militarily or supports intervention by another. In this connection it may be noted that the U.S. would find it very difficult to provide necessary logistical support for a large deployment of U.S. forces into the Gulf region unless some countries en route were willing to cooperate.

A collective security aspect to OPEC might not be negotiable in advance in view of Iran's differences with the Arabs, but it might be tacitly understood and a collective response could be quickly carried out.

The Gulf states can therefore quite easily make the costs of a foreign military takeover of their oil production capacity prohibitively high. These direct costs are in addition to the difficulties of full agreement among OECD countries, the risks of Soviet intervention, and the adverse impact on industrial country relations generally with the less developed countries. Taken together, these factors appear to effectively rule out a Western military takeover of oil fields in the Persian Gulf region as a rational course of action.

Access to markets. An exporting country's interest in guaranteed access to foreign markets is the reciprocal of an importer's interest in access to energy resources. In a seller's market, of course, buyers want long-term contracts at guaranteed prices, but in a buyer's market it is the suppliers that want firm arrangements. Over time, however, an exporter's perception of its security interests may change even though the world market remains quite favorable to the seller.

For example, an oil exporter with a large population is likely to plow back most of its oil revenues into domestic industrialization. As this process advances and gains momentum, the country may become more, rather than less, dependent on a stable flow of oil revenue. Strong dependence on foreign exchange earning may continue until the modernization process is complete and a fully diversified economy is in being. In such circumstances an exporter may consider an assured outlet for oil to be a direct security concern. Here we have a security problem that grows out of economic success.

An exporter may seek to guarantee its access to foreign markets through any one or more of the interdependent arrangements we considered earlier from the importer's view-point. Long-term supply contracts may be negotiated, invest-ments may be made downstream, and so forth.

The important point is that once an energy exporter per-ceives that its particular security interests are served by pur-suing interdependence, there will emerge a wide area for fruitful negotiation with importers which similarly perceive their security interests. Such a common perception seems most likely to emerge between the industrial countries of Western Europe and Japan, on the one hand, and the more populous and rapidly developing OPEC countries, on the other.

*   *   *

The relationship between energy and national security is a vital concern to the world community. But there is no set of energy security principles applicable to every country. Energy self-sufficiency, sovereignty over energy resources, and inter-dependence are general concepts that lead to quite different results depending on the specific circumstances of the country applying them.

Since every country will have a vital interest in its energy security and yet each will view the matter differently, at-tempts at large solutions are likely to fail. The energy security of the world community as a whole may be improved if national governments recognize the need for a particularized approach not only to their own energy security problem but also to every other country's. In a world without a central government, there is no substitute for national self-restraint in the pursuit of security.

Chapter 4

Energy and the World
Economy

THE WORLD ECONOMIC STRUCTURE has evolved beyond the
nation–state, though some national governments may attempt
to deny it. A world economy of sorts exists, although the destructive behavior of an insecure nation or group of nations
may still pull it apart. It would be very difficult to describe
the "world economy" accurately or in detail. But for our
purposes the term includes the aggregate of the national
economies of the noncommunist industrial countries. It also
embraces the economies of those less developed countries that
are in fact advancing. The East European communist countries are beginning to participate in the world economy, while
some of the less developed countries are losing ground.

In the context of an evolving world economy, there are
four key energy issues: the economic efficiency of energy use,
the role of energy in economic development, the role of private
multinational corporations in the energy sector, and management of the financial aspect of the international oil trade.
The fact that has pushed these four issues to the forefront is

OPEC's quadrupling of world oil prices in 1973–74. This chapter discusses them in turn, not in a technical sense, but rather to perceive their political implications. A related issue, energy conservation, is considered in Chapter 5.

If the order of presentation indicates priority, then many experts would argue that it should be reversed, or at least that financial issues should be moved to the top. If urgency were our criterion, the experts would be correct. The monetary and investment problems must be currently managed or the other issues may never be reached. Oil import bills may bankrupt some of the weaker national economies, thereby threatening the interdependent structure of the world economy as a whole. However, our purpose is to gain a sense of direction for the long run. We have stated the issues in a reasonable order to develop a broader understanding of underlying causes and conflicting interests.

Energy Efficiency

The earth is plentifully endowed with a rich variety of energy resources. What is an efficient way for the world community to develop and use these resources? This is the basic economic question. The direct answer is: The most efficient way is whatever way incurs the least cost. In economic terms, efficiency equates with costs, and the problem of doing anything efficiently becomes a problem of doing it in the least costly way possible.

The major (though not the only) factor contributing presently to an inefficient use of the world's energy resources is the price of oil. Oil prices now bear no relation to costs. The costs of producing oil from OPEC's developed reserves have not increased substantially. Only the price has increased.

In this section, therefore, we first explore the basic problems in determining costs and a variety of other approaches to energy efficiency. Then we consider the risks and costs of the inefficiencies that may flow from current world oil prices.

ECONOMIC EFFICIENCY

Whether a society is structured according to capitalist or socialist principles, the economic objective is the efficient use of resources to achieve whatever ultimate values the society establishes. The capitalist argues that a private market in which buyers and sellers freely exchange money for goods and services is the most efficient allocation mechanism. Of course for a free market to function efficiently, buyers and sellers must be guided by perfect information and disciplined by pure competition. On the other hand, the socialist argues that state ownership of the means of production and government planning of the output of goods and services results in the most efficient use of resources. Government omniscience and benevolence must be assumed. Governmental benevolence in the socialist economy thus substitutes for competition in the capitalist market, but both rest on an assumption of more knowledge than is humanly possible to obtain.

Simply outlining the two conflicting ideals suffices to show how far they both are from achievement in the real world. Nevertheless, the point remains that cost is the primary measure of efficiency in either a market or a planned economy.

The efficient development and use of the earth's energy resources involves a continuous effort aimed at the low-cost alternatives. If oil is cheaper than coal for electric power generation, oil will be used. But if and when electricity can be produced more cheaply with nuclear fuel than with oil, nuclear power will replace oil-fired generation. Costs tend to rise as nonrenewable natural resources are depleted. However, such increases may stimulate a search for additional resources of the same fuel or for a different fuel that is a substitute. Moreover, technological improvements may reduce costs. Over time, technological change may or may not fully offset cost increases resulting from resource depletion and other factors.

Energy costs must also be viewed in relation to other cost trends in the economy. For example, if energy costs are increasing, but more slowly than other factors determining the cost of food, then it would be efficient to use more energy in food production.

Cost as the criterion of economic efficiency is a simple concept that becomes both complicated and imprecise in its application. We only outline a few of the more important difficulties below.

First, marginal or incremental costs should be used to determine efficiencies, not original or historical costs. In choosing the most efficient pattern of energy development and use, we should face future, not after-the-fact, costs. Therefore, in deciding whether to develop additional oil production capacity in the Persian Gulf or on the Alaskan North Slope, we base the choice on a comparison of the total costs associated with an additional increment of production from each source.

Marginal costs as a basis for resource allocation are thus estimated, not actual, or incurred. Such estimates often prove to be substantially inaccurate. Therefore, the practical application of marginal cost principles involves assumptions about an uncertain future, with the degree of uncertainty being reflected in cost as a risk premium.

Second, we face a difficult and elusive problem in determining what items are to be included as costs. Of course we consider all operating costs and capital charges. This includes a reasonable return on capital investment. But we should also take account of so-called "externalities," or social costs, such as environmental pollution and health and safety hazards. Externalities may be internalized more or less fully, by either performance standards or taxing schemes. Thus quantified, they are reflected in costs fully or in part.

But societies are often slow to recognize the existence of externalities. Even after a harmful environmental effect is recognized, a society may choose to tolerate the burden or only reduce it slightly. Rarely is an environmental or social cost fully internalized. Moreover, the quantification of social costs is an imprecise art. Thus there will usually remain ample room for debate about which energy choice is the more efficient, even after detailed cost comparisons are available.

A third cost problem is time horizons. Investments in energy resources are long term, and many of the costs associated with energy production and consumption are also long term. The owner of a depletable resource such as oil will produce a barrel of oil today if the profit he expects to make from it, including the return on investment of the proceeds of sale, exceeds the profit he would expect if he were instead to produce that barrel any time in the future. Present values may be imputed to future benefits and costs through the use of discount rates.

The choice of discount rate is often decisive in determining whether a particular long-term investment in energy is worthwhile and also in determining how much of an energy resource to produce currently. Yet the appropriate rate is a factor on which reasonable men may and do differ.

Finally, economic efficiency is in theory indifferent to the problem of income distribution. The chips fall where they may. If this results in a pattern of wealth distribution that is deemed undesirable, redistribution may be effected through mechanisms such as income taxes and subsidies. The redistribution of wealth through energy prices that are either too high or too low in relation to costs is, however, an economically inefficient use of energy resources.

Government regulation in the United States, which favored the consumer, kept the price of natural gas artificially low during the 1960s. Regulatory policy stimulated demand, reduced incentives to discover and develop additional supplies, and was thus a major cause of the current gas shortage. In retrospect, the post-World War II development and use of natural gas in the United States appears to have occurred in an inefficient manner. The OPEC cartel is now setting the world price of oil artificially high. This too is resulting in gross inefficiencies.

Despite the difficulties involved, applying least cost as the criterion of efficiency helps to discipline our thinking about energy matters. For example, a heat pump is not necessarily more efficient than another type of space-conditioning system simply because the pump requires less energy input per unit of energy output than the other system. Rather, comparative efficiency depends on which system results in the lowest total cost—capital and operating—over the lifetime of the system involved. Similarly, solar heating is not more efficient than electric or gas heating simply because it draws upon a zero-cost, renewable energy resource. Rather, the question is whether solar heating is the cheapest alternative in terms of its total costs, including the high cost of solar collectors and the cost of stand-by electric or gas utility service for use in bad weather.

Difficulties with the cost criterion have led to suggestions of a variety of other approaches to energy efficiency. At one extreme is the large-scale relationship between energy consumption and gross national product (GNP). According to this criterion, an economy with increasing energy efficiency would be indicated by a decreasing ratio between the growth rate in energy use and the growth rate in GNP. Increasing energy efficiency would thus be shown if the growth rate in energy use declined in a decade from 4 percent to 3 percent while the GNP maintained a constant growth of 4 percent over the same period.

The energy/GNP ratio may be useful in the context of a mature industrial economy with relatively stable price relationships. However, it does not apply to a developing economy. In a move from a simple agrarian society to a modern mechanized agricultural society, energy requirements are likely to grow faster than total output. In further development from a predominantly agricultural into an industrial society, energy growth is likely to outpace the GNP to an even larger extent.

Even in a mature industrial economy, preferences for environmental quality, such as less air pollution, or technological barriers, such as the metallurgy of steam turbines, can cause a declining energy/GNP ratio to reverse. However, the shift from heavy industry toward a service-oriented economy may reduce energy input per GNP output by an amount that is large enough to cancel out or cover the fact that energy efficiency is declining within the industrial sector alone.

At the other extreme is the criterion of energy resource use as a measure of the efficiency of specific processes or activities. Stated most simply, the argument is that less is better. Applying the energy use criterion to transportation, for example, and judging efficiency by the relationship between miles traveled and fuels consumed per traveler, the bicycle appears to be more efficient than the bus or train, either of which is more efficient than the airplane. Such an approach ignores the opportunity cost of the time needed to go from suburb to city on a bicycle. It is true, of course, that there are much more efficient ways of moving people than by the private automobile, especially the American behemoth. Energy efficiency is a much more complex matter, however, than simple application of a "less is better" criterion.

The large, heavy cars of the early 1970s were in part due to affluence and widespread desires for the comforts that large horsepower could provide, but they were also a consequence of low and historically falling real prices for gasoline. The overall efficiency of private automobiles versus public transportation must in any event be determined on a broader basis than merely the single criterion of energy use. The configuration of population settlements in a vast country such as the United States may tend to produce a transportation system more dependent on individual automobiles than a compact and densely populated country such as Belgium.

Efficiency considerations also apply to energy production. From the physical characteristics of an oil or gas reservoir we may calculate a rate of production that will result in maximum recovery over the lifetime of the reservoir concerned. This is known as the maximum efficient rate of production. However, considerations beyond the maximum efficient rate may enter into decisions regarding actual production rates. In a noncompetitive market such as petroleum, it may pay an oil exporter to reduce production in order to maintain a high price. If foreign supply is interrupted, it may pay an importing country to exceed the optimum production rate from domestic wells to meet demand. Similarly, flaring of natural gas associated with oil may be reasonable economic behavior, though the flared gas is lost to future generations, as long as there is no nearby market for the gas or there is no technology available for transporting the gas to a distant market for delivery to customers at competitive costs.

Finally, per capita energy consumption is sometimes used as the basis for comparing efficiency of energy use in various industrial countries. Per capita energy consumption in the United States is currently about twice that in several large West European countries. This fact leads to the question, Is the quality of life in America twice as good as in Western Europe? Or, are the people living on the western shore of the North Atlantic twice as happy as the people on the eastern shore? In many cases, differences in such indicators as per capita energy consumption may be traced to specific economic or structural factors. Much is explained by income disparities between countries. Those who have more money to spend can buy more energy.

The important point is that the relationship between levels of energy use and quality of life is far from clear. A very broad frame of reference is necessary to evaluate the role of energy in society.

INEFFICIENCY OF WORLD OIL PRICES

As of mid-1975, the multinational oil companies were paying roughly $10 per barrel for oil from Persian Gulf sources. The cost of production is 10 to 20 cents per barrel, and the rest of the $10 price is government revenue. The shocking discrepancy between cost and price colors the entire world energy scene. The current level of oil prices is causing inflation and recession in all oil-importing countries, is retarding economic development and reducing food supplies in poor countries, and is converting an oil weapon into a money weapon.

Yet the world's known reserves of low-cost oil appear adequate to meet projected worldwide demand for a few decades at least. If the governments of the main exporting countries are able to maintain the OPEC cartel, the high oil price may, by restraining demand, stretch the lifetime of low-cost oil reserves even further. In these circumstances, pressing for substantially lower world oil prices is more than a short-term expedient. Indeed, it may be viewed as a long-term economic strategy. How might such a strategy be carried out?

One way would be to discover additional oil provinces that are comparable in magnitude and production costs to those centered in the Persian Gulf. In 1974 many new oil discoveries were reported, adding billions of barrels to oil reserves outside the OPEC countries. These discoveries may add significantly to world oil production capacity by 1980. But despite these new finds, the Persian Gulf remains unique in the world as the location of enormous reserves of oil (and natural gas) with very low costs of production.

A second way to lower oil prices would be to break down the OPEC cartel and restore price competition in the world market for crude oil. The U.S. government argues that the OPEC price agreement could be breached by concerted action of the OECD countries to restrain demand and develop alternative supplies. Others assert that indirect attacks on the producers' cartel would be more effective.

One idea is to fix an absolute ceiling on oil imports and auction off import tickets through secret bidding. This would provide a way for oil exporters to lower their prices without fear of disclosing their identities, and the seizure of such opportunities by exporters would create competitive pressure downward on oil prices. Another suggestion is to break up the integrated operations of multinational oil companies downstream from the wellhead. Such action would be intended to achieve a more competitive industry structure overall, and would make it more difficult for the OPEC country governments to exert monopoly power by making the oil companies in effect their agents for collecting rents or taxes from the consumers.

In the meantime, exorbitant world oil prices will have a relatively small effect on the demand/supply balance in the short run. The quadrupled oil price merely flattened the forecast demand growth; demand has not fallen off substantially. Nor have the increased oil prices drawn forth large additions to currently producible supplies. In the economist's language, both oil demand and supply are relatively price inelastic in the short run. "Short run" here could mean a painfully long period of at least five years. This is because on the demand side we are locked into a whole stock of energy-using facilities and processes that cannot be changed rapidly. The stock can only be run at less than full capacity.

On the supply side, at or near current world oil prices a range of alternative fossil energy resources may become economical. These include oil and gas resources under the outer continental shelves and in arctic regions, natural gas liquefaction, and long-distance transportation, coal gasification or liquefaction, and oil extraction from tar sands and shale. However, a significant response in terms of increased fossil energy supplies at higher costs cannot be expected for at least a decade. Moreover, high oil prices would tend to accelerate the installation of nuclear power, but this effect in the short term has been more than offset by reduced demand for electricity due to the general economic slowdown and by financial difficulties in electric utility industries arising largely out of general inflation.

Thus there is no shortage of paths to pursue to bring large supplies of energy within reach, assuming the benefits are deemed to outweigh the risks and costs. However, the outstanding fact about these options is that it will require large investments of capital and many years before any of them will make a substantial difference in the world energy picture. Moreover, many of them require the development of new technologies before commercial exploitation can proceed. Finally, the environmental costs of many of the options appear substantially greater than use of existing low-cost fossil fuel resources.

The potential development of solid hydrocarbons in the U.S. serves as a good illustration of the large inefficiencies that current world oil prices lead toward. Many countries that lack indigenous oil and gas supplies have solid hydrocarbon resources—coal or oil shale—that they could develop. Few countries have deposits that approach the quality of those in the United States. Therefore the U.S. is in as strong a position as any of the noncommunist industrial countries to become substantially independent of oil imports from the Middle East. But the price would be very high.

U.S. achievement of energy self-sufficiency would entail, among a variety of measures, the increased use of coal. Where coal can be burned directly, as in current electric power generation, it can be used with about the same efficiency as oil. Where liquids or gases are required or preferred, coal may be converted to either form. If coal is either gasified or liquefied, however, 20 to 35 percent of the energy content is lost in conversion, depending on the type of gas manufactured and the process used.

Synthetic fuels made from coal or oil shale, using resources of the highest quality, may have a price almost as high per heat unit obtained in combustion as the current price of world oil. A synthetic fuel industry would be very capital intensive. A plant to make 100,000 barrels of liquid fuel per day (less than 1 percent of domestic petroleum demand) may cost about $1 billion. Research and development may reduce the costs of synthetics somewhat, but not bring them close to the costs (as distinguished from the current prices) of Middle East oil.

It seems unlikely, short of a wartime commitment, that as much as 10 percent of U.S. petroleum demand in 1985 could be met by synthetic fuels production from coal and oil shale. And even though a major effort would produce only a small percentage of U.S. energy requirements, there would be massive environmental problems to overcome. These problems are taken up in Chapter 5.

One final point about the development of high-cost energy resources, such as solid hydrocarbons, must be made. It will drive home the character and magnitude of the inefficiencies that are likely to flow from the current high OPEC oil prices.

It might appear that the availability of higher-cost energy resources would reduce demand pressures in the world oil market and pave the way to OPEC's break-up. The cost of effective substitutes for Persian Gulf oil does establish a ceiling on the monopoly price that OPEC may extract. However, the OPEC monopoly price, or a price somewhat below it, may also be viewed as a floor on which private investments in alternative energy resources must rest. Governments will either have to underwrite private investments and guarantee them against a future reduction in oil price or make direct investments themselves in the development of higher-cost energy resources.

The costs of these actions will be high, and they will ultimately be borne by consumers in the prices or taxes they pay. Thus U.S. achievement of energy self-sufficiency or implementation of comparable plans by other countries will result in irrevocable commitments on a large scale to an inefficient pattern of world energy use.

Is it therefore clear that the world would be much better off if much lower oil prices were reestablished? The primary beneficiaries would be the present generation of consumers in both rich and poor countries. Prices derived from costs rather than monopoly power could, however, induce a growth rate in world demand for oil that would drain even the Persian Gulf's low-cost reserves in a few decades. Then, with a much larger population, the world would face the painful adjustment process that is now under way.

Economic Development

The 1973–74 oil price increases halted economic development worldwide except in the OPEC countries, where development was rapidly accelerated. The general inflation–recession effects of current oil price levels have been especially severe in industrial countries with already weak economies, such as Great Britain and Italy, and in less developed countries (LDCs) apart from OPEC members. In this section we consider economic development options for oil-importing LDCs and development policy for oil-exporting LDCs, a group composed of essentially all the OPEC members except for the sparsely populated Arab countries.

Oil-Importing LDCs

In oil-importing LDCs a high oil price makes a direct hit on the economic vitals, agriculture and industry. There are few if any nonessential uses of energy in LDCs. High oil prices translate directly into higher costs for the fuel and fertilizer required for domestic food production, and into higher costs for boiler fuel needed for industrial production and electric power generation. Moreover, high oil prices have undesirable indirect effects in the Third World. The prices of LDC imports from industrial countries are increased by the inflationary effects of oil price increases. The market for LDC exports in industrial countries is shrunk by the recessionary effects of high oil prices. And finally, the flow of long-term development aid from industrial countries to the LDCs is likely to be reduced.

The abrupt world oil price increases of 1973–74 hit LDC's that were in various stages of economic development and confronted by a wide variety of development obstacles. A country-by-country breakdown is beyond our scope. However, it is useful to think in terms of LDCs that have "taken off" in the economic development process, LDCs where the oil price may abort a take-off, and LDCs where the oil price will worsen an already deteriorating situation. In addition, we must take account of an LDC's indigenous energy resources and capabilities.

Such a categorization hinges on a definition of "take off" in economic development, and there is also the problem of drawing a line between developed and less developed countries. However, such a classification provides a basis for priorities. With limited assistance available, it is better to concentrate on countries where foreign aid can make a difference rather than spread available assistance so thinly that no country is substantially helped.

Faced with a quadrupled price, an oil-importing LDC has three basic options. First, it may simply absorb curtailed imports through a reduction in its gross national product (GNP). Second, it may attempt to offset the increase in its oil import bill with increases in the prices for its exports. And third, it may seek increased development assistance from foreign sources. In the context of any of these options, an LDC may redesign its development plans specifically to emphasize energy conservation.

Reduction in GNP. Some reduction in GNP is almost certain in every oil-importing LDC. The extent will vary widely, depending on particular national economic circumstances.

If an LDC's economy has already taken off, the high oil import prices may cause it to crash-land. The constraints imposed by very high energy costs may make it impossible to recapture development momentum after an initial adjustment period. The country's development strategy may rest on assumptions that are wiped out by high energy prices. Moreover, the government may be too weak to take the decisive actions required to meet the challenge.

However, an LDC would be starting into the new energy situation from a much narrower base and with more flexibility than an industrial country, and it may be able to adjust more easily and quickly. An LDC government may thus perceive in the new situation an opportunity to narrow the gap between it and the industrial world. To have much chance of success, the government would need to be firmly in power and willing to adopt policies that would attract substantial private foreign investment. Nevertheless, the high oil price might stimulate modernization in an LDC in order to resume overall development as soon as possible. This could include adoption at the outset of energy-conserving forms of industrial technology, as well as development of any high-cost domestic energy resources that were available, and perhaps heavy emphasis on nuclear power.

An LDC that had not yet reached the economic take-off stage when the oil crisis hit may be better off in some ways than one that had already felt the exhilaration of a few development successes. The government would not have committed itself to a particular development strategy, and popular expectations of more in the future would not have been aroused. Underlying assumptions could be reexamined, strategy changed, and future effort and priorities reallocated without affecting vested political interests. In such circumstances, the LDC's choice may now be whether to attempt a leapfrog over the energy-intensive steps in economic development or to settle permanently for some form of subsistence level society. The leapfrog approach would involve basing economic development on social service delivery systems that require much less energy input than the systems presently used in industrial countries. In this sense the question is whether an LDC might invent a development approach that would bypass industrialization and yet achieve a high standard of social welfare for its people.

Finally, some LDCs were caught in a process of economic deterioration even before the oil price increases. The crisis has accelerated deterioration, but the effect on long-run development prospects is unclear. A country may sink beneath the subsistence level. Or an acceleration of economic deterioration may be a catalyst for political change. The change may produce a more effective national government and consequently a somewhat brighter economic outlook.

Offsetting increases in LDC export prices. An LDC may attempt to offset the increase in its oil import bill with increases in revenues earned on its own exports. In the past the LDCs have vigorously pressed claims for higher prices for their commodity exports and for preferential access to industrial country markets. In this regard oil has been the most dramatic success story so far. It seems unlikely, however, that LDCs will now be generally successful in charging the industrial countries a great deal more for their commodity exports. Indeed, many commodity prices slumped in early 1975. Several Central American countries, for example, attempted to impose a large export tax on bananas to compensate for higher oil prices. But there is substantial excess banana production capacity in Ecuador, an OPEC member. Moreover, bananas are not considered an essential food and there are many substitutes.

The prices of LDC exports may, of course, reflect increased energy costs, just as the prices of industrial country exports. But an attempt to charge even more in order to compensate the entire LDC economy for the increased oil import bill is not likely to succeed. Faced with severe problems with their own economies, the industrial countries may be less inclined now than previously to grant import preferences to the LDCs. In any event, demand in the industrial countries for imports from the LDCs will tend to be less as a result of the wealth being siphoned off by OPEC.

Increases in foreign aid to LDCs. A particular LDC or the LDCs as a group may seek to offset increases in oil import bills by increases in the flow of development aid granted on concessionary terms. The LDCs may turn toward either the industrial countries or the OPEC oil exporters for assistance. And, of course, they may try both.

The industrial countries recognize that the new energy situation raises special problems for the LDCs. However, industrial country governments are largely preoccupied with their own economic difficulties. The most they have been able to accomplish is to prevent substantial cutbacks in the flow of development aid. Meanwhile, inflation is reducing the real amount of aid being transferred.

In these circumstances, if the industrial countries are unable to cope with their own economic difficulties, the LDCs may be hurt badly. If the industrial world enters a prolonged depression, the LDCs will be cut off from both concessionary development assistance and markets for their exports.

Whether the LDCs will get more assistance from the industrial countries by pressing their claims individually or as a group is difficult to judge. An individual approach may pay larger dividends in enough cases to make questionable the desirability of action in concert. In this respect current LDC diplomacy may be out of phase.

The LDCs now have a clear majority in the United Nations and the specialized UN agencies. As a group they have over the years increasingly coordinated their activities and escalated their demands. In 1974 this culminated in the adoption by the UN General Assembly of a Charter on the Economic Rights and Duties of States, a document that is quite uncompromising in its formulation of the Third World position on the major contentious issues. Now, when the LDCs can act effectively as a diplomatic majority, the world economic situation is changed profoundly. The industrial countries are themselves politically incapable of an affirmative response to many of the LDC demands, regardless of their sympathies toward the plight of the Third World countries.

OPEC may thus prove to be a better source of help for the oil-importing LDCs than the industrial world. Following their triumph in the oil price revolution of 1973–74, many OPEC countries quickly recognized a special duty to aid the hard-hit oil-importing LDCs. In this assistance, political self-interest was perhaps a stronger factor than humanitarian motives. Various OPEC members could easily perceive opportunities to use aid to enhance their power regionally as well as within the Third World generally. In this respect OPEC donors of development aid may not be expected to behave very differently from industrial country donors.

Venezuela has aimed a special assistance program toward Central America initially and a broad economic development plan at Latin America generally. Iran has focused on India and Pakistan. The Arab Gulf sheikdoms have been primarily interested in helping out the rest of the Arab world, while Nigeria has extended aid to other countries in black Africa. The magnitude, scope, and effectiveness of these assistance programs remain to be seen, and the "strings" are unclear. But it seems likely that total aid from all sources flowing to the LDCs will still decline rather than expand in the years immediately ahead.

Oil-importing LDCs may seek either oil at concessionary prices or short-term financial assistance that would enable them to pay their oil import bills. A number of OPEC members have reportedly lowered their prices for certain LDC importers.

It is not likely, however, that OPEC will formally adopt a "two tier" pricing system—one price for industrial countries and another for LDCs. Drawing a line between the two categories of importers would involve the cartel as a whole in a series of difficult and disagreeable decisions. Moreover, individual OPEC countries might lose in two-tier pricing much of the political leverage they would otherwise gain through a series of ad hoc aid programs. Finally, even as to their individually sponsored aid programs, the OPEC countries may reject price breaks and opt instead for forms of aid where more strings can be attached.

Despite the damage that OPEC's exorbitant oil prices is causing to their economies, the oil-importing LDCs have thus far sided with OPEC against the industrial countries. The LDC stance may be based on a political calculation such as the following: For the first time in history, a nonindustrial group of countries has forced the noncommunist industrial world into a redistribution of wealth on a large scale. Politically, the fact that the redistribution is occurring is more important than the fact that a large number of LDCs are being hurt while only a few, the OPEC members, are being benefited enormously. The possibilities for obtaining compensatory or concessionary aid from OPEC are greater than the prospects for obtaining more aid from the industrial countries in a world economy where inflation was rampant well before the oil crisis.

LDC OIL EXPORTERS

While the oil price rise slowed—indeed reversed—economic growth in the rest of the noncommunist world, it dramatically accelerated development in the OPEC countries. In considering economic development within OPEC itself, we must bear in mind that today none of the OPEC members have modern industrial economies.

The country that comes the closest is Venezuela. Before the 1973–74 oil price increases Venezuela's per capita income was the highest in Latin America, but it was only one-fifth that of the U.S. Even before the oil price revolution, the sparsely populated Arab oil sheikdoms enjoyed high per capita incomes. This handful of countries, most of them newly formed from former British colonial possessions, are now recording the highest per capita income statistics in the world, and their governments are rapidly becoming the world's bankers. Yet over half the adult population in some of these same countries cannot read or write.

One useful way to categorize the oil-exporting LDCs is according to the capacities of their respective economies to absorb oil revenues at current price levels. In this respect OPEC includes countries that can productively absorb all present and future oil revenues and countries that are piling up large surpluses. Only a few OPEC countries are in the surplus position, and they are all Arab. Countries with sufficient absorptive capacities may be further divided into those that can absorb all their oil revenues and, other things being equal, still remain poor; those that can develop a viable and stable national economy; and those that have the potential for affluence.

OPEC countries may also be classified according to the extent of their oil resources. Here we find that only a few countries have known reserves that may be viewed as providing them with a basic resource beyond the twentieth century (assuming conservation is practiced). Even the vast resources of countries in this category, including Saudi Arabia, could be pumped dry in a few decades if their oil production capacities were to continue to expand to meet the rate of growth in demand that was experienced before the 1973–74 oil price increases.

An oil-exporting LDC may seek to develop into a modern industrial state. This will require a long-term effort, however. A viable industrial economy presupposes a relatively high level of literacy and education among the people. Such a level may take a generation or more to achieve, even with a massive effort. Moreover, if some West European country of today is chosen as its model, the LDC may well achieve an obsolete and uncompetitive form of economy for itself a generation from now. Thus an LDC with an enormous source of new wealth may choose to base its development strategy on its own particular circumstances and social aspirations, rather than measure itself by existing Western standards.

A number of intriguing possibilities arise with respect to industrial diversification within an oil-exporting LDC. A diversification plan may be across the board, or it may build on energy-intensive industries and petrochemicals. Thus a large share of the world's output of refined metals, such as steel or aluminum, and petrochemicals, such as fertilizer, may in the future come from the oil-exporting countries.

For example, at present Saudi Arabia exports some oil to the U.S., which is used to make fertilizer, which is used to grow food, which is given to Bangladesh to reduce starvation among its people. Instead, Saudi Arabia might use that amount of oil to manufacture fertilizer, which could then be given (or sold) to Bangladesh, which could use it to increase its domestic food production. The U.S. could then import less oil and give away less food.

It is also interesting to recall that the nineteenth-century Industrial Revolution in Western Europe and America was centered on coal deposits. An increasing fraction of the world's petroleum is being used as industrial feedstocks and lubricants—more valuable uses than primary fuel. Rather than transport the raw materials to factories in the United States and Western Europe, the industries may be attracted to where the basic resources are located, especially when ample labor is available at the same location.

Some oil-exporting countries may reject Western notions of development, attempting to retain their Arab traditions and culture intact. This would mean either leaving their oil in the ground or producing it and making sure that the wealth is invested overseas so as not to disrupt domestic society. Until recently several of the Arab sheikdoms seemed determined to do this. But it now seems unlikely that an Arab oil exporter, no matter how conservative its regime, will be able to resist rapid and potentially destabilizing change.

In any event, the LDC oil exporters will have a choice in emphasis in their economic planning between economic self-sufficiency and interdependence. We discussed this choice in Chapter 3 in the context of energy security. Self-sufficiency would stress the development of a balanced and diversified economy, while interdependence would stress economic specialization, comparative advantage, and efficiency. Interdependence may make the world community as a whole better off. However, in the absence of a practical and effective international mechanism for wealth redistribution, self-sufficiency may be worth the price. Moreover, a degree of self-sufficiency is necessary for bargaining in an interdependent relationship.

The Role of Private Multinational Oil
Companies

Until the early 1970s the major multinational oil companies—Exxon, Gulf, Mobil, Texaco, Standard Oil of California, British Petroleum (which is 50 percent government owned, but privately managed), Royal Dutch Shell and Compagnie Française des Petroles (which is partly owned by private interests, but largely government controlled)—were the most powerful actors, politically and economically, in the world petroleum market. The flow of oil in the noncommunist world was controlled by a worldwide integrated industry that was primarily under private ownership.

The OPEC governments are now in the process of completing their takeovers of crude oil production. An increasing share of world refinery capacity may, in the future, also be located in the producing countries. Thus on the OPEC side, the private company will serve primarily as a contractor supplying technical know-how, marketing skills, and transport, though some OPEC countries are acquiring tanker fleets and may encroach upon the latter function.

The remaining unresolved issues are largely on the buyers' or consumers' side of the world oil market. Nationalization of the production phase has had large effects on operations downstream in the fuel cycle. It has also perhaps accelerated the trend within the petroleum industry to diversify. Even while OPEC is divorcing the private oil companies from their ownership of low-cost crude oil resources, the expropriated companies are pushing hard into other energy fields. The major multinational oil companies are recycling their own petrodollar earnings, not only by developing new oil and gas reserves but also by investing large sums in coal mines, oil shale leases, and nuclear power. Thus most of them are evolving from oil companies into energy companies. This development, if maintained and extended, could have implications as far-reaching for the world energy situation as the emergence of the OPEC cartel.

If vigorous global competition could be assured among a limited number of giant energy companies, each with its own strategic position in most phases of almost every fuel cycle, it might be a desirable outcome for energy consumers throughout the world. The costs and benefits of various energy resources could be assessed and fully rationalized, across the board, within the corporate hierarchies. Meanwhile, competition among the few gigantic firms would keep energy prices ultimately charged to consumers as low as practicable. All of this would be achieved by the private sector with a minimum of government intervention.

The transformation of the multinational oil companies into energy companies would make it even more difficult for new firms, private or public, to enter the field to challenge the majors. But the majors would be quite capable of challenging competitively or controlling indirectly a number of other large industrial sectors such as electric and gas utilities and electric equipment manufacturing. Furthermore, the few giant energy companies might seek to avoid the rigors of competition, preferring instead the cooperative pursuit of monopoly profits. Finally, transnational economic and political power would be further concentrated at the top of a few multinational entities, a trend that has already made some national governments feel sufficiently threatened to impose curbs on foreign companies and to extend preferences to domestic corporations operating on their territories.

Present importing country–multinational oil company relationships are very complex. The mixture of rewards and punishments and of subsidies and regulatory controls for private activity varies from one country to another. The basic choice now before every importing country is, however, the same: whether to move toward greater or less government intervention. In this respect the world oil market and the various domestic energy markets are inseparable. Moreover, there is a widespread tendency toward greater government intervention.

Consumers and the public generally want more and stricter regulation in order to assure that oil company profits are kept within reason, and also in the belief, perhaps unfounded, that energy security will be increased if their government takes an active part. The private multinational oil companies also want government intervention, but of a different sort. In the face of potential competition from low-cost Middle East oil, the private companies want government subsidies and guarantees before gambling their stockholders' money on investments in high-risk, high-cost energy supplies.

In the direction of increased government intervention, a variety of specific steps may be considered. On the demand side, these include price controls and various rationing schemes in the short run, and public utility–type regulation of oil prices in the longer term. On the supply side are research and development subsidies, financial assistance for demonstration projects, tax incentives for energy investments, guaranteed prices for output, and protection against competition from cheaper foreign energy supplies.

Beyond measures that government may apply to private industry are steps to give the government a proprietary role of its own. These range from the establishment of a government corporation that would compete with private industry to outright government takeover of oil industry operations.

But a government may consider less, rather than more, intervention in energy markets. Possible actions in this direction include decontrol or deregulation of prices, such as the wellhead price of natural gas, and repeal of tax advantages, such as depreciation allowances, deductions for intangible drilling expenses, and tax credits for what are in effect royalty payments to foreign governments.

More broadly, the structure of the energy industry may be reviewed from the antitrust policy viewpoint. First, should the trend toward the formation of energy companies be stopped? Should it be reversed by requiring oil companies to divest themselves of existing interests in coal mines or nuclear power? Second, now that multinational oil companies no longer control the main sources of foreign crude oil supply, should the disintegration process be carried further? Should, for example, refineries and pipelines be separated from marketing operations? The government–industry relationship may be considered separately with respect to each part of the petroleum fuel cycle—namely, exploration and development (outside OPEC), production, transport, refining, and marketing refined products.

Most importing-country governments have been cautious so far in their actions toward the private multinational oil companies in the new situation. This is understandable in view of the high stakes, not only for the world energy markets but also for domestic politics and foreign relations among the importing-country governments. Considerable restraint in consumer country government policy toward the multinational oil companies seems desirable.

This does not mean maintaining the status quo permanently. The industrial importing countries may have a mutual interest, however, in seeking a common understanding concerning what values presently contained in the private sector of the world oil industry are worth preserving.

The main values in the private multinational oil companies seem to be know-how and capital. If those values were lost or dissipated in the near future, they would be difficult, if not impossible, for the world community to replace.

In determining the future worldwide role of the private multinational oil companies, the U.S. will have a large influence for a variety of reasons. The ownership of most of the companies, both the majors and the smaller independents with international operations, is U.S. based. The U.S. has a large installed domestic oil production capacity. It is by far the largest market for petroleum products. And furthermore, the private oil industry has traditionally wielded a large influence in U.S. domestic politics.

The key issues appear to be these: Will the present tax incentives for American companies to operate outside the U.S. be abolished in an effort to focus the efforts of American companies on domestic energy resource development? Will the ground rules for domestic energy investment be sufficiently clear and favorable to attract private capital? Will the U.S. government apply antitrust policy in an effort to break up the American-owned "majors"?

Aside from the U.S., most of the other industrial countries have already launched national oil companies which are now competitors of the private multinational companies. In the case of France and Italy, these companies have a long history. In Japan and West Germany, national oil companies are new endeavors. Actually, the government and the private sector participate jointly in the oil operations through the structure that is formed.

Such national oil companies will take time to acquire a position to effectively challenge the majors. In the meantime, the country concerned faces the risk that a private company will cut back its supplies if its national oil company behaves too aggressively. For these reasons, the governments of Western Europe and Japan are likely to move in small steps, rather than make a decisive leap, in restructuring their particular relations with the large multinational companies.

On the issue of the future role of private multinational oil companies, the LDCs are likely to be the most vocal countries and yet have the least influence on the outcome. Compared with the industrial countries, the LDCs form a relatively small fraction of the world market. Moreover, they lack the technical and managerial skills to mount an efficient government-owned competitor to the private multinational companies. Nevertheless, relations between foreign oil company suppliers and LDC country governments may be quite hostile, simply because of the continued dependence involved.

Petrodollar Flows

As pointed out at the beginning of this chapter, we might well have begun our discussion of energy and the world economy with the money problem. Certainly this is the most immediate and urgent world economic problem created by current OPEC oil prices. How we evaluate the options for managing the flow of petrodollars depends, however, on how we view the issues discussed previously, as well as on the issues generated by the money problem itself.

The basic facts of the petrodollar problem may be simply stated:

Prior to the Arab–Israeli war in October 1973 the OPEC governments' revenues were less than $2 per barrel of oil produced. In 1972 the oil bills of the two largest importers, the U.S. and Japan, came to $3.9 billion each. In that year, the oil revenues of the two largest oil exporters, Saudi Arabia and Iran, amounted to $3.1 billion and $2.4 billion, respectively.

At the end of 1974, the OPEC governments' revenues were more than $10 per barrel, and during that year almost $90 billion flowed from the rest of the world into OPEC treasuries in payment for the cartel's oil output. Of the $90 billion in revenues, the OPEC governments spent about $30 billion in 1974 on everything from guns to butter, leaving them with a surplus of about $60 billion.

In 1974 the biggest spenders on oil imports were the United States—$24 billion; Japan—$18 billion; West Germany—$11.3 billion; France—$9.5 billion; the United Kingdom—$8.5 billion; and Italy—$7.5 billion. The biggest earners were Saudi Arabia—$20 billion; Iran—$17.4 billion; Venezuela—$10.6 billion; Libya—$7.6 billion; Kuwait—$7 billion; Nigeria—$7 billion; Iraq—$6.8 billion; and the Union of Arab Emirates—$4.1 billion.

This was only the first full year of the new oil price era. The massive transfer of wealth from the rest of the world to OPEC continues in 1975 largely unabated, and it will continue until something occurs to restrict or alter the flow.

The international monetary problem created by the 1973–74 oil price revolution and options for managing it are considered below, first from the oil importer's viewpoint and then from the exporter's.

OIL IMPORT PAYMENTS

The importing country's money problem is essentially how to pay for oil purchased from foreign sources for domestic consumption. The problem arises not because oil is imported or because the importer must pay for it. Rather it arises because oil accounts for a large fraction of the importer's total imports, because the price of oil has quadrupled suddenly, and because there is no conceivable way for the importer to cut its imports to one-fourth their previous level (thus spending the same amount for foreign oil) without economic and political chaos. The difficulty of solving the oil payments problem in a particular country will depend on the overall strength of that country's economy, as well as the size of its oil bill.

Assuming an oil-importing country pays its debts currently, the immediate effect of the oil price rise is suddenly to enlarge the flow of money from that importer to its OPEC suppliers. If nothing else happens, consumers in the importing country will have less money to spend on other goods and services. Consumer demand will drop, and as this occurs, production will drop and unemployment is likely to increase. At the same time, prices will increase for all products in which oil is a factor. Consumers will be able to buy even less, and producers will therefore reduce output further and more unemployment will occur.

The government of the importing country now faces strong recession–inflation tendencies introduced by the oil price rise and various multiplier effects throughout the economy. The government also sees money that was previously in circulation in the domestic economy, thus enhancing the national welfare, now flowing in enormous amounts into OPEC's coffers. Faced with this depressing set of circumstances, what options does the importing country's government have?

In the first place, it can do nothing and let the national economy adjust to the higher oil prices. This will be a viable option only for a country with an exceptionally strong and flexible economy and a highly mobile work force. Nevertheless, it is important to bear in mind that all other options, aside from doing nothing, are basically measures to ease the shock effect of the abrupt oil price rise and to smooth out the economic adjustment process. The importing country cannot escape the adjustment unless, of course, the price of foreign oil falls to its former level or the importer discovers undeveloped domestic sources of low-cost oil.

Assuming action is necessary, the government of the importing country may move in one or more directions: it may cut other imports, increase exports, incur budgetary deficits, increase domestic investments, print more money, postpone its oil payments, or repudiate its foreign debts. We will discuss each of these possibilities separately. But it is important to understand that they interrelate. Government trade, fiscal, and monetary measures to deal with the oil payments problem will constitute a complex and changing blend that will be adjusted frequently in light of the dynamic economic situation as a whole.

First, the government of an oil-importing country may be strongly tempted to offset the increase in oil payments by reducing imports of other goods, especially imports of goods for which there are domestically produced substitutes. It may try to do this by increasing tariffs, imposing quotas, or erecting other more subtle and hidden trade barriers. Hopefully, consumers would spend the amount saved by the government's import control program on domestically produced goods and services. The import control program would also help to protect jobs and businesses from foreign competition. The higher price for oil and the scarcity of certain imported products would, of course, cause demand patterns to shift. But the government may see that the adjustment to higher oil prices, though painful, is necessary.

So far so good in the importer's adjustment process. But how would the government of a second oil-importing country view the first country's import controls? If the second country's exports were adversely affected, it would view the controls with grave concern for two reasons. First, the effect would be to disrupt the second country's balance of trade. And second, the import controls which restricted the second country's exports to the first would occur at the worst possible time, namely, when government of the second oil importer was attempting to solve its own money problem created by its increased oil import bill. Therefore, unilateral action by the government of one oil importer to restrict other imports as a means of coping with its oil payments problem may lead to retaliation by its trading partners with potentially widespread repercussions on world trade generally.

If an oil importer cannot reduce its other imports, then why not increase exports? Its government may encourage this by increasing the subsidies available for exports, or the international prices of its exports may be reduced by a currency devaluation.

Once again, however, the importer's efforts will be viewed with alarm abroad. At the very time when consumers in other oil-importing countries are themselves spending enormous amounts on oil imports, they are being induced to spend more on imports from the first oil importer because its goods are now more attractively priced.

Thus export promotion, like import controls, may be fine for one country but very bad for the world economy in general. Both types of action would have the unwelcome effect of dumping one country's oil payments problem in the laps of its trading partners.

We turn, therefore, to consider options to deal with the problem at home. The government may finance its country's oil bill by deficit spending. The government spending program may be designed to pump back into the domestic economy roughly the same amount as the foreign oil payments are draining out. Consumer demand would remain at the same level, production would continue as before, and unemployment would not increase. Domestic inflationary effects could be minimized if government deficit spending put back into circulation only enough money to offset the out-flow to OPEC.

The government spending program may be used to soften or postpone an adjustment to the oil price increase by sub-sidizing the sale of oil in the importing country at the old price levels or only slightly higher levels. Alternatively, the spending could be aimed to achieve various social welfare goals apart from the energy problem, while permitting the oil price adjustment to proceed. Perhaps the simplest distri-butional device would be a tax cut.

There is a catch, however. In order to run a deficit, the government of the importing country has to borrow. If it borrows from its own economy, this will drive interest rates up, making it more difficult and costly for other large borrowers like the energy industry to obtain the investment funds they need to operate or expand their activities.

To avoid competing with its own private sector for scarce money, the government may seek to borrow money abroad. Leaving aside for the moment the possibility of borrowing from OPEC to finance oil import bills, the importer country government would be entering the international finance market at a very awkward time. Will other oil importers help finance the first importer's deficit when they may be having difficulty financing their own? Up to some limit, the answer is likely to be yes, in support of the common interest in main-taining an interdependent world economy. But that limit may be far short of what the first importer needs from external sources in order to finance its deficit.

Another option the government may consider is to stimu-late domestic investment. The purpose would be to increase the productive capacity of the economy by an amount suffi-cient to generate the additional income required to make the oil payments to its OPEC suppliers. Although current con-sumption would be reduced by the increased investment, economic growth would provide the eventual solution to the oil payments problem. Tax incentives, lower interest rates, and various subsidies may be used as investment stimulants. But none of these devices are cost free. In particular, it may be difficult to lower the interest rate to encourage investment while at the same time the government is borrowing to finance a deficit. Another problem is the lag between investment and actual production increases.

Domestic investments would have to be economically efficient and internationally competitive, or the government might be trapped into later erecting trade barriers in order to protect the very investments it had previously encouraged. Of course, domestic investments in high-cost energy resources will require protection against the potential competition of low-cost OPEC oil. Finally, domestic investment as a long-run solution to the oil payments problem will require capital and confidence, both of which may be currently in short supply in the importing country.

The feasibility and effectiveness of the measures discussed so far depend largely on the economic strength of the country concerned. What may a government be forced to do if the oil payments problem remains unresolved and the national economy continues to weaken, or if the importing country went into the oil crisis with an economy that was already weak? The government may increase the money supply. This may stimulate domestic demand in the short run, or it may merely inflate the economy further. It would reduce the foreign exchange rate for the importer's currency, having an effect comparable to devaluation. Printing more money to pay for oil bills would not work very long, and the consequences would be devastating for the country's economy.

The government of a country with a seriously weakening economy may seek to postpone payments for its oil imports. This is the same as requesting a loan from its OPEC suppliers. The suppliers may or may not be willing to underwrite a bail-out. Finally, there is the possibility of repudiating for-

eign debts and trying to start over. But how forgiving will
the international community be, and where will the energy
come from to restart the economy?

PETRODOLLAR RECYCLING

Having considered the importing country's oil payments
problem and options, let us now turn to the OPEC oil
exporter's investment problem and options. In the earlier discussion of economic development, investment options for
domestic development were considered. We are now concerned with investment of surplus funds, that is, oil revenues
in excess of an exporter's capacity to absorb them into its
own economy.

At the outset it is important to note certain aspects about
a country's absorptive capacity. The 1973–74 oil price revolution is almost as much of a shock for the exporters as for the
importers. Many were caught without well-developed plans
for domestic investment. Therefore during the initial years
following the price revolution many OPEC countries will
have temporary surpluses, even though they may subsequently
be able to absorb their increased revenue in domestic investments. Once a development plan takes off, however, the
absorptive capacity will continue to increase indefinitely.

For the sparsely populated, large oil-producing countries,
the problem of investing surpluses will continue to grow indefinitely. If surplus oil revenues are invested wisely, they too
will soon begin to yield substantial returns. These returns on
petrodollar investments, as well as revenues realized from
current oil production, must then be spent, reinvested, or
given away.

This leads us to a central question: Why would a country
produce more oil than necessary to generate the revenue it
currently needs for its own economy? In other words, why
would a country produce oil at a rate which would create
surplus revenues, except perhaps as a temporary measure

pending completion of its domestic development plan? The incentive is that the producer expects to receive a higher return on petrodollar investments than from oil produced later instead of currently. Therefore the main economic incentive for some of OPEC's largest producers to continue to produce oil despite the surpluses they are piling up is the expectation that there will be ample attractive investment opportunities somewhere in the world economy.

Unfortunately, the government of an oil-exporting country faces an array of difficult investment options, none of which appear very attractive as of 1975. It is helpful to recall in this regard that the exporter is swapping oil, its precious national heritage, for a lot of pieces of curiously printed paper.

What then may the government do with the paper money filling up its treasury? In considering investment opportunities for surplus oil revenues, as in our earlier discussion of the oil payments problem, it must be understood that government investment policy is likely to be a complicated and shifting mixture of some or all of the options outlined below.

One option is for the oil exporter simply to let its foreign currency reserves pile up. This will happen to some extent as a result of lags between oil revenue receipts and the exporter's domestic expenditures or foreign investment. But the government may prefer to pile up really huge reserves rather than gamble those reserves on risky investments abroad. If a foreign currency reserve position indicates strength, then Saudi Arabia, Kuwait, and the other Arab states on the Gulf will soon be the financial superpowers of the world. The problem is that the larger the reserves, the more vulnerable they become to losing their value through inflation or devaluation. Therefore the exporter government can only accumulate so much foreign currency without grave risks of seeing the values behind the bits of paper wiped out.

Once the government with surplus funds from oil revenues decides to limit its cash on hand, it faces the problem of foreign investment in a world economy that is shaky at best.

As with any investor, the government's investment objectives may be to maximize either its returns or security. Alternatively, the government may, for various reasons, wish to help other countries in need of assistance.

To obtain maximum security, the exporter would remain as liquid as possible and invest in government or private short-term debt, such as U.S. Treasury obligations and certificates of deposit issued by banks. This type of short-term lending will go only so far. Foreign banks will be reluctant to accept unlimited petrodollars in exchange for short-term claims, since this will impose undue risks on their own long-term lending activities.

In the longer term, OPEC surplus oil revenues may be invested in countries with strong industrial economies or in projects in developing countries. Probably some investments will be made in countries of each type. Reasons for investment in relatively strong industrial economies, such as West Germany, Japan, and the United States, may be the likelihood of a reasonable rate of return, the needs of these economies for financing their own oil-induced payments deficits, and the dependence of the world economy as a whole on the continued viability of these national economies. On the other hand, reasons prompting investment in developing economies in Latin America or Africa may be the potential for relatively high returns and the needs of the developing countries concerned for capital development assistance. Indeed, the opportunities for realizing a high return may be greater, with no appreciable increase in risk, in a resource-rich developing country such as Brazil than in a fully developed country such as the U.S.

Some OPEC surplus funds are being funneled to less developed countries as aid on concessionary terms. This flow of development assistance may continue and enlarge in the future. For example, the Arab OPEC members that are running large surpluses may give strong emphasis in development assistance to helping other Arab countries or the Moslem countries generally in order to strengthen the bonds of nationalism or religion. There is no doubt that the non-oil-producing parts of the Arab and Moslem worlds can absorb all the aid the oil-rich sheiks can provide and more. Venezuela is already embarking on a major economic development assistance plan for the Latin American region based on its oil revenue surpluses, as discussed previously.

The main point here is that those OPEC governments which run large surpluses in the years ahead have an enormous opportunity. Through their investment policies they may perhaps realize substantial returns. But they also may have the leverage to reshape the world economy along lines that are more favorable for the less developed countries generally.

The industrial countries may themselves be better off in the long run if generous proportions of the OPEC surpluses are directed toward investments in less developed countries. To advance their own welfare, after all, the industrial countries will need expanding markets for their goods and services and a relatively open world economy. Evolution in this direction requires the creation of purchasing power in the less developed countries, as well as the maintenance of consumer spending and current living standards in the industrial countries.

* * *

Exorbitant world oil price levels will, if maintained, lead to a use of the world's energy resources that is grossly inefficient from an economic viewpoint, just as surely as if energy prices were kept artificially low. There is no way for the industrial countries to adjust to $10 per barrel oil prices without reducing their living standards appreciably. The central task of political leaders in the industrial countries is to convince their people of the need for austerity and to adapt their national economies to the new world energy situation in ways their people believe to be fair.

Deeply troubled by the oil crisis, many people have a desire to find a scapegoat, and the most popular candidate for this role seems to be the private multinational oil companies.

The capital and know-how that these companies command, however, seems essential to a solution of the current energy crisis in an open world economy. Nevertheless, the role of the multinational oil companies requires substantial adjustment to fit the new circumstances.

The rulers of a very few Middle East countries must now be numbered among the trustees of the world economy—if any such economy is to continue to develop. This is so whether current world oil prices are maintained, increased, or somewhat reduced in the future. Limited experience, as well as fears for the security of their thrones, may lead some of them to a narrow or short-sighted view of the future. Nevertheless, the enormous challenge before the Middle East monarchies is to help to ensure the survival of the industrial world and, simultaneously, to provide leadership in forging a new, more equitable relationship between the industrial countries and the Third World.

Chapter 5

Energy and the Global
Environment

As WE HAVE SEEN, the world political community is fundamentally unstable and insecure, and the world economy is far from perfect and complete. Within existing social structures, drives for either energy security or low-cost methods of energy use may cause widespread and perhaps irreversible environmental damage. The impact of energy-related activities on the global environment, therefore, requires special attention.

In this chapter, we first develop a general approach to the international environmental implications of energy production and use. Thereafter, we outline briefly the issues raised in applying that approach to particular problems: certain risks of catastrophic accidents; land use; air and water pollution; radioactive waste storage; and climatic disturbance. Finally, we take up energy conservation, a way to reduce environmental problems and to extend the time to deal with them. But before focusing on these energy-related matters, we need to orient our thinking about the environment generally.

141

The General Problem

Human beings quarrel endlessly amongst each other over the division of nature's treasures and about social ends and means. Throughout all this turmoil, one purpose of the human race remains constant: survival. No law of nature, however, guarantees mankind's survival. Human life depends on nature's mercy.

Men pursue knowledge through science and make practical use of much of that knowledge through technology. Technological man has thus accumulated an awesome array of powerful means to achieve human ends—some good, some evil.

Man's own inventions can compound his problem of survival. It is conceivable that men now have in their hands instruments capable of destroying not only an individual or a group or a nation, but the entire human race. It is also conceivable that human activity may cause global catastrophes not only consciously, through thermonuclear wars, but also inadvertently, through damage to the life support systems of the biosphere.

In saying this, it is important to stress the word "conceivable." Some of the human race would be likely to survive a large-scale thermonuclear exchange between the United States and the Soviet Union or a melting of the polar ice caps. But the survivors might well envy the dead. And the thought that man, by misusing technology, may threaten his own survival as a species seems no longer to be a wild flight of imagination.

Whether or not human survival actually hangs in the balance, the process of harnessing ever more powerful technologies raises a central problem for the world community as a whole. The problem has two aspects.

One is the gap between man's ability to cause events and his ability to fully comprehend the effects of those events.

Whatever the objective, the development of a powerful new technology usually requires great effort. That effort is mainly focused on achieving efficient performance according to the economic ground rules then in force. Once successfully developed, a new technology can be used with more or less predictable performance in relation to the objective specified. However, the side effects will be relatively unknown.

With technology that is not very powerful, there is ample opportunity to learn from experience, though a few individuals may be hurt or killed in the process. As technology increases in power, the opportunities to learn from experience become more limited and the costs of experience increase, and there is not necessarily a corresponding increase in before-the-fact knowledge of side effects. The gap between the power to cause and the comprehension of effects may thus be widening dangerously.

The risks may be acceptable as long as the zones of irreparable damage are relatively small in area or numbers of people affected. The eutrophication of Lake Erie, though lamentable to the Americans and Canadians living in the region, may be tolerable and constitute a valuable learning experience for the world community as a whole. A comparable disaster to the oceans would be neither tolerable nor a useful learning experience. In short, some technologies are so powerful, or their applications are so widespread, that they may set in motion environmental disasters of global magnitude before the knowledge needed to avert catastrophe is available.

The other aspect of the problem posed by increasing technological power is the gap in attitudes. People feel differently about, and behave differently toward, environmental and health hazards. Attitudes vary widely within one country and also between the peoples of different countries. A coal-fired power plant belching smoke into the atmosphere may be a sign of deterioration in an industrial country and of progress in a less developed country. Nuclear power reactors in the United States are required to be surrounded by massive dome-like containment structures to prevent release of radioactivity in the event of an accident, whereas similar reactors in the Soviet Union operate without containment.

Countries also differ according to the fragility of their natural environments. For example, Canada and the Scandinavian countries occupy fragile arctic zones. People living in these countries may feel more compelled than others to take strong action, unilaterally if necessary, to control vast areas outside their generally recognized political boundaries in order to protect their environments. Differing attitudes, shaped by particular environments, thus compound the difficulty of managing technology so as to avoid damage to the earth's biosphere.

Like the cause–effect knowledge gap, the attitudinal gap may well be widening. Consciousness of environmental risks is becoming more widespread. Yet the squeeze on finite resources also increases pressures to take environmental risks in order to avoid economic hardships.

In facing long-term environmental risks, like any other set of implications or projections about the future, we confront basic uncertainty. Some of our present uncertainty about environmental risks is due to the fact that many of them have been recognized only recently. However, some of the most important environmental consequences of human activity may prove to be not much more predictable than the political or social consequences.

A decisive policy issue regarding the environmental implications of human activity thus concerns presumptions. Confronted by uncertainty, is a particular human activity presumed safe or unsafe? Most activity is not presumed environmentally harmful. However, in a number of circumstances the presumption has been reversed. The trend toward greater caution has followed not only from an expanding public concern about environmental degradation but also from the knowledge that pollution thresholds—the point at which

forces are set in motion in an irreversible direction—are difficult, if not impossible, to anticipate.

Activities related to fossil energy production and consumption have proceeded thus far primarily from an after-the-fact
understanding of environmental effects. For decades the
normal conduct of energy industry operations has been
deemed presumptively beneficial. Those alleging injury to
themselves or to the natural environment have borne a heavy
burden of proof. Often this burden was simply too heavy, and
the environmental and health issues were not raised. Now
the risks are becoming more apparent and the presumption
appears to be shifting—at least in the industrial countries.

Activities related to nuclear energy, however, have proceeded on a different premise and for a very dramatic reason.
The nuclear age had a violent birth. The effects of uncontrolled releases of nuclear radiation were all too evident in
the dead at Hiroshima and Nagasaki, and the survivors have
been available for scientists and doctors to study over the
years. We may wonder what maximum permissible levels of
radioactive releases from nuclear power plants would be prescribed if an atomic bomb had never been exploded in a war.
But in any event, the nuclear power industry now bears a
heavy burden of proof that radioactive emissions from anywhere in the nuclear fuel cycle do not constitute an environmental or health hazard.

Environmental Approach

Conceptually, the environmental implications of the world
energy situation may be analyzed in terms of particular
events and their effects and causes. What events resulting
from energy-related activities are environmentally significant?
What are the effects of these events? What are the causes?
All three questions must be tackled in the management of

environmental problems at any level of government—local, national, regional, or world. Moreover, action may be necessary on the basis of imperfect or partial answers.

Two categories of environmentally significant events concern us here: those that may occur accidentally in the energy industry, such as an oil tanker collision, and those that occur in the normal course of energy industry activities, such as operation of a power plant. The main political problem with respect to accidents is to determine an acceptable probability of occurrence, while the chief problem for normal industry operations is to establish a permissible level of emissions.

ACCIDENTS

With respect to the environmental implications of the world energy situation, we are concerned with accidents which alone or cumulatively may cause unusually severe damage. Most safety risks are viewed in probabilistic terms. We evaluate risks and lower them or raise them over time through experience. Technological change in a particular area of activity may alter the accident risk associated with the activity, and attitudinal change within society may alter the accident rate that is deemed tolerable. But we continually view most accident risks in terms of the likelihood of the occurrence, and such a view is based largely on an evaluation after the fact of operational experience.

We also tend to distinguish the risks of accidents on the basis of whether individuals can voluntarily decide for themselves whether or not to undertake the activity involved, or whether the risk is imposed involuntarily on individuals or groups in society. A higher accident rate is usually considered acceptable for an activity that people can more or less freely choose to undertake than for an activity they are compelled to engage in.

With respect to energy industries, we are concerned primarily with risks of accidents that may cause very large damage. These risks are involuntarily imposed by the industry, with government approval, on society as a whole. The risks range from supertanker wrecks, to natural gas explosions in the atmosphere, to nuclear power plant "excursions" with release of radioactivity off-site. Dealing with this class of risks poses several special problems.

First, probabilistic evaluation does not work very well in many cases. The probability of an accident may be very low, but never zero. Yet even a near zero accident rate may be viewed as intolerable because of the catastrophic consequences. In such circumstances, experience may not be an acceptable means for deriving an acceptable level of risk. We must predict possible accidents almost infallibly and avoid them almost entirely. However, prospective analysis of very low-probability, large-damage risks is necessarily speculative. With little or no experience as a guide, controversy is bound to swirl around both potential effects of accidents and possible causes. In short, the experts will disagree on what is credible.

Second, if a single accident does occur, it may have a very large impact on the energy industry as a whole. The *Torrey Canyon* wreck in 1967 had a major impact on international oil tanker regulation, and the Santa Barbara oil blow-out in 1969 halted temporarily most offshore oil drilling in the U.S. In this connection, it is essential that the nuclear power industry continue, as it expands, the remarkable safety record it has compiled so far. A major power reactor accident in any country would have worldwide ramifications.

Normal Operations

In the normal operation of various energy industries a large number of events have already been identified as significant in relation to the environment. Fossil fuel combustion normally results in gaseous and particulate emissions into the atmosphere. Energy resource extraction, refining, and transportation normally result in irreversible changes in land and in the release of effluents into rivers and oceans. Nuclear fission normally results in very small radiological releases into the surrounding environment. Every human activity contributes heat to the biosphere, and many energy-related activities inject very large amounts of heat. Moreover, the number of events of potential environmental significance continues to grow both as knowledge of causes and effects expands and as the sensitivity of measuring instruments increases.

Major concern about the environmental effects of many energy industry operations arose long after political and economic commitments to basic technology were made, and after enormous industrial momentum had built up in the deployment and use of that technology. If we had known then what we know now, we might have done things differently.

In the real world, therefore, the first step in recognizing an environmental problem is usually detecting a harmful environmental or health effect. This step frequently occurs only after large-scale application of a particular energy technology has occurred over a period of time and the particular environmental effect is quite widespread or intense. Indeed, it is growth in numbers or in the scale of energy industry operations that causes most emissions to become environmentally significant.

In assessing the significance of environmental effects of emissions in the normal course of energy industry operations, we confront at the outset the problem of thresholds or tolerance levels. The effects of a particular emission on humans are a primary concern because of the high value we place on human life. Health effects may be distinguished from effects on welfare or aesthetics, although the borderline is vague. For most emissions, there will be a wide variation among individual tolerance levels, since some persons are much more sensitive than others. This makes the setting of primary air and water quality standards—namely, those standards which may not be exceeded without undue risk to human health—an extremely difficult political task.

An emission from the energy industry such as heat may affect an entire life support system within the earth's biosphere, such as the oceans or atmosphere or climate. Here the problem of thresholds or limits confronts us with a vengeance. In order to protect human health, we can set environmental and safety standards which may be adjusted in light of experience. But we may not have a second chance in the case of the carrying capacity of global ecological systems or the tolerance levels of essential life support systems within the biosphere. Nature may endlessly forgive man's insults on a small scale and yet not tolerate even one mistake on a large scale or in a vital part.

As discussed above, harmful environmental effects of normal energy industry operations are likely to be detected quite late in the game. Thus the effects lead us to the trigger events, usually in the form of emissions, and the events to the causes. It is only after causes are identified that we can take action to prevent or reduce the harmful effects, or to prevent or delay further damage to the environment.

But where does an effort to trace the chain of causation lead us? Human activity may be the sole cause of a harmful environmental effect or merely a contributing cause. When it is the latter, the problem of setting permissible emission levels is more complicated. Frequently human activity contributes to a natural, or background, effect. The earth absorbs a good deal of nuclear radiation from the sun. The small amount of radiation released by a nuclear power plant is added to the background radiation. Oil seeps into the marine environment through natural cracks in the ocean floor, and it also spills from tankers traversing the surface.

However, sometimes human activity results in a substantially new effect. Man is the only living creature so far to have contributed to the environment a variety of substances that are not biodegradable. Thus the Biblical phrase "ashes to ashes, dust to dust," applies to man himself, but it may not apply to what he leaves behind.

In addition to natural and human causes of environmental effects, we must grapple with combined effects of synergism. A particular emission may be relatively innocuous itself but become deadly if it combines with other emissions. Automobile smog is one well-known illustration of this problem. If an effect becomes dangerous through synergism, the problem of causation becomes much more difficult to solve.

Even where it is established that human activity is obviously the sole or main cause of a harmful environmental effect, the problem of causation is still not resolved. The sources of a particular type of environmental pollution may be few or many, and they may be concentrated in certain locations or widely dispersed. Moreover, the particular pollutant may flow from one type of activity, such as the energy industry, or from different kinds of activity—for instance, sulphur oxide emissions from coal burned to generate electricity and to make steel.

After the causes have been identified, an acceptable level of emissions from the human-caused activities may be established. The resulting standards would, in effect, distribute the costs of environmental controls and permissible emissions between the energy industry and society as a whole.

Environmental standard setting may be viewed as a two-part process: first, the establishment of general criteria, and second, the formulation of particular standards which are deemed to fulfill the criteria. General criteria are usually qualitative expressions, whereas standards are quantitative. The former are often, though not always, contained in legislation enacted by political bodies, while the latter are usually set forth in regulations promulgated by expert agencies. Both parts of the standard-setting process involve striking a balance between competing interests and thus are inherently political acts. Moreover, the balance must often be struck on the basis of conflicting evidence.

An alternative to the establishment and enforcement of environmental quality standards is the taxation of pollution-causing activities. The higher the tax levied on a particular level of emissions from an industrial operation, the more money the owners of the operation would presumably be willing to spend instead of paying the tax. A pollution-taxing scheme may permit those causing pollution considerable flexibility in choosing how to reduce the harmful emissions from their operations to socially acceptable levels. The problem of establishing an appropriate level of taxation to achieve a desired reduction in pollution, however, is likely to be at least as difficult as standard setting.

Finally, environmental administration involves monitoring and inspection to ensure compliance with established standards and enforcement in the event of noncompliance. Administration also completes the loop by providing data and experience that may be fed back into problem assessment and standard-setting activities. Administration is a technical operation, but it may quite easily become politicized. For example, if the administrative organization is inadequately funded, implementation of a comprehensive scheme will become uneven and holes will appear.

From the preceding discussion, we conclude that efforts to deal with the environmental problems may be divided into three generic areas: problem assessment, standard setting, and administration.

INTERNATIONAL ENVIRONMENTAL MANAGEMENT

In dealing with particular environmental problems related to world energy production and consumption, national governments will play the primary roles in the foreseeable future. On the one hand, government regulation is the only way to ensure that energy industries will internalize environmental costs to an acceptable degree. On the other hand, national governments will be reluctant to delegate to supranational authorities the power to make binding decisions regarding environmental standards. They may be more willing to enable international organizations, such as the Inter-governmental Maritime Consultative Organization (IMCO) or the International Atomic Energy Agency (IAEA), to make recommendations which are optional or which may become binding only upon consent of the government concerned.

Therefore the main international issues with respect to environmental problem assessment, standard setting, and administration are the following: What is the appropriate allocation of authority among national governments and international or supranational bodies? And how are the international or global dimensions of energy-related environmental problems to be managed? We consider these questions in the context of several major environmental areas below.

Catastrophic Accidents

As discussed previously, the energy industry contains a variety of risks of accidents of potentially catastrophic magnitude. A very large crude carrier (VLCC) may break up near a beautiful coastline or in arctic waters, natural gas may leak from a liquefaction plant into the atmosphere and explode causing a firestorm, or a nuclear power plant malfunction may result in the contamination of a large area with radioactive debris. The risks of such accidents in the energy industry cannot be reduced to zero. Nor can they be reduced to very low levels without, in many cases, incurring substantial costs.

The problem of ensuring public and environmental safety against catastrophic accidents in the energy industry is complicated by a number of factors when it is dealt with in an international setting. In sum, these factors exemplify the problem of attitudinal differences we noted previously.

Governments hold widely differing views about the probability of occurrence of particular catastrophic accidents and the amount of compensation required in the event an accident occurs. The energy industry thus faces less stringent safety requirements in some countries than in others. In the event of a catastrophic accident, those injured will receive more adequate compensation in some countries than others. Unfortunately, low safety standards tend to coincide with low compensation levels, thus compounding the problem from the viewpoint of the individual citizen.

A government may be too safety conscious, however, and impose costly requirements on the energy industry to guard against incredible accidents. If this occurs, rather than public exposure to an undue safety risk, the result is payment of unnecessarily high energy prices.

In an international market, stringent domestic safety requirements imposed on energy equipment manufacturers may penalize them in competition for export sales in countries where standards are lower. However, the reverse effect may also occur. Safety measures incorporated in energy technology in order to meet high standards in one large national market are likely to be included in similar technology when it is used in countries with lower standards. Thus leveling-up as well as leveling-down tendencies may exist in an international setting.

Large disparities in attitudes toward safety and the willingness to run risks of catastrophic accidents in the energy industry are likely to persist among peoples and their governments. Minimum safety requirements for oil tankers are being slowly developed internationally through IMCO, but standards for most other energy technology capable of causing widespread accidental damage are being developed nationally. Here is an area where the multinational energy industry may itself lead the way. Rather than argue about competitive disadvantage and thus level down, the industry as a whole may develop a common interest in leveling up.

Land Use

In the energy field, two strategic land use decisions are resource extraction and facilities siting. These decisions are usually viewed as matters solely within national jurisdiction. But they have major environmental ramifications for the entire world. Moreover, the energy industry is moving more and more of its activities offshore from the continental land masses and into the oceans beyond the traditional limits of national jurisdiction.

RESOURCE EXTRACTION

Natural forces in previous geological eras determined the distribution of energy resources in the earth's crust. Men, however, make decisions to extract the resources they discover. The impacts of energy resource extraction decisions are truly momentous for the entire global environment, as well as for national security and economic development.

For example, government regulation of the strip mining of coal in the North Central Plains in the United States will have a major impact on the economy of the entire country and its natural environment. Large areas may be removed from food production, temporarily or permanently, depending on the stringency of the government controls. Moreover, the use of nuclear power will be accelerated or decelerated, and U.S. oil imports will go up or down, depending on whether coal production is restrained or pushed ahead.

But the U.S. decisions as to the development and production of its coal reserves will also have ramifications for other countries. A decision to prevent or delay U.S. coal resource development in order to preserve the environment would affect not only the world economy, because of the impact on world fossil energy prices, but also international security, because of the impact on the world petroleum and nuclear markets.

Despite their far-reaching international implications, resource extraction decisions are the jealously guarded prerogative of the resource owner, whether Texas cattle rancher, Arab sheik, or socialist state. Economics and politics aside, the Texas cattle rancher may simply enjoy his present life style and decide to leave the oil he owns in the ground for his children or grandchildren to produce. The Arab sheik may leave his oil in the ground because of love for the desert or hatred of Zionism.

Regardless of the identity of the resource owner, the environmental implications of decisions regarding onshore energy resource development will be assessed, and standards will be established and administered, at the national level or below. It is unlikely that a national government would permit any outside interference with its sovereign prerogatives on environmental grounds. The rest of the world so far has no alternative but to trust the good judgment of the resource owner.

However, international environmental regulation of offshore extraction of energy resources seems feasible. The oceans, over which no nation has unfettered sovereignty, will be directly affected by offshore production of energy resources. Moreover, the potential for use of the overlying waters for other purposes will be restricted. There is no environmental rationale for any particular boundary line on a continental shelf or ocean floor in order to divide national from international regulatory regimes. A line is a political necessity, however, and coastal states are tending to exert control over a widening band of the most productive ocean areas. Concurrent national and international authority may be a sensible approach to environmental regulation of a substantial part of offshore energy resource extraction in areas where coastal states are granted primary control over exploitation.

Problem assessment might be carried out with the coastal state playing a leading role and an international body reviewing and commenting. An international body must also provide a mechanism for countries to share their findings in the course of many different assessments of particular offshore developments. International regulations might establish minimum environmental standards, while the coastal state or states could establish more stringent standards. Administration could be primarily left to the coastal states concerned, with a supervisory role for the international body.

FACILITIES SITING

Large energy-processing or conversion facilities have major impacts on the local environment. In addition, such facilities can be sources of air and water pollution that in the aggregate adversely affect the entire global environment. In many industrial countries, energy facility–siting decisions have become very difficult to make.

In considering the environmental implications of energy facility siting, a two-way perspective is useful. First, the particular facility may be viewed in the context of the entire fuel cycle of which it forms an integral part. Second, the facility may be perceived in the context of a pattern of industrial development.

With respect to fuel cycle analysis, an energy facility may be located and the localized environmental costs incurred near the place of resource extraction, near the place of consumption, or at some convenient location in between. A coal-fired electric power plant may be located at the mine mouth, in which case long-distance electric transmission is required, or near a load center, in which case long-distance transport of coal is required. Which location is chosen will affect regional air quality and also the railroad or pipeline industry. A large oil refinery center may be located either close to the producing or close to the consuming region, or somewhere between, such as the Caribbean. Which location is chosen will affect the local environment and also local energy demand, since refining is an energy-intensive process.

As to industrial development, concentration and dispersal have very different implications. Heavy industry, including energy processing and conversion, has tended to concentrate in various enclaves in an industrial country. Whether planned or left to unregulated economic forces, the result has been largely the same. In the future, an industrial country may decide to continue to encourage industrial growth within already polluted areas on its own territory, or it may decide to encourage industrial development on a more dispersed basis.

From an environmental viewpoint, the international ramifications of an energy facility–siting decision are complex. Decisions that appear to be purely national affairs may contain strong international components. For example, the transportation of oil from Alaska to the lower forty-eight U.S. states inevitably affects Canada's environment. A pipeline might have been used to transport the oil down from the Arctic through the McKenzie Valley in Canada into the Midwest. However, the U.S. chose a different alternative. Thus supertankers will carry the oil from the south end of the trans-Alaska pipeline, down through the island chains off the coast of British Columbia to the west coast of the U.S. Though the United States consulted Canada, the U.S. government never viewed the decision as a joint one. Canada was never permitted a choice as to where to incur the environmental costs of U.S. oil transport, much less a right to object to the entire development on the grounds of the potential environmental damage to Canadian territory.

A region within a country, or an entire country, may also refuse on environmental grounds to permit construction of an energy facility. Consumers in the region or country involved are still likely to want the output of the facility that is rejected. The failure of repeated proposals to locate oil refineries on the Atlantic coast of the United States is a prime example. The assumption, of course, is that the facility will be constructed in a timely manner elsewhere. This type of exclusion is most likely to occur in highly industrialized and affluent regions and countries, or in pristine areas which derive considerable economic benefit from recreational activities.

From an environmental viewpoint, if the facility is not built and energy use therefore declines, the result may be beneficial. However, if the consequence of failure to build the facility is simply to force a shift in energy demand to a more polluting form of energy, then the result is likely to be detrimental. Often the result will be to shift the needed facility to some other location where is is politically acceptable.

The issue of pollution havens in less developed countries arises here. Shifting pollution sources from industrial to less developed countries implies reducing pollution concentrations in industrial countries and dispersing pollutants globally over a much wider area. It also implies industrialization and economic growth for less developed countries. Industrial countries need not become more and more polluted while less developed countries remain pristine and poor.

One issue to consider in this regard is whether the particular facility would fit well into a larger industrial development plan of the less developed country. Another issue is whether advanced technology would be used so that environmental impact in the less developed country would still be as low as practicable. To encourage less developed countries to use the best available environmental control technology, financial and technical assistance may be necessary. Perhaps a form of international subsidy could be arranged analogous to fast tax write-offs or tax-exempt bond financing for pollution control equipment in the United States. In the long run, therefore, a stalemate in the conflict within industrial countries over siting energy facilities may be environmentally beneficial for these countries and economically productive for the less developed countries.

A final issue with international ramifications concerns the offshore location of energy facilities, such as superports and nuclear power plants. As with drilling platforms and offshore oil and gas development generally, the ocean location of such facilities will restrict the use of the oceans by other nations and will have environmental impacts on coastal waters, which are among the biologically richest and most vulnerable areas of the marine environment.

The governments of coastal states may take adequate account of international concerns in their environmental problem assessments, standard setting, and administration of these facilities by agreeing to a regime of concurrent jurisdiction. This would involve, for example, adherence to minimum, internationally established measures for pollution prevention and control, and acceptance of some form of international supervision of their administration.

Air Pollution

We all breathe the same air. Fossil fuel combustion causes an environmental problem of global dimensions, although most acute effects are likely to be felt locally or regionally. Depending on the amount and nature of industrial activity in a particular region and the number of separate countries involved, air pollution may be more or less effectively dealt with at the national level.

Air pollution generated in the United States, the Soviet Union, China, or India may primarily afflict the citizens of the country that is the source. But much of the sulphuric acid in rainfall over Scandinavia is injected into the atmosphere in Great Britain and the Benelux countries. To what extent can countries be left to themselves to manage the global air pollution problem on a decentralized basis? Alternatively, to what extent are international authority and action required?

As a step toward an answer, countries may be classified into three categories: those in which atmospheric emissions create substantially harmful effects that are confined largely within the country's own territory; those whose emissions create substantially harmful effects in other countries; and countries where emissions result only in certain localized problems. One difficulty with such a classification is that emissions from one country may worsen an existing air pollution problem in another country. A second difficulty arises with a country such as the United States, from which atmospheric pollution along the Atlantic coast is swept out to sea, where there are harmful impacts on the marine environment. Nevertheless, the classification is helpful in ordering priorities from an international viewpoint.

Whether a country considers its air pollution problem as primarily national in scope or as caused by external sources and thus international, there is much to be gained through international cooperation in problem assessment. This may be done with varying degrees of formality in particular cases, but the common purpose would be to achieve a full exchange of information regarding effects, cause–effect relationships, and monitoring and evaluation techniques. The industrial countries may play the leading role in international air pollution problem assessments, but less developed countries with existing or emerging localized problems may find participation useful.

Standard setting is a function of the source country unless harmful effects substantially and adversely affect another country. Rather wide variations in acceptable air pollution levels may exist among industrial countries. In Europe, however, international cooperation in establishing air quality standards appears necessary. Similar cooperation seems required in any heavily industrialized transnational region, such as along the Great Lakes between Canada and the U.S.

If air quality standards are nationally established, it is, of course, up to the national government concerned to implement them. In the case of a large country with widely varying levels of air quality such as the United States, the Soviet Union, or Canada, considerable delegation of administrative authority from national to subnational levels of government seems appropriate. Where standards are internationally established, as possibly in Europe in the future, administration may still be delegated to the participating countries, with an international body having a supervisory role.

In coping with air pollution problems and meeting air quality standards, industrial countries face certain strategic choices. First, they may choose between, on the one hand, the development and deployment of less polluting fossil fuel combustion technology for industry and, on the other, encouraging the transfer of industrial activities to pollution havens in less developed countries. If an industrial country opted for more advanced technology, it would increase the cost of its industrial output, making a less developed country's comparable output more economically competitive. If an industrial country opted to accelerate the shift away from an industrial and toward a service economy, the less developed country might obtain the advantage of a new basic industry. Either way the less developed countries would benefit economically, though perhaps more so under the second alternative.

Second, industrial countries may choose between emphasis on less polluting private automobiles and emphasis on mass public transit. Of course, a large country such as the United States may choose both. Either way may deal with air pollution problems, but emphasis on public transportation may be much more beneficial in reducing energy consumption.

Third, industrial countries may choose to rely primarily on nuclear fission instead of fossil fuels, for electric power generation. The shift to nuclear-electric power, in addition to reducing air pollution, would conserve large amounts of fossil fuels for other uses. However, as previously discussed, nuclear fission poses a variety of unique environmental, public health and safety, and security problems.

Fourth, industrial countries may choose to adopt comprehensive energy conservation strategies and to accelerate efforts to make available low-pollution energy sources, such as solar energy. Energy conservation is discussed further below.

Where does this leave the less developed country with respect to air pollution? In effect, such a country remains free to choose for itself between more polluting technology, which could free up resources for other forms of investment currently, and less polluting technology, which may yield considerable economic benefits in the long run, since it is often cheaper to prevent environmental problems than it is to remedy them.

To the extent that industrial countries are concerned about exceeding some maximum acceptable level of air pollution on a global scale, they might consider two alternatives: they could reduce their own emissions by the additional amount necessary to offset increases from sources in less developed countries, or they could subsidize the use of the best available pollution control technology by less developed countries. Either alternative would, of course, effect a transfer of wealth.

Water Pollution

Some countries are landlocked, while others are ribbons stretching for thousands of miles along a coastline; some are dotted with freshwater lakes, others are treeless deserts; some are bounded by great rivers, others are fenced off by high mountains. For each country, water and water pollution are problems that arise out of its peculiar circumstances. Nevertheless, the oceans are the source of rainfall that replenishes lakes and rivers everywhere, and all the great oceans mix with each other ever so slowly.

In the basic approach to global control issues, water quality has much in common with air quality. As with air quality, it is useful to classify countries according to whether they have a primarily national water pollution problem, or whether they are the source of a problem for one or more other countries. Here again the need for action is likely to be acute in industrial countries, and the need for action on an international basis is likely to exist in Europe and in areas where large water bodies are enclosed by more than one country.

Two energy-related water quality problems that merit particular international attention are thermal pollution of rivers by electric power generation and oil pollution of oceans by tankers. Thermal pollution is a major international problem when a large river, such as the Rhine or Danube in Europe, flows through more than one country. Probably, thermal discharges will be only one of a variety of pollutants that must be dealt with in the environmental management of an international river. Environmental assessment, standard setting, and administration are likely to be accomplished by the countries directly concerned, rather than by a broadly based international body.

Oil pollution of the oceans presents a different type of problem. Though the largest sources of marine oil pollution are land-based activities, considerable pollution results from oil transport. There are strong economic incentives to transport oil across the oceans as cheaply as possible.

Increasing ocean pollution by oil tankers, coupled with growing recognition of the economic disincentives for effective environmental controls, has led to increasing interest in stronger regulation. The basic issue is how regulatory authority should be allocated among flag states, where oil tankers are registered, coastal states, which are located along tanker routes, port states, where oil transported by tanker is unloaded, and an international body.

A flag state may have little incentive to establish environmental controls on ships under its registry. Moreover, standards which are internationally developed tend to reflect weak compromises, especially if the organization used for this purpose is substantially controlled by maritime interests, as is presently the case with IMCO. On the other hand, a coastal state's claim, on environmental grounds, of broad authority to regulate tankers in transit off its shores is likely to be rejected by the shippers and the oil importers as well. The port state may well be able to enforce its own environmental requirements as to spills from tankers entering its harbors or unloading oil at its offshore superports. However, the oil importer would seem to be in no position to insist that all tankers destined for its ports meet certain safety requirements, such as double bottoms or twin screws, that it might believe necessary for adequate environmental protection of its coastal waters.

Given the array of conflicting interests, there seems to be no alternative to international problem assessment and standard setting. Moreover, the administrative role of the international body would have to be stronger than in the case of many other environmental problems. Nevertheless, authority to take enforcement action against tanker polluters is likely to remain primarily with the flag state.

Beyond particular problems, pollution of the ocean environment raises three fundamental issues very clearly. These issues are also embedded in other environmental problems, but it will be useful to highlight them here.

One is the problem of management of a valuable resource that no one owns. As with land, men have fought and died and empires have risen and fallen in past efforts to appropriate the oceans for exclusive use or to deny others a comparable right. Over the years, however, it has become gradually established that the oceans are a common heritage of all mankind. All countries enjoy a right to freedom of the seas, and each may exercise that right, subject only to noninterference with the exercise of comparable rights by others.

The principle of freedom of the high seas is subject to qualifications in the case of waters close to shorelines, and the width of so-called "territorial seas" that are claimed varies from place to place and government to government. Free use of the oceans has served many nations very well, especially those maritime powers, such as Great Britain, which had the capabilities to exploit their rights more fully than others.

From an environmental viewpoint, however, whenever a resource is shared by everyone, there are incentives to misuse it. Some countries overfish an ocean, while others turn it into a cesspool. Those exercising self-restraint in the common interest simply lose out to those that do not. There is every incentive to despoil man's common heritage and none to preserve it. The oceans thus exemplify what is aptly termed "the tragedy of the commons."

A second issue is how to manage a valuable resource for which there are multiple and often conflicting uses. The same body of water may serve as a commercial thoroughfare, a scientific laboratory, a food factory, a theater of war, a mining venture, a garbage dump, and a vacation paradise. How do we allocate among ourselves the right to use the oceans for particular purposes, and how do we decide among uses when they are in conflict? A national government has difficulty in deciding how to use publicly owned natural resources within its jurisdiction. The oceans challenge us to solve this most difficult political problem at the international level but without institutions capable of decision making.

The third issue exemplified by the oceans is how to manage on an international scale increasingly powerful technology. Oil tankers have grown into VLCCs, offshore drilling depths have increased from tens to thousands of meters. Meanwhile, fishing boats have become fish factories and diesel-powered submarines have been transformed into nuclear-powered undersea launchers capable of thermonuclear destruction of cities thousands of miles away.

With hopes of developing acceptable solutions to these complex problems the United Nations launched the current efforts to develop a new international agreement on the law of the sea. Unfortunately, prospects are not good for reaching any new agreement, let alone an environmentally sound agreement, under the auspices of the Third United Nations Law of the Sea Conference scheduled for completion in 1975.

Radioactive Waste Management

The high-level radioactive wastes from nuclear power programs will pose what would appear to be the ultimate in a long-term management problem. The international issues raised have two basic dimensions, space and time. Where may radioactive wastes be placed, and under what conditions, so that containment or isolation from the biosphere is achieved? And for how long must isolation be assured?

Nuclear weapon production programs in the United States and the Soviet Union account for the vast bulk of high-level radioactive wastes produced so far in the world. The U.S. government's record of radioactive waste management so far leaves something to be desired. Storage tanks at Hanford, Washington, have leaked repeatedly. Furthermore, a proposal for permanent storage of nuclear power industry wastes in a salt dome at Lyons, Kansas, proved to be ill conceived and politically unacceptable. Little is known of Soviet radioactive waste management practices. The early practice of a number of countries was to dispose of their relatively small amounts of radioactive wastes by placing them in cannisters and dumping them into the oceans.

The radioactive wastes, which are an inevitable result of nuclear power, create three distinct problems. First there is the problem of temporary storage of wastes that are separated from plutonium and uranium during the chemical reprocessing of irradiated nuclear fuels. Next the problem of permanent storage of wastes arises after sufficient decay of materials with short radioactive half-lives has occurred. Then there is also the problem of the radioactive component parts of nuclear power plants and fuel cycle facilities after they are retired from use and torn down.

Temporary storage of high-level waste must occur at the chemical-reprocessing plants where the waste is first separated because the materials involved are too "hot" to do anything else. During such storage, the materials must be carefully monitored and the heat that is generated during radioactive decay must be removed. The time period involved is five to ten years.

One environmental risk arising during temporary radioactive waste storage is local and the other global. The local risk is that materials may accidentally leak into the surrounding environment. The global risk is that the storage facilities may be blown up in a war or terrorist attack. A large explosion in a temporary storage facility might inject into the atmosphere an amount of radioactive debris equivalent to the detonation of nuclear weapons having a total yield of tens of thousands of megatons.

The entire world community thus has an interest in the implementation of strict safeguards in the design and operation of temporary storage facilities for high-level radioactive wastes at chemical-reprocessing plants. How keenly that interest will be felt and how vigorously it will be pursued by various governments will depend primarily on their assessments of trends which are not necessarily tied to the world energy situation, namely, the likelihood of warfare or terrorist activity in the vicinity of nuclear fuel–reprocessing plants and the credibility of particular sabotage scenarios.

Self-interest may move those countries which have or plan to build chemical-reprocessing plants to play the leading role in coming to grips with this international environmental risk. These countries may cooperate in initiating a problem assessment. Depending on the particular country and the chemical-reprocessing plant location, neighboring countries might be more or less affected by a major mishap. The governments of the countries with reprocessing plants and temporary waste storage facilities are not likely, however, to accede to an international body when it comes to standard setting, although a strong case can be made for internationally prescribed minimums. Administration will probably be carried out by the national governments concerned, although here again international observation seems warranted.

Turning to permanent radioactive waste storage and disposal methods, a wide variety of techniques are currently being studied. These range from solidification and storage in underground salt formations, to solidification within glass and storage in drums spaced out on the surface in remote, protected desert areas, to using rockets in order to shoot wastes into deep space or the sun. One or more of the earthbound techniques seem likely to prove feasible.

Various countries will be in very different positions as to long-term storage of radioactive wastes from reprocessed nuclear fuels. Many countries with nuclear power programs may ship their irradiated fuels to another country for reprocessing, thereby shifting the waste disposal problem to the recipient. However, some countries with chemical-reprocessing plants are likely to have difficulty finding permanent waste storage sites on their territories. For example, Japan is geographically small, highly industrialized, densely populated, and earthquake prone. Yet it has a large nuclear power industry. The Soviet Union, however, has vast areas of relatively uninhabited lands and a smaller nuclear power program. Radioactive waste disposal on its own territory may be very difficult for Japan but quite easy for the Soviet Union.

Future generations in the world as a whole are likely to be safer if permanent disposal sites are established in a few remote locations under optimum conditions. This assumes, of course, that safe methods of transportation between temporary and permanent storage facilities are practical. The best disposal sites may not be in countries with chemical-reprocessing facilities.

International cooperation may thus be highly desirable in all phases of management of this environmental problem, including problem assessment, standard setting, and certain aspects of administration. The lead might be taken internationally by countries with existing or planned commercial-scale fuel-reprocessing plants, especially countries such as Japan, Belgium, and Britain, which have severe geographic constraints as well.

Nuclear facilities with highly radioactive structural components, such as power reactors or chemical-reprocessing facilities, are likely to dot the landscape long after their useful lives (approximately thirty years) have ended. This will be necessary in order to permit some radioactive decay to proceed. What will thereafter be done with the radioactive junk? Perhaps these structures will be perpetual monuments to the nuclear age. Active custodial care may be necessary in order to ensure that future generations do not blunder into them.

The problem of radioactive junk disposal will not arise on a large scale in the nuclear power industry for perhaps two decades. There will be a strong international interest in assuring that no nation adopts junk disposal methods which might cause a radioactive hazard outside its territory. Moreover, if radioactive junkyards are eventually established, any country is likely to demand a high price for international access to one on its territory.

So far we have focused on the spatial dimension of the radioactive waste management problem. The time dimension is at least as troublesome. Depending on the characteristics of the waste involved and the disposal technique adopted, radioactive material may be a lethal hazard for any life coming in contact with it for hundreds, or thousands, or hundreds of thousands of years. Lethality for only a few hundred years would exceed the expected lifetime of all governments and many nations. Lethality for thousands of years would transcend civilizations, and hundreds of thousands of years may reach into a different geological era.

All governments and private industries which use nuclear power thus assume what is virtually an eternal obligation to assure that radioactive wastes are effectively isolated from the biosphere and do not somehow find their way back to poison life. Given the moral awesomeness of this obligation, it is remarkable how easily we seem to have assumed it.

Heat Discharge Limit

As outlined in Chapter 2, there is a limit to the amount of heat that human energy consumption can add to the environment without serious disturbance to the earth's climate. The limit is contained in a physical law that men may try to avoid but cannot repeal.

A substantial change in the earth's climate would inevitably force a worldwide political, economic, and social upheaval. We can adapt comfortably to large seasonal temperature variations, and we can endure occasional painfully hot, cold, wet, and dry spells. All human institutions rest, however, on the underlying balance of the world's climate.

The thermal limit may be exceeded through the affluence of a growing world population that has happily avoided thermonuclear war and famine and that has kept its air and water quite clean (except for the heat input). Thus climatic change may occur and social upheaval ensue at a time when both the world's population and per capita standards of living are at their all-time highs.

A thermal limit to energy growth exists, but we do not yet know what the limit is. Two questions thus arise: What is the limit? And how do we avoid transgressing it? The first question may be tackled as a matter of high priority and pursued until a satisfactory answer is found. The task is likely to be difficult, prolonged, costly, and perhaps inconclusive. The second question may perhaps be approached in more leisurely fashion. Nevertheless, serious speculation is warranted.

When we finally discover the thermal limit, we may find ourselves already quite near and approaching rapidly. We may not then have much time to prepare for the momentous choices required in order to avoid exceeding it. If we find the limit and also discover to our horror that we have already transgressed it, our earlier speculations may be helpful in the even more painful choices we will then confront in the struggle to adapt and survive in the midst of rapid climatic change.

Finally, it may be that in a speculative, but serious, search for ways to avoid the thermal limit we will come across ideas that are worth pursuing in a different context. A wide variety of other limits to growth may conceivably exist. We may encounter one or more of these before the thermal limit. If so, the thermal limit will turn out to be irrelevant, but thinking about how to deal with it may be usefully applied.

Ascertaining the Thermal Limit

It is difficult to imagine an environmental problem assessment activity in which the stakes are higher than they are in ascertaining the thermal limit. Since so much of the future human condition may hang in the balance, we would like to know the limit with great precision. Yet the world community may have to make the momentous political decisions necessary to avoid transgressing the thermal limit on rather vague grounds.

The problem may simply prove too tough to solve with any precision, or it may be insoluble without actually observing the limit from the other side. When and if a limit is defined, it may look more like a wide fuzzy band than a thin bright line. Finally, the world's inertia behind the growth rate in energy use and its rate of closure on the thermal limit may mean that the most painful decisions will be necessary when we are still rather far beneath whatever limit exists and perceive it only dimly.

Ascertaining the thermal limit will thus be a mixed scientific–political matter. It will be as important for the results of scientific research to be politically accepted as for the results to be scientifically accurate.

In assessing the thermal limit problem, the industrial countries are likely to play the leading role. The main impulse may come from Europe, since Western Europe is today the world's most advanced "heat island." Thus Europe has an immediate regional interest in understanding the problem.

Deciding What to Do

If and when a thermal limit is established, the world community may face social changes in trying to avoid it which may be almost as profound as turmoil that would flow from a substantial alteration of the earth's climate. Procrastination would itself be a very effective form of decision. Furthermore, if we want the possibility of choice, we will have to develop in time the international political institutions which will give us the capacity for decision. Such institutions do not exist today.

If we opt for managing the problem ourselves rather than for risking nature's solution, the next issue is to draw a line. Even though the scientifically established thermal limit may be airy and uncertain, a politically sanctioned limit would have to be clear and precise. Moreover, the consensus behind the agreed limit would have to be wide and deep.

Assuming a limit were fixed, what then would be the alternative ways of adjusting to it? A few main ideas are set forth below.

If a ceiling were agreed for the total heat from human activity put into the biosphere, the basic question would be how to allocate the total. Thermal discharge permits might be fixed globally according to the amounts discharged in some base period. A system of priorities might be established and adjusted from time to time. Or discharge permits might be auctioned and sold to the highest bidder. An international authority might make thermal discharge allocations among countries, leaving each government free to decide how to use its allocation. Alternatively, the authority might make allocations directly to major economic sectors or even to groups or individuals. Difficult questions would arise concerning allocations between existing activities and proposed new activities.

In general, thermal efficiency would be a primary criterion in development of energy technology. Moreover, there would be a large incentive to find a way to escape the thermal limit. One conceivable escape would be to transfer industrial activities into space or onto the moon. Solar energy might be used to provide power for activities outside the biosphere. The moon's resources might be mined and thereafter processed on the moon or in space between the moon and earth. Development of the technological capabilities to actually use such an escape from the rigors of the earth's heat balance would require large efforts over decades with no assurance of success.

Though extremely speculative, the preceding discussion illuminates the basic nature of the world's dilemma if increasing energy use pushes us closer and closer to the thermal limit. Any global allocation scheme covering the international distribution of thermal discharge rights would require for its implementation a supranational authority with enormous political capacity. The international political system and world economy would pivot around the decisions of such an authority. At least within its jurisdiction, the supranational body would need plenary and unchecked powers for its decisions to be effective.

Viewed from the present, of course, it seems almost inconceivable that such a supranational institution will be created. An alternative to an unpalatably strong dose of world government, however, may be substantial self-restraint and self-discipline on the part of the largest energy users. This leads us to consider energy conservation.

Energy Conservation

We discussed energy rationing in the context of national security in Chapter 3. In this section, we focus on energy conservation as an element of a long-term strategy to deal with the world energy situation.

The economist will argue that optimum energy use, including conservation, would result from the operation of a market with efficient prices based on full costs. But an economically efficient pricing mechanism does not exist, and therefore a specially developed energy conservation effort is justified. Throughout the following discussion we should be aware that national economies generally function in ways that do not adequately account for environmental values and social costs. But we should also be concerned that particular steps to conserve energy do not result in the misallocation and waste of nonenergy resources.

Energy conservation efforts may have multiple pay-offs. First, conservation can ease national security problems by reducing energy import requirements, though the security benefits of conservation will accrue mainly over the long term. Second, the lifetime of energy reserves will be extended and resources that are conserved may be consumed later in uses for which there are no substitutes. For example, oil not burned currently in automobiles or industrial boilers may be used later as a lubricant or in plastics. And third, energy conservation reduces the environmental effects not only of energy consumption but of the totality of energy industry activity to support that consumption. In short, energy conservation may be a way for industrial countries to eat their cake and still have it—to increase their security and preserve their environment.

But what will be the economic effects? To the extent that conservation efforts reduce actual waste, the efficiency of a national economy will be improved. However, to the extent that such efforts lead to overconsumption of nonenergy resources or overinvestment in capital equipment, energy conservation will reduce economic welfare.

Whether or not conservation is beneficial to the economy as a whole, it will lead to temporary dislocations in certain industries and sectors. Offsetting the dislocations, however, is the fact that some conservation measures will produce jobs and stimulate economic growth. For example, building insulation requirements, though adding to the costs of housing, would expand the output of insulating materials and require growth in the number of installers employed.

A domestic political difficulty with developing a strong energy conservation effort, therefore, is the need to make decisions which override, or buy off with some form of subsidy, the sharply focused complaints of adversely effected interest groups in order to achieve diffuse (though large) gains for society as a whole. But in the long run economic growth does not necessarily depend upon corresponding growth in energy use. This is illustrated by the fact that Denmark, West Germany, and Sweden have per capita gross national products comparable to that of the United States, although each of these countries uses only about 40 to 50 percent of the energy per capita that is used in the United States.

The time scale for energy conservation efforts to have a significant impact upon demand would depend on the nature of the efforts undertaken and the overall context of the country involved. For example, primary reliance may be placed upon energy prices and the marketplace or on government intervention through a series of coordinated conservation measures. The degree of "fat" in the energy economy involved would vary from one country to another, as well as the political acceptability of the dislocations which might be necessary. Mandatory restrictions on energy use can clearly have immediate results, but obtaining political acceptance for such measures and the possibilities for acute economic dislocations present serious difficulties.

In an industrial country where an energy-intensive economy has developed over the years in response to low prices, there are likely to be opportunities for significant and immediate reductions in energy demand which would not entail any substantial economic disruption. For example, certain industries have recently been able to reduce their energy use by 10 to

30 percent through inexpensive alterations in production processes or equipment.

The large energy conservation gains will be realized over the long run, however. The benefits of many important measures will take five to ten years to show up because of the large existing stock of energy-consuming technology in every industrial country. Some of that stock may be retrofitted and made more efficient. Homes may be insulated, for example. However, much of it cannot be altered to consume less energy. There is no practical way to get 25 miles per gallon with a heavy American car. Similarly, there may be no practical way to retrofit a large San Francisco skyscraper so that its windows can be individually opened to substitute outside air for centrally conditioned air.

An ambitious energy conservation strategy in such conditions may therefore require substantial changes in the technological base and overall direction of the national economy. What is involved in energy conservation is thus a substantial change in direction for an entire national economy. The new direction would be away from energy-intensive processes and products and toward more durable products and, perhaps, a service-oriented economy. Thus the world energy situation may accelerate the emergence of a postindustrial society.

It is important to note here that a less developed country may not confront directly, or to the same extent, the obstacle to energy conservation that is posed in an industrial country by an energy-intensive economic base. Thus a less developed country may have the option to devise a development plan which minimizes energy inputs and maximizes use of available energy-efficient technology. In this way it may be able to avoid, or at least reduce, the type of energy–environment and energy–security problems that now face industrial countries. The extent to which a less developed country will be able to leapfrog such problems, however, may be significantly hindered by the lack of presently available alternatives to the energy-intensive technologies which have been previously developed in the industrial countries.

From an international viewpoint, there are very strong incentives in the current situation for industrial country energy conservation. Energy prices are very high. Moreover, conservation is the only way an importing country can increase its security and protect its environment at the same time. Despite the incentives, the industrial countries have been slow to develop and implement meaningful conservation programs.

An array of measures have been proposed: truth-in-energy disclosure; building insulation requirements; miles per gallon standards on automobiles; energy efficiency standards for appliances, such as air conditioners, refrigerators and water heaters; restrictions on electric outdoor advertising; and reformation of electric utility rate structures. These and various other energy conservation proposals now need to be developed into coordinated strategies for the long run.

Establishing conservation goals and means for their implementation is a complex and highly charged political process. Each country has, of course, a distinctive economic organization and social structure. It can be assumed that each country will formulate an energy conservation strategy that suits its own circumstances. Indeed, within many countries conservation goals may be set at the national level, but decisions as to how those goals are to be reached may be delegated to each sector of the economy or even to individual consumers.

Flexibility is also likely to be the hallmark of efforts at the international level to achieve energy conservation. For example, in addition to demand restraint in the event of supply interruptions, the International Energy Program contemplates that the participating OECD countries will develop cooperative programs to exchange information on energy conservation and to study ways to reduce the growth of energy consumption. Whether or not specific conservation objectives are developed, this kind of cooperative effort can at the least improve the dialogue among industrial countries and the information base upon which national policies are based.

One final point about energy conservation is essential to an understanding of this problem in a worldwide context. Industrial country energy conservation will not necessarily benefit the less developed countries or provide the poor of the world with more energy. This is so whether the conservation effort is voluntary or mandatory and whether it is imposed by the industrial country's government or some combination of external factors. The problem of the less developed countries and of the world's poor generally is that they do not have enough money to buy what they need. If industrial countries conserve energy, the less developed countries will not have as a consequence more money to pay their oil import bills with. In fact, if industrial country energy conservation efforts lead to a general economic slackening, the less developed countries may suffer the most. If we are concerned about the plight of the poor in the new world energy situation, the way to help them is not through energy conservation, but through a redistribution of wealth and income which command energy and other resources.

*　*　*

Energy production and use is and will continue for the foreseeable future to be a major contributor to environmental degradation throughout the world. Growing awareness of the energy–environment relationship has called into question the wisdom of past policies designed to emphasize energy use with little concern for environmental consequences. There is a continuing need to evaluate energy as a system, considering impacts throughout entire fuel cycles, as well as upon other scarce resources. There is also a need to improve the means for identifying, as well as controlling, internationally significant environmental problems.

Existing world political institutions contain obvious short-comings for dealing with environmental problems in the long run. In the near term, however, much can be done within those institutions to learn more about the global problems and to evolve ad hoc solutions to acute national and regional problems.

We may come more effectively and quickly to grips with the international dimensions of environmental problems if we proceed, politically, from particular interests to a broader understanding of the general interest. If human civilization is a race between education and disaster, largely as a result of the world energy situation, the perennial race is now sharply focused on man's relationship to the thin layer of the earth's biosphere.

Chapter 6

Energy and International Politics

THE WORLD COMMUNITY has entered a new era of interdependence on a global scale. However, we lack the international institutions that are necessary to guide us safely in such an era. A large and growing number of actors are capable of gravely threatening the international political and economic systems that now provide what small measure of stability and order there may be. The human problems that demand international solutions—energy, food, population, economic development, environment, war and peace—continue to increase in magnitude and complexity.

The tension between the particular interests of nation-states and the general interests of the international community, between the principles of interdependence and independence, is manifest in every aspect of the world energy situation—oil prices, production levels, and embargoes, for example. Consumer nations are inclined to characterize the producers' behavior as myopic, parochial, and nationalistic. The oil producers generally look upon their own actions as vindicating sovereign rights which were trampled by the multinational oil companies and the industrialized world for over a quarter century. The same tension lies at the heart of nuclear power development, where, due to the close connection between nuclear power and nuclear weapons, one nation's pursuit of self-sufficiency may threaten international stability and security.

In their efforts to deal with the energy crisis, many national leaders have preached interdependence and practiced independence; they have advocated multilateral cooperation and made bilateral deals. Such contradictory behavior simply reflects the unresolved tensions between the specific political interests of nations and the broader interests of the world community. Yet the world has no institutional framework within which the tensions can be resolved and the conflicting interests harmonized. In the final analysis, therefore, the energy crisis is an institutional challenge.

The Priority Task

International institutions may serve as structures to achieve agreement among nations defining areas of common interest, as structures within which nations may cooperate in the pursuit of defined common interests, or as structures for the settlement of disputes among nations when their interests are conflicting. All three potential functions—definition of common interests, cooperation to pursue those common interests, and dispute settlement—are interrelated and important.

Will a priority effort aimed at institution building meet the institutional challenge the energy crisis poses? If OPEC's power continues and the OECD's International Energy Agency becomes a counterweight, is the next step to meld the producer and consumer groups into a World Oil Organization? Alternatively, should the IAEA's worldwide nuclear energy responsibilities be expanded to include a set of functions for the fossil fuels?

Since World War II all sorts of international organizations have been built to float above national interests. There are enough of these already. The world is crowded with international agencies, many of them eager to do what they can to help solve the world's energy difficulties. These organizations, however, can in fact do very little because they lack an essential ingredient: political capacity.

Premature efforts at building new international energy institutions could create dangerous illusions of progress. At best, the development of a new World Energy Organization would be a pleasant diversion from the painful necessity for nations to widen the area of common interest in the energy field. The scope of common interest must first be defined in order that it may thereafter become possible to endow an international institution with the political capacity to harmonize national interests with certain overriding general interests.

The priority task, therefore, should be to lay a foundation for institutional development in the solid rock of well-defined, clearly perceived, common interests of the nations involved. This task will require slow and painstaking exploration through the labyrinth of conventional, largely bureaucratic diplomacy. The problems have too many important details and they engage too many weighty domestic interests to be solved by a few strokes of high-level statesmanship, no matter how brilliant.

A Transition Period

Energy has become the cutting edge of a broad transition in international politics. The transition was brought on by the successful culmination of the main historical trends of the first quarter century after World War II: the growth of affluent consumer societies in the Western industrial countries; the growth in military power and industrialization of the communist countries; the rise of nationalism and recognition of the political value of natural resources in the less developed countries; and the stalemate of the Cold War between the United States and the Soviet Union. In the energy field, the transition is exemplified by the growing politicization of energy, as consumers and resource owners alike have realized the vital dependence of modern societies on abundant energy supplies; the end of rapid growth in energy demand based on declining prices relative to other goods and services; the introduction into commercial use of nuclear power as the primary alternative to fossil energy; and the emergence of deep concern about the environmental impacts of energy production and use.

Implicit in a period of transition is choice. In the energy transition, we must decide what dangers we want to avoid: The Western industrial countries tumbling into chaos and pulling the rest of the noncommunist world after them? One Western European democracy after another opting for the extreme right or left politically to cope with domestic social disintegration? Famine, triggered by inadequate fertilizer and energy, engulfing one poverty-stricken country after another while the industrial and the resource-rich countries turn their backs and continue to play power politics with each other? The use of armed force to pump oil out of the Middle East? The use of an oil embargo to strangle the industrial countries until the U.S. no longer insists on the survival of Israel? Terrorist violence using nuclear explosives made with fuels stolen from nuclear power industries? Or is the world community even now so close to killing the earth's oceans or so rapidly approaching the earth's heat limit that other potential catastrophes look pale in comparison?

We must also choose what goals are worth striving for: The industrial countries becoming postindustrial societies in which the raw materials they use will no longer increase exponentially, though their economic and social growth continues? Continuing evolution of Soviet–American détente and the increasing consumer orientation of communist societies? Worldwide wealth redistribution, not just to stave off starvation, but to spread purchasing power so that the poor countries too have a political stake in international stability? Widespread acceptance of an obligation to prevent or minimize the adverse environmental effects of energy-related activities? Acceptance at last of appropriate limits on national sovereignty in an interdependent world community?

A Common Goal

The energy crisis is both cause and effect of the transition in international politics. Given the opportunity which the transition creates, what do we want as an outcome?

An attempt to develop an overall policy goal in a field as broad as energy can do little more than state the problem. Nevertheless, such attempts are an important ingredient of international diplomacy. Without too much complication, a common energy goal for the world community might be stated as *assured supplies of sufficient energy at equitable prices with acceptable environmental consequences.*

The term "assured supplies" evokes two thoughts: security against intentional interruptions and reliability against accidental interruptions. The first has political and the second primarily technical implications. Both, of course, usually result in increasing economic costs.

Settling for "sufficient" rather than pressing for "abundant" energy supplies perhaps implies a shortfall from common aspirations. However, most people elsewhere in the world would probably be quite content with half the energy now used per capita in the United States. From a global perspective, it seems desirable in the long run to push for a concept of sufficiency in planning levels of energy production and consumption.

There are two reasons why it is better to think in terms of "equitable prices" than "reasonable cost." First, the world's energy difficulty in the short run arises out of the exhorbitant prices the OPEC members can and do charge for their crude oil. These prices are largely monopoly rent. The word "prices," rather than "costs," highlights the continuing need at every step in each of the various fuel cycles—fossil and nuclear—for prices charged to bear a reasonable relation to costs. This would include, of course, an appropriate rent to the owners of resources and return on the capital invested by the operators of transport, processing, and conversion facilities.

Second, the qualification that energy prices should be "equitable," rather than "reasonable," implies not only a reasonable relationship between prices and costs but also a notion of distributional justice. Hence in allocating energy resources throughout the world, it may be desirable to consider factors other than ability to pay the asking prices.

Finally, the term "acceptable environmental consequences" is included as an integral part of a world energy goal. Many persons may presume that an equitable energy-pricing scheme would include a mechanism for internalizing environmental and social costs—so-called "externalities." However, there is substantial evidence of a tendency to ignore or suppress concern for environmental values in developing crash programs to solve energy problems. Major risks will be incurred if environmental and social costs are not adequately taken into account. Therefore it is appropriate to make environmental considerations an explicit concern of energy policy.

Is our energy policy goal biased in favor of energy consumers and against producers? "Assured supplies of sufficient energy at equitable prices with acceptable environmental consequences" may at first glance appear to tilt toward consumer interests. However, "assured supplies" for consumers implies assured markets for producers; "equitable prices" implies a balancing of interests on both sides; and "sufficient energy" signifies not only that consumer countries have a legitimate interest in the production policies adopted by exporting countries but also that producer countries have a reciprocal interest in the energy conservation policies of importing countries.

We have now played with words long enough to understand how each term begs a variety of questions and masks a number of deep-seated value conflicts. Such word play can be an important game, however, in clarifying intentions and communicating effectively in international political processes. Thus it is a useful preliminary to deeper probing.

National and International Interests

To probe more deeply, let us turn from the abstractions of diplomatic rhetoric to the realities of concrete national security, economic and environmental interests. In this context, we must examine the variety of energy goals that nations may adopt, depending on their particular circumstances, and the various ways these goals may fit together into a pattern of international relations.

ENERGY SECURITY

In a world that lacks central government, the ultimate in national security is freedom of action, but the essence of international security is stability. It is important to view energy security with this fundamental tension in mind. It is also helpful to analyze the problem in terms of great powers, major powers, and lesser powers.

A great power conceives its national security interests in global terms. It may guarantee the political security of other countries, some very far away. A great power should be largely self-sufficient in energy resources. Otherwise its energy deficiencies will be especially potent leverage points, and therefore tempting targets for political pressure. If a great power permits itself to become substantially dependent on foreign energy supplies, it will thereby expose not only itself but possibly the entire world community to major security risks. The great power may be less reliable as a guarantor of another country's security, since its own security problem will be so much more complicated; it may be more of a security risk to other countries because of the possibility of its using force to secure access to energy supplies; and it may be more of a danger to itself due to the greater risk of miscalculation and escalation in a clash of interests with another great power.

At present there are two countries in the world with the attributes of great powers: the United States and the Soviet Union. The United States' claim to great power status rests on both economic and military grounds, whereas the Soviet Union's still rests mainly on its military might.

For the first quarter century after World War II both great powers were largely self-sufficient in energy resources. In the early 1970s the U.S. lost its position of substantial self-sufficiency in oil as consumer and environmental interests challenged national security interests in the U.S. governmental decision-making process. In a few short years the U.S. became the world's largest oil importer, though still continuing to be among the largest oil producers.

In particular, U.S. oil imports from Middle East sources reduced international security overall. The U.S. itself became vulnerable to the Arab oil weapon because of its commitment to Israel. Moreover, the oil supply security of the major industrial countries in Western Europe and Japan was threatened not only by U.S. competition for scarce supplies but also by the possibility of an Arab embargo against the allies of the U.S. in an effort to reach the U.S. indirectly. Thus the U.S. shift from self-sufficiency to foreign dependence in oil threatens specifically the energy security of the very countries whose overall political and military security the U.S. guarantees.

The Soviet Union's international energy position may also be in the process of change. There is no immediate prospect of Soviet reliance to a dangerous degree on foreign sources of supply for essential fuels. Substantial reliance on Western energy technology and capital seems possible, however. Would such a major departure from self-sufficiency make the Soviet Union less secure? Probably not.

It would seem easier for the Soviet Union to adjust to politically inspired interruptions in the international transfer of technology or flow of capital than for the United States to adjust to a prolonged oil embargo. Moreover, a deal to exchange technology and capital for a share of future energy resources production would be more or less fully performed on the Western side before performance would begin on the Soviet side. Therefore, energy deals with the West would not adversely affect the Soviet Union's national security or fundamentally compromise its position as a great power. Indeed, it is the Western suppliers of technology and capital that would run the highest risks in such deals.

Unlike a great power, a major power will not have global security responsibilities. It will conceive its national security interests in regional terms primarily. Like a great power, a major power may well have worldwide economic interests. Many major powers cannot, however, be self-sufficient in energy resources.

There are now two groups of major powers: the industrially developed and the resource rich. Energy self-sufficiency is not a practical possibility for most of the industrial countries in Western Europe and Japan. A few industrially developed major powers, such as Canada and Australia, are also resource rich; and the resource-rich countries with large populations, such as Iran and Brazil, are industrializing rapidly.

Major powers may seek energy security largely through interdependence. Indeed, most of them have no other choice. But the bargains struck between the industrial and the resource-rich major powers will be bargains among equals. This signifies a major shift in global political power away from the industrial countries and toward the resource-rich, nonindustrial countries.

Before World War II, industrial countries kept power balance in their favor through coercion and colonial empires. Though many of the empires were lost, the economic predominance of the industrial countries was largely restored after World War II, and it was thereafter maintained for a quarter century through the interaction of multinational corporations with relatively weak national governments in the resource-rich countries.

The global power shift in favor of the resource-rich countries was caused by the success of the industrial countries in creating affluent consumer societies with enormous demands, the success of nationalism in strengthening governments in the resource-rich countries, and widespread international recognition of the impermissibility of the use of force to gain access to natural resources in foreign countries.

Power has not, however, shifted all the way from the industrial to the resource-rich countries. Instead, the center of political gravity now lies in a zone somewhere between the two kinds of power centers. Neither the industrial nor the resource-rich major powers will succeed in realizing their national aspirations without cooperation from the other group of countries. The common interests of both groups in the cooperative exchange of industrial technology for energy resources run very deep. Indeed, the common interests between the two groups are strong enough so that long-term exchange relationships may, as they develop, increase international stability and hence security.

What about energy security for the rest of the countries in the world? If the great powers are reasonably independent in their energy postures and the industrial and resource-rich major powers are strongly interdependent, the result will be a much more stable international energy situation than at present. In such circumstances, the smaller advanced countries too may be quite secure. And the resource-poor, less developed countries will exist in a political environment that is more supportive of their own struggles for economic and social development.

We must also inquire about the security implications of dependence on a great power for energy supplies. Either type of major power or a less developed country may be substantially dependent on a great power for energy resources or technology. Indeed, Eastern Europe is fundamentally dependent on the Soviet Union for its oil and gas supplies, although the pattern appears to be shifting gradually. Moreover, all noncommunist countries with nuclear power programs are primarily dependent on the U.S. for uranium fuel enrichment, and many countries have looked to the U.S. for power reactor technology. The U.S. enrichment monopoly will come to an end, but not until the early 1980s. Are the great powers secure sources of energy supply for other countries?

A great power may be expected to put its own interests first, like any other country. But if West Germany and Japan, which substantially rely on the U.S. for their military security, also depend on it for nuclear fuel, are they less secure than otherwise? The industrial major powers generally believe their energy security interests would be substantially strengthened by a reduction in their nuclear dependence on the U.S. Similarly, the East European countries might feel more secure if they were able to be less dependent for oil and gas on the Soviet Union.

As to international oil security, from the preceding discussion it is clear that the U.S. occupies a pivotal position. If the U.S. rapidly reduced its oil imports from the Middle East to a very low level, Arab ability to use oil as a weapon directly against the U.S. could be ended. The credibility of a continued U.S. policy of strong support for Israel would thus be enhanced. The oil supply security of Western Europe and Japan might also be increased, depending on the outcome of negotiations among the major powers—industrial and oil rich. More generally, by minimizing its own oil vulnerability, the U.S. would regain a substantial amount of freedom of action as a great power.

There are, however, potential risks as well as benefits in U.S. oil independence from Middle East sources. A major incentive for the U.S. to push Israel toward a compromise political settlement with the frontline Arab countries would have been removed. Given the increased U.S. capacity to act decisively in support of Israel from an oil-independent position, the West European countries might feel safer in trading their own diplomatic support for the Arab cause for increased oil supply security. The U.S. might thus become even more isolated than currently in its support for Israel.

If the U.S. remains substantially dependent on oil imports and becomes increasingly entangled in a network of interdependent relations in the Middle East, how might the Soviet Union respond? To the extent that U.S. reliance on Middle East oil imports leads to strong cooperative relationships with Iran and the Arab countries, Soviet influence in the Middle East may be diminished. On the other hand, the Soviet Union may view the U.S. oil dependence as a vulnerability it can exploit in the long run, especially if the present conservative monarchies of the Persian Gulf states are replaced by radical governments.

On the dark side, if détente is reversed in the future, the Soviet Union may be tempted to step up its support for guerrilla activities of the more radical Arab groups. But on the bright side, the Soviets may grow more consumer oriented and, consequently, more interested in importing Western technology than in exporting the Marxist–Leninist revolution. If so, Soviet behavior may adjust toward more complex interdependent relations with the West European countries and Japan, even as the United States pursues interdependence with the Middle East kingdoms.

Turning to international nuclear energy security, the major industrial countries are in the pivotal role. A number of less developed countries with substantial nuclear power programs will also have important roles to play. The basic issue is whether the spread of nuclear power will substantially increase the likelihood of nuclear violence.

The choice facing the major industrial countries, which will largely influence the security outcome, is whether to pursue nuclear energy self-sufficiency or interdependence. The major powers have a choice in nuclear energy, unlike oil, because of their ability to stockpile several years' supply of nuclear fuel; the long-term possibility of dramatically reducing nuclear raw materials requirements via development of breeder reactors; and the nuclear export policies they might adopt.

The major industrial countries of Western Europe and Japan are in a position of leadership because these countries will be the first, aside from the United States, to require large-scale enrichment, fuel fabrication, and chemical-reprocessing plants for nuclear power purposes. The choice of nuclear energy self-sufficiency or interdependence is implicit in decisions as to whether these strategic facilities are to be owned and operated nationally or multinationally.

The United States and the Soviet Union, either together or separately, will have limited influence on the outcome. To encourage a multinational approach, the U.S. might provide its uranium enrichment technology on favorable terms to multinational enrichment ventures. This could be part of a broader initiative to encourage the multinational ownership and operation of large-scale nuclear fuel cycle facilities and their colocation on a relatively few sites in various countries. If implemented, this approach would substantially increase the nuclear fuel supply security of the rest of the world in a way that would keep the risk of nuclear weapon proliferation as low as practical.

The two great powers will remain largely self-sufficient in nuclear energy. Their nuclear power independence will not necessarily increase the risk of nuclear violence, assuming they implement effective national safeguards against nuclear theft, since both the United States and the Soviet Union already have more than enough nuclear weapons to destroy themselves and many other countries.

If, however, a substantial number of non-nuclear-weapon countries opt for maximum independence in their nuclear power industries, the risks of nuclear weapon proliferation, both to governments and to terrorist groups, will increase dramatically. The possibilities for theft and the development of a black market in nuclear materials, or crude explosives manufactured with stolen materials, will increase if the facilities where these materials are located are widely dispersed and the transportation links between them are stretched out. The availability of large quantities of nuclear explosive materials in civilian industry would pose a grave internal security risk in a country with an unstable government or in the midst of political revolution. Finally, a government may feel itself compelled to choose between a costly civil nuclear power race and preemptive acquisition of nuclear weapons in order to offset the threat perceived in a large nuclear industry in a hostile neighboring country.

If the major industrial powers enlist the broadest possible cooperation from other countries and strongly pursue nuclear energy interdependence themselves, the future development of nuclear power need not be a major source of international tension and insecurity. Several countries, however, have already opted for nuclear energy independence—India, Argentina, and South Africa, for example. Thus nuclear interdependence is likely to be an imperfect worldwide strategy for security.

In conclusion from the overall energy security viewpoint, a reasonably harmonious pattern of international relations could rest on two underlying premises, great power self-sufficiency and major power interdependence. To permit such a pattern to emerge, the U.S. would have to regain its self-sufficiency in oil or at least its independence of Middle East supply sources. The industrial and oil-rich countries would have to weave their own web of long-term interdependent oil relations, approaching the complex negotiations with a good deal of pragmatism and flexibility. The industrial major powers would also take the lead in developing nuclear energy interdependence outside the United States and the Soviet Union. This would be accomplished through multinational ownership and operation of large-scale nuclear fuel cycle facilities, co-located in appropriate regions, and providing fuel and processing services to nuclear power plants in countries throughout the respective regions.

ENERGY ECONOMY

The essence of economy is the efficient use of resources over time, and economic efficiency equates with least cost. The political structure that constrains economic activity raises insurmountable barriers to economic efficiency on a world-wide scale. Therefore, in the evolving world economy, no nation or private enterprise should expect to achieve the economic optimum in using up the earth's stock of non-renewable energy resources. As a practical matter, a rough approximation of efficiency, in which economic calculations are tempered by political judgments, is the best we should expect, and even this will be difficult to achieve.

High rent to energy resource owners seems acceptable, especially since many of them are presently less developed countries. In producing its energy resource, a less developed country may be exchanging oil or uranium, which yields no return except when sold, for a development project, which will increase its national productive capacity in the long run. To the extent that the resource owner's rent accelerates economic development within its own boundaries or in some other less developed country, it is arguable that the wealth redistribution is beneficial to the world economy as a whole.

Furthermore, some compromise in economies of scale seems acceptable in order to fit a particular energy facility into the economic framework of a small or less developed country. In this respect, reductions in scale that will not endanger security, such as a small oil refinery, may be distinguished from reductions in scale that will be destabilizing from an international security viewpoint, such as a small nuclear fuel–reprocessing plant.

Before the 1973–74 price revolution, oil provided a price floor, and international and interfuel competition tended to drive energy prices generally down toward it. Since the revolution, the world oil price set by OPEC has served as a ceiling, and the multinational energy industry has been pushing other fuel prices up toward it.

Energy prices in general are now so high that they may lead to a world oil glut. Moreover, if early-1975 energy prices are maintained, many countries which left their high-cost fossil energy resources unexplored and untapped until the 1973–74 crisis may eventually achieve self-sufficiency. Or the OPEC producers may lower the oil price just enough to keep the importing country governments from making the firm decisions required to attract the capital and support the investments needed to develop large additional energy supplies. Or the costs of most new energy supplies may turn out to be much higher than expected and make oil at $10 per barrel appear more attractive.

A few years ago we faced the economic future with a set of historical trends from which we could extrapolate with some confidence. Artists of extrapolation, many of them economists, painted bright or gloomy pictures of the future which we could appreciate and talk about. The historical economic trends have now been interrupted. The artist of extrapolation can no longer project with confidence, and our current experience gives us no real basis for appreciation of his work.

Viewed in this light, the main question is: If nations pursue their particular economic interests, how far will the result be from a rough approximation of an efficient use of the world's energy resources? The answer, of course, depends on what various nations will perceive their economic interests to be and how they will pursue them. As with security, it is useful to classify countries as great powers, major powers—industrial and resource rich—and lesser powers. As to lesser powers, we will discuss only the less developed countries that are resource poor.

There is only one great power in the world, economically speaking, and that is the United States. In terms of the size of its national market, its gross national product, and foreign trade and investments, the United States is in a class by itself. The Soviet Union's economy, which is the second largest, is only a little more than half the size of the U.S. economy. Moreover, it is still largely self-contained, except for strong interaction with the economies of the East European socialist countries. With regard to the world energy economy, therefore, we will limit our discussion of the great powers to the United States.

We should note at the outset that a large economy is not necessarily a healthy or even a wealthy economy. But size is the distinguishing characteristic of a great power in the world economy. Due to its size, the state of the U.S. economy and U.S. international economic behavior will necessarily have a decisive influence upon the future evolution of the world economy as a whole.

The United States, with its enormous oil consumption, large current import levels, and undeveloped fossil energy resources, and Saudi Arabia, with its enormous oil production capacity, low-cost oil reserves, and surplus revenue position, are the major factors maintaining the oil demand/supply balance at current price levels. The key question is whether the current world oil price will, if maintained, lead to a reasonably efficient or a grossly inefficient pattern of use of world energy resources. This question may be dealt with in operational terms.

There is little doubt that at current or somewhat lower world oil prices, the United States has very large reserves of fossil energy that could be economically developed. These include offshore oil and gas, coal (including coal-based synthetic fuels), and perhaps shale oil. What then would be the long-run impact on economic efficiency if the U.S. were to push hard toward self-sufficiency in oil by expanding its own fossil energy production capacity?

If the current world oil price is anywhere close to an efficient price, then the result of the United States' developing its high-cost fossil fuel resources will be strongly in its national economic interests. And if, instead, the current world oil price is actually exorbitant, then the strongest possible action the U.S. can take to drive the world price down is to remove itself as rapidly as possible from the world market. Whether and how far the oil price would fall as a result of withdrawal of the largest oil importer from the world market would depend primarily on how far the oil producers with large petrodollar surpluses, such as Saudi Arabia and Kuwait, would cut back their current production in order to avoid an oversupply.

A possible outcome of U.S. withdrawal from the world oil market might be a return, part way, to the basic economic relationships that existed before the oil price revolution. The U.S. domestic oil price, or prices for synthetic substitutes, might again, as before the 1973–74 oil price revolution, provide a ceiling for the world oil price, while the Persian Gulf price would be the floor. There would, however, be less room between the ceiling and the floor than before the 1973–74 price revolution.

An additional economic reason for getting out of the world oil market would be the possibilities for improvement in the U.S. balance-of-payments position. The U.S. foreign exchange advantage might be viewed as an offset to the commercial competitive advantage the major industrial countries would enjoy as a result of lower oil costs as a factor of their production. But if U.S. withdrawal from the world oil market caused the bottom to fall out and the price dropped to quite low levels, the issue would arise as to how much pressure from consumer and manufacturing interests the U.S. government could withstand before the U.S. once again moved into the world market as a large oil importer.

Thus we are led to a twofold conclusion: First, U.S. pursuit of fossil energy independence may well be in its national economic interests. And second, U.S. withdrawal from the world oil market seems quite clearly to be in the interests of the world economy as a whole. On balance, such U.S. action could substantially help to achieve a rough approximation of an efficient use of the world's fossil energy resources.

We must recognize, however, that in order for the U.S. to move decisively away from the world oil market and toward extensive development of its own high-cost fossil energy resources, the government may have to place a floor under U.S. energy prices or provide other incentives and guarantees for energy industry investments. The domestic political decisions required to move in this direction may prove to be too difficult to make in the final analysis.

Turning to nuclear energy, the United States has a national electric power market that is more than ample to take full advantage of the economies of scale inherent in nuclear fuel cycle operations. Moreover, the U.S. has sufficient uranium reserves and, as a by-product of its weapons program, a very large stockpile of fertile uranium-238 that can ultimately be converted into plutonium and used as breeder reactor fuel. The most economically efficient U.S. nuclear energy policy, therefore, is self-sufficiency.

The U.S. would do well to avoid becoming substantially dependent on foreign sources of uranium ore. Until recently all uranium ore imports were prohibited in order to protect the domestic mining industry in a situation where there was excess production capacity worldwide. This embargo on uranium imports is being phased out gradually between now and the mid-1980s. As with U.S. oil before the price revolution, U.S. uranium prices are now somewhat higher than world prices. However, as mentioned previously, the world's known low-cost uranium reserves are highly concentrated in a few countries. If it fails to develop its own reserves adequately, the U.S. is likely to become the largest buyer in the world market because of its very large nuclear power capacity relative to the rest of the world. Uranium prices would rapidly escalate (as they are beginning to), although the risks of cartelization would not seem very large.

A U.S. move into the world uranium market would force higher prices upon the major industrial countries which lack uranium reserves of their own, such as West Germany and Japan. Moreover, the U.S. would have an unhealthy domestic uranium-mining industry to fall back on if it later wanted to withdraw from the world market. The U.S. and general world economic interests will thus be advanced if the U.S. maintains a posture of nuclear power independence, including self-sufficiency in uranium.

The major powers are roughly in the same roles economically as in relation to energy security. Therefore, the same two categories are useful: industrial and resource rich. If the major economic powers pursued their national interests, how far would the probable outcome be from a roughly efficient use of the world's energy resources?

As to oil, the degree of departure from an economic efficiency norm would depend largely on the success of the major industrial countries in negotiations with the OPEC members. The main objective would be agreement on a system of oil prices and production policies that would serve as a basis for industrial countries to make long-term economic adjustments and for oil exporters to fund long-term economic development plans. The major industrial countries would, of course, be seeking a reduction in the monopoly rent which constitutes most of the current OPEC oil price.

Whether the major industrial countries would be substantially successful in their negotiations with OPEC would depend largely on the relative bargaining power of the two sides. The parties at the negotiating table would be an important factor in determining the bargaining power of the major industrial countries. Until recently the major private multinational oil companies (five out of eight of which are American owned) have negotiated with the OPEC governments, thus in effect representing the interests of the major oil-importing countries of Western Europe and Japan. If the multinational oil companies continue to occupy the front row seats at the conference table, there is likely to be no negotiation, but rather a continuation of OPEC dictation. The OPEC governments would try to capture in the price of crude

oil not only the rents inherent in their monopoly of oil production but also as much as possible of the rents chargeable
because of monopoly power the multinational oil companies
may possess in their downstream marketing operations.

The bargaining power of the industrial countries is likely
to be greater if their governments face the OPEC governments across the conference table than if the private sector
continues to represent them. But what will be the effect on
the position of the major industrial countries of the U.S.
government's direct participation in the negotiations?

If the U.S. government casts itself in a leading role, the
bargaining power on the industrial country side as a whole
may be reduced because of the weakness generated by the
deep U.S. entanglement in the Arab–Israeli conflict.

Therefore, from the viewpoint of the major industrial countries the best negotiating situation with OPEC would be
created if the U.S. were firmly committed to regaining its own
energy self-sufficiency and were absent from the major power
negotiations. As long as the U.S. remains a large oil importer,
the major industrial countries would appear to be better off
with the U.S. participating in, but not leading, the negotiations than if the U.S. were on a separate negotiating track
of its own with OPEC.

This leads to the question whether the major industrial
countries would be in a stronger position if they negotiated
together and from a common position or pursued individual
tracks themselves with various OPEC members. Especially
if the U.S. acquiesced and let the other industrial importers
take the lead, the major industrial countries would seem to be
stronger by bargaining as a group than individually. In
Western Europe and Japan there would seem to be a substantial congruence in the oil interests of the individual countries.
Thus a solid common position would not be difficult to
develop.

This might not be the case, however, if the United States
were a leading member of the importer group. Both energy
postures and Middle East political involvements would pro-

duce substantial areas of conflicting national interests as between the U.S. and the major industrial countries, thereby weakening any common position.

Price stability would be as important as price level to the major industrial countries and to the general functioning of the world economy. It would be important for the major industrial countries not to seek such a reduction in price that the U.S., having at considerable cost extricated itself from the world market, would turn around and plunge in once more, pushed by its insatiable consumers. Indeed, U.S. government awareness of this problem seems to be one of the main reasons behind its proposals in early 1975 for agreement among the industrial countries on an oil price floor. If an oil agreement were worked out between the two sides, it would also be important that separate barter agreements, swapping technology and development assistance for oil, did not undermine the basic agreement.

In conclusion, the best chance for a rough approximation of efficiency as between the major industrial consumers and the oil-rich producers lies in direct bargaining, with the U.S. in the background. With the U.S. headed toward energy self-sufficiency, there would seem to be no clash of basic economic interests between the major industrial countries and the U.S. However, the oil-rich OPEC countries would lose the advantage of having the U.S. ensnarled in the negotiations.

With regard to nuclear energy, the departure from an economic efficiency criterion if the major economic powers pursue particular national interests will depend on a variety of factors. If oil supply security increases, then governments may, on reflection, develop nuclear power programs with efficiency more in mind than security of fuel supply. A more important factor will be the balance between incentives and disincentives to acquire nuclear weapons.

The government of a major power may want a secure nuclear weapons option as a national security hedge against a very uncertain future even though it is not in favor of weapons manufacture immediately. Such a secure weapons option will be inherent in a self-sufficient nuclear power fuel cycle. The costs of self-sufficiency could be very large, however, in terms of lost economies of scale in fuel cycle support facilities, unless a country's operable nuclear power capacity exceeded about 10,000 megawatts.

Among the countries which have not yet acquired nuclear weapons, only West Germany and Japan are likely to have nuclear power capacities above this threshold in the next decade, and both these countries are heavily committed so far in the post-World War II era to the achievement of world power status in primarily economic, not military terms.

Thus economic efficiency in most national circumstances is likely to be incompatible with nuclear power self-sufficiency for some years. Technological developments may, however, change the situation. In the near term, gas centrifuge technology may be used in economically efficient uranium enrichment facilities that are substantially smaller than the enormous gaseous diffusion plants presently in use, but commercial centrifuge plants would still be quite large. But the successful development of laser methods of enrichment would make operations on a very small scale highly efficient. Therefore technological developments may make self-sufficiency in uranium enrichment and a secure nuclear weapons option an efficient mode of nuclear power development on a relatively small scale.

When we turn from the major powers to the less developed countries, we immediately confront the problem of balancing efficiency and development. If the economic efficiency criterion is applied with the same rigor in a less developed country as in a rich industrial country, the less developed country may never reach the take-off point in its own process of industrialization. The gap between the scale of most industrial operations that is efficient in the world economy and the scale that is practical within a less developed country is likely to be unbridgeable.

In order to help bridge this gap, the industrial countries have manufactured reactors in small, less efficient sizes, suitable for incorporation into small electric power grids, and have subsidized their reactor exports to less developed countries through the extension of easy credit terms. Although the evidence is somewhat unclear, the OPEC oil producers may now be easing oil import problems of a few of the less developed countries by an informal two-tier system of prices and by accepting some payments in inconvertible currency.

Will a two-tier pricing system whereby the less developed countries pay a substantially lower price for their oil imports than the industrial countries lead to an inefficient outcome? An LDC importer may argue that a lower oil price for poor countries is justified and not a form of subsidy. In a two-tier system the OPEC countries will simply be charging the rich countries a monopoly rent, whereas they will be charging the poor countries an economically efficient price for their oil. If a two-tier system is developed, however, the less developed countries would do well to make sure it is a long-term arrangement. Otherwise their national economies will respond to the prices by relying too heavily on oil, and their ultimate adjustment will be more difficult.

Should the industrial countries continue to assist nuclear power development in the less developed countries? Of course the international security implications of such assistance would be a large factor in an overall answer to this question. From an economic viewpoint, small power reactors would probably be competitive with oil-fired power plants in many less developed countries at current oil prices. In terms of economic efficiency, there seems to be a trade-off. Less developed countries may use small nuclear power reactors efficiently but rely on foreign suppliers for fuel and reprocessing services. This type of reliance would minimize the risk of diversion of nuclear materials, and would thus go far toward overcoming the security difficulties raised by the acceleration of nuclear power development in the less developed countries.

On balance, therefore, if countries pursue their particular economic interests, as we have conceived them in the preceding discussion, the resulting pattern of development and use of the world's energy resources would not appear to be grossly inefficient.

We have left to the end two major problems: the role of the multinational oil companies and the investment of surplus oil revenues.

The private multinational oil companies contain invaluable assets in the capital and know-how they control. These assets should be preserved and efficiently used in the world energy economy. Furthermore, the multinational oil company has traditionally served as the middleman in the world oil market, performing the operations that lie between oil in the ground and oil in the gasoline tank or furnace. This is another value in the private multinational oil companies that governments would do well to preserve, at least until they have developed and tested a more effective substitute. Despite government takeovers at the production end, the world market would simply cease to function if there were no middleman.

An energy economy is always permeated with politics, regardless of the government–industry relationship. However, if government-to-government bargaining largely determines world prices and production, the politicization of the world economy will be increased substantially. If there is to be stability, energy will have to be viewed by governments more technically than it is at present.

One option is to have the decisions made by government technocrats. Another option is for governments on both sides to conceive of the private companies as, in part, a device for depoliticizing their own decision making. Instead of each side's attempting to make the company into an agent of its own, the private multinational company might play a very important dual role as a joint agent for the performance of specific functions in the world market and as an intermediary or buffer between governments on each side of the supply/demand balance.

The efficient operation on a global scale of any fuel cycle, whether nuclear, oil, or gas, would require highly centralized, expert management at the top. The private multinational corporation offers an option for centralized economic management within a decentralized political system. Furthermore, this is an option that is already intact.

Turning to the problem of investment of surplus oil revenues, we must recognize that these revenues are the result of economic inefficiency. They are the consequences of the exercise of monopoly power. The oil-rich countries have the power to tax the wealthy industrial countries, and a few of the oil-rich countries are through taxation accumulating enormous wealth beyond their current needs. Once accumulated, it is important that the surplus oil revenues be invested in a way which would make a maximum contribution to economic welfare.

Should the poor two-thirds of the world receive special consideration in the investment of surplus oil revenues? With the past record of generosity by the affluent industrial countries before them, should we expect a handful of Middle East monarchs to distribute their surplus wealth like beneficent and far-sighted trustees for the benefit of the world's poor?

Even though presently burdened by oppressive OPEC taxation, the wealthy industrial countries would do well to recognize as a distinct possibility that their welfare in the long run hinges on two developments. The first is the creation of enough purchasing power outside the present industrial world to avoid widespread social chaos and revolutionary violence. The second is the acceleration of their own evolution from industrial societies, with high and apparently insatiable demands for raw materials, into various forms of more service-oriented postindustrial societies. In both these developments, at least one of the great powers, the United States, is in a position to play a leading role, along with the major industrial countries.

Neither the United States nor the other affluent industrial countries nor the oil producers with large financial surpluses are likely to provide assistance to the poor countries on the scale required to keep the development option open in the future unless the effort is made cooperatively. In this regard, the World Bank's role may be substantially enlarged and its expertise fully used. Through such an existing institutional structure, the economic aid of Middle East monarchies and Western democracies may be effectively commingled and channeled to poor countries in order to give them a fair opportunity to take off into economic development.

ENERGY AND THE ENVIRONMENT

Human activity involving the production and consumption of energy is by far the largest cause of environmental pollution. At the core of every environmental problem lies a question of human consciousness. Is the human being fully conscious of his role as trustee of the biosphere? Until recently, men could reject stewardship in favor of exploitation and spoliation with little danger to the biosphere. Now that has changed.

Man has thrust himself into the role of trustee over nature by the force of his own social evolution. He is the only living being with the power to make the earth unlivable. The awesome responsibility cannot now be cast off.

Fortunately, nature offers man considerable leeway in the discharge of his trusteeship duties. The basic life support systems have pollution-carrying capacities that are quite large in relation to man's reasonable needs, and they also have the ability to sustain localized catastrophes and recover eventually. But the scale of human activity resulting from multiplying

—total population times technological power times material affluence—has now reached the threshold of danger.

What will happen to the global environment if nations continue to pursue their particular interests without any overriding concern for the biosphere as a whole? In other words, will life on earth be safe if man, the trustee, deals with the earth's life support systems mainly from his existing political frame of reference, the nation–state system?

The safety of dealing nationally with problems, such as air and water pollution, that inevitably have global effects will depend largely on whether concentrated local effects will necessarily become very hazardous to human health before dispersed global effects reach any threshold that, if crossed, would cause major damage to any life support system. Intuitively, we seem to be in roughly the following position: it is dangerous to assume that action to assure reasonable protection to human health from local environmental pollution will take care of any global environmental risks, but individual nations are reluctant to establish strong international mechanisms for management of such risks.

The political acceptability of international mechanisms to deal with environmental problems will depend largely on their functions. International agencies charged with gathering information and monitoring the environmental effects of energy-related activities would be more easily accepted than mechanisms charged with establishing pollution prevention and control requirements, even if the governments of the countries involved reserved to themselves, individually, the power to administer and enforce the requirements that were internationally developed.

Similarly, acceptance of internationally established measures is likely to be influenced by the extent to which they are perceived to encroach on traditional areas of national jurisdiction. For example, internationally established standards for activities conducted in the ocean—traditionally treated as an area outside national jurisdiction—may be more readily adhered to than similar standards for land-based activities. Moreover, requirements that are essentially procedural in nature, such as environmental assessments of energy-related activities or consultation with other countries concerning potentially transnational problems, may be more acceptable than substantive requirements such as emission limitations.

International cooperative efforts are more likely to receive a high priority when the boundaries of the environmental problem can be circumscribed and the potential impacts on participants are relatively clear. Bilateral or regional machinery and agreements built around common problems may assist in developing a base of international support for broader oversight of environmental implications of energy policy, eventually on a worldwide basis.

Nations have not been insenitive to the need for international efforts to deal with the environmental effects of energy use and production. The 1972 United Nations Conference on the Human Environment expressly recommended that an international mechanism be established for exchanging information on energy, including data on the environmental consequences of different energy systems. The United Nations Environment Program has undertaken these, as well as other responsibilities, and places particular emphasis upon establishing monitoring systems.

With this international view in mind, let us turn to what may happen if the great powers, major powers, and less developed countries pursue their particular national interests instead of deferring to any global environmental interest.

Whether or not it is a great power, a country that is largely self-sufficient in energy will strike its own balance between environmental preservation and energy development. Yet where such a country strikes the balance will affect the global environment. If it favors strong measures to protect its own environment, so much the better for the rest of the world.

Energy resources will be conserved and the amount of that country's contribution to global pollution levels will be reduced.

As to the great powers, the Soviet Union, with its huge land mass, may deal with its environment as it wishes in the next decade or so, and the global effects are not likely to be threatening. However, the United States is in a more problematic position. It confronts a series of environmental choices that can no longer be postponed.

One of the reasons the U.S. entered the world oil market was an inability to resolve its domestic energy–environment conflict. What would be the environmental consequences of continued U.S. reliance on foreign oil supplies at current levels? How do those consequences compare with U.S. pursuit of fossil energy self-sufficiency?

For the U.S. itself, continued substantial reliance on foreign oil would appear preferable in terms of air pollution levels and land degradation to moving strongly ahead with energy self-sufficiency, which would require substantially increased reliance on coal. However, the dollar outflow to OPEC would continue to bleed the U.S. economy, and a general weakening of the economy would reduce the ability and general willingness to finance the cost of effective pollution control.

If the U.S. were to move to regain fossil energy self-sufficiency, large-scale drilling for oil and gas offshore in frontier areas would occur; extensive coal deposits under the North Central Plains would be strip-mined; and the U.S. nuclear power program would be accelerated. A number of environmental standards may be eased temporarily. Despite any lofty ideals concerning environmental stewardship, will the energy industry welcome or resist reimposition of environmental controls once they have been lifted? If environmental controls are relaxed, such action should be limited in time and scope. The period during which standards were eased could be used to reassess the control approach and to develop improved control technology. But strict environmental standards should be replaced as soon as practical.

In the long term, the global environment will probably be better off if the U.S. opts for self-sufficiency, especially if the U.S. also adopts a strong conservation policy in order to minimize environmental damage to itself. Indeed, long-term conservation, without an undue departure from economic efficiency, would provide a way for the U.S. to protect its environment while enhancing its national security.

The major industrial countries are in a different position toward the energy–environment conflict than either of the great powers. Pollution problems associated with energy consumption are as intense in many parts of Europe and Japan as in the United States. But Europe in particular lacks a political framework large enough to deal with them. In Europe international standards would appear necessary to keep total environmental effects in every country—effects that originate from foreign as well as domestic sources—below acceptable levels. For this purpose, the two political halves of Europe—West and East—should cooperate.

The international significance of environmental problems associated with energy supply and use is clear. Similarly, there can be little doubt that international cooperation in all phases of environmental management—problem assessment, standard setting, and administration—would facilitate the efforts of nations individually and collectively to cope with these problems in an adequate and timely fashion. The industrial countries, as the major pollution sources and repositories of experience with environmental problems, may be expected to take the lead in developing worldwide cooperation and international machinery.

Four energy-related environmental problems with global dimensions deserve priority attention. These are impacts on the marine environment of energy supply and use (for example, offshore oil and gas development); air pollution and land degradation associated with coal utilization; radioactive waste management; and the heat limit. Moreover, means for achieving energy conservation warrant treatment at the international level, since reductions in demand for energy provide perhaps the best means to minimize environmental problems associated with energy use.

Trade-offs

The essence of the political process at any level of government is making trade-offs. Yet trade-offs between values like national security, economic efficiency or development, and environmental protection are extraordinarily difficult to make clearly or effectively. During normal times the business of politics is to balance conflicting values in a manner that will be widely accepted within society. In extraordinary circumstances, however, political leaders must make essential trade-offs more decisively, yet in a manner which mobilizes more intense public support than when conditions are normal.

As we enter the last quarter of the twentieth century, the world energy situation confronts political leaders in a large number of countries with extraordinary circumstances. In many of these countries the decisive trade-offs are yet to be made. The leaders of a country may feel they lack the popular mandate, or the government machinery, or the confidence of the people, that is needed to make the hard choices and make them stick. The people may feel that their leaders are corrupt or lack vision, or that the functioning of their government results in unfairness.

Regardless of the causes, if a country cannot make the political trade-offs required to deal with energy problems decisively, the consequences of indecision may be fatal to its economy and perhaps to its security. Moreover, because of economic interdependence, the effects of political indecision or ineptness in one country will inevitably spill over into others. No international institutions exist that have the political capacity for either striking a balance clearly or ordering priorities decisively as to any country's energy policy, much less for the world community as a whole. No such institution is likely to emerge in the near future to rescue national governments from the necessity of choice as to their basic energy policies.

In a national context, there may seem to be potential conflict among the three major values: security, economy (whether efficiency or development takes priority), and environment. The pursuit of energy security will be costly in terms of the most efficient use of resources. Moreover, security and environmental values may conflict, especially if security means intensive domestic development and use of solid hydrocarbons rather than foreign oil. To complete the circle, environmental and economic values are likely to collide wherever environmental costs have not already been fully internalized.

But do all these hypothetical conflicts arise in the real world? Or are nations actually constrained by their particular circumstances rather narrowly, so that their real options are limited?

* * *

If we would apply one lesson from history to the current world energy situation, it would seem to be self-restraint. Lacking political institutions to define the general interests of the world community as a whole, national self-restraint is mandatory. With restraint, there is opportunity: the world energy situation will be manageable in the short run, and it will also be feasible to lay the foundations for more effective institutional structures that will surely be needed in the long run.

The energy crisis clearly challenges nations to develop a common understanding of the interdependence of all human life, and then to develop the present discord among the world community into a more harmonious whole.

Bibliography

As INDICATED in the Introduction, there is a vast and rapidly growing literature about energy and energy policy. The following bibliography is highly selective. It includes the sources found to be especially helpful in preparing this book, certain works which may be used as points of departure for further study, and a variety of other material representing differing points of view about the problems discussed. Since most of the entries are entitled topically and contain material that is relevant to more than one chapter, the bibliography is divided into books, articles and pamphlets, and official documents.

Many of the entries predate the new energy situation that emerged following the 1973–74 OPEC oil price increases. Of course the projections these publications include are out of date, but they nevertheless continue to provide valuable insights into basic issues and underlying problems.

Books

ADELMAN, M. A. *The World Petroleum Market.* Baltimore: The Johns Hopkins University Press, 1972.

213

BOHI, DOUGLAS, and MILTON RUSSELL. *Policy Alternatives for Energy Security*. Baltimore: The Johns Hopkins University Press, 1975.

BROWN, SEYOM. *New Forces in World Politics*. Washington: The Brookings Institution, 1974.

BRUBAKER, STERLING. *To Live on Earth: Man and His Environment in Perspective*. Baltimore: The Johns Hopkins University Press, 1972.

CALDWELL, LYNTON K. *In Defense of Earth: International Protection of the Biosphere*. Bloomington, Ind.: Indiana University Press, 1972.

CAMPBELL, ROBERT W. *The Economics of Soviet Oil and Gas*. Baltimore: The Johns Hopkins University Press, 1968.

COCHRAN, THOMAS B. *The Liquid Metal Fast Breeder Reactor: An Environmental and Economic Critique*. Baltimore: The Johns Hopkins University Press, 1974.

CONNELLY, PHILIP, and ROBERT PERLMAN. *The Politics of Scarcity: Resource Conflicts in International Relations*. London: Oxford University Press, 1975.

DARMSTADTER, JOEL. *Energy in the World Economy*. Baltimore: The Johns Hopkins University Press, 1971.

ENERGY POLICY PROJECT OF THE FORD FOUNDATION. *A Time to Choose: America's Energy Future*. Cambridge, Mass.: Ballinger Publishing Company, 1974.

ERICKSON, EDWARD W., and LEONARD WAVERMAN, eds. *The Energy Question: An International Failure of Policy*. Vol. 1, *The World*; vol. 2, *North America*. Toronto: University of Toronto Press, 1974.

FALK, RICHARD A. *This Endangered Planet*. New York: Random House, 1971.

FISHER, JOHN C. *Energy Crises in Perspective*. New York: John Wiley & Sons, Inc., 1974.

FREEMAN, S. DAVID. *Energy: The New Era*. New York: Walker & Company, 1974.

GOELLER, HAROLD E., et al. *World Energy Conference Survey of Energy Resources*. New York: United States National Committee of the World Energy Conference, 1974.

GORDON, RICHARD L. *The Evolution of Energy Policy in Western Europe: The Reluctant Retreat from Coal.* New York: Praeger Publishers, Inc., 1970.

HAMMOND, ALLEN L., WILLIAM D. METZ, and THOMAS H. MAUGH, II. *Energy and the Future.* Washington: American Association for the Advancement of Science, 1973.

HARTSHORN, J. E. *Politics and World Oil Economics: An Account of the International Oil Industry.* New York: Praeger Publishers, Inc., 1967.

HEALY, TIMOTHY J. *Energy, Electric Power and Man.* San Francisco: Boyd & Fraser Publishing Company, 1974.

HOTTEL, H. C., and J. B. HOWARD. *New Energy Technology: Some Facts and Assessments.* Cambridge, Mass.: The M.I.T. Press, 1972.

JACOBY, NEIL H. *Multinational Oil: A Study in Industrial Dynamics.* New York: Macmillan, 1974.

KNEESE, ALLEN V., ROBERT U. AYRES, and RALPH C. D'ARGE. *Economics and the Environment: A Materials Balance Approach.* Washington: Resources for the Future, Inc., 1970.

LANDSBERG, HANS H., and SAM H. SCHURR. *Energy in the United States: Sources, Uses and Policy Issues.* New York: Random House, Inc., 1968.

LONGRIGG, STEPHEN. *Oil in the Middle East: Its Discovery and Development.* London: Oxford University Press, 1968.

MANNERS, GERALD. *The Geography of Energy.* London: Hutchinson University Library, 1971.

MASSACHUSETTS INSTITUTE OF TECHNOLOGY. *Man's Impact on the Global Environment: Report of the Study of Critical Environmental Problems.* Cambridge, Mass.: The M.I.T. Press, 1970.

MIKDASHI, ZUHAYR. *The Community of Oil Importing Countries.* London: George Allen and Unwin Ltd., 1972.

MIKESELL, RAYMOND F., WILLIAM H. BARTSCH, et al. *Foreign Investment in the Petroleum and Mineral Industries: Case Studies of Investor–Host Country Relations.* Baltimore: The Johns Hopkins University Press, 1971.

NATIONAL ACADEMY OF ENGINEERING. *U.S. Energy Prospects: An Engineering Viewpoint,* report prepared by the Task Force on Energy. Washington: National Academy of Engineering, 1974.

NATIONAL ACADEMY OF SCIENCES–NATIONAL RESEARCH COUNCIL. *Mineral Resources and the Environment.* Washington: National Academy of Sciences, 1975.

NATIONAL ACADEMY OF SCIENCES–NATIONAL RESEARCH COUNCIL. *Resources and Man.* San Francisco: W. H. Freeman and Company Publishers, 1969.

NATIONAL ACADEMY OF SCIENCES–NATIONAL RESEARCH COUNCIL. *Understanding Climatic Change.* Washington: National Academy of Sciences, 1975.

NATIONAL PETROLEUM COUNCIL, COMMITTEE ON ENERGY PREPAREDNESS. *Emergency Preparedness for Interruption of Petroleum Imports into the United States.* Washington: National Petroleum Council, 1973.

NATIONAL PETROLEUM COUNCIL. *U.S. Energy Outlook.* Washington: National Petroleum Council, 1972.

NAU, HENRY R. *National Politics and International Technology: Nuclear Reactor Development in Western Europe.* Baltimore: The Johns Hopkins University Press, 1974.

ODELL, PETER R. *Oil and World Power: A Geographical Interpretation.* Harmondsworth: Penguin Books Limited, 1970.

PENROSE, EDITH. *The Large International Firm in Developing Countries: The International Petroleum Industry.* London: George Allen and Unwin Ltd., 1968.

PENROSE, EDITH. *The Growth of Firms, Middle East Oil, and Other Essays.* London: Frank Cass Ltd., 1971.

RAMAZANI, ROUHOLLAH K. *The Persian Gulf: Iran's Role.* Charlottesville: The University Press of Virginia, 1972.

SCHURR, SAM H., ed. *Energy, Economic Growth, and the Environment.* Baltimore: The Johns Hopkins University Press, 1972.

STOCKING, GEORGE W. *Middle East Oil: A Study in Political and Economic Controversy.* Nashville, Tenn.: Vanderbilt University Press, 1970.

TANZER, MICHAEL. *The Political Economy of International Oil and the Underdeveloped Countries.* Boston: Beacon Press, 1969.

WEINTRAUB, ANDREW, ELI SCHWARTZ, and J. RICHARD ARONSON, eds. *The Economic Growth Controversy.* White Plains, N.Y.: International Arts & Sciences Press, Inc., 1973.

WHITE, IRVIN L., et al. *North Sea Oil and Gas: Implications for Future United States Development.* Norman, Okla.: University of Oklahoma Press, 1973.

WILLRICH, MASON. *Global Politics of Nuclear Energy*. New York: Praeger Publishers, Inc., 1971.

WILLRICH, MASON, ed. *International Safeguards and Nuclear Industry*. Baltimore: The Johns Hopkins University Press, 1973.

WILLRICH, MASON, and THEODORE B. TAYLOR. *Nuclear Theft: Risks and Safeguards*. Cambridge, Mass.: Ballinger Publishing Company, 1974.

YAGER, JOSEPH A., and ELEANOR B. STEINBERG. *Energy and U.S. Foreign Policy*. Cambridge, Mass.: Ballinger Publishing Company, 1974.

Articles and Pamphlets

ADELMAN, M. A. "Is the Oil Shortage Real? Oil Companies as OPEC Tax Collectors," *Foreign Policy*, no. 9, pp. 69–107 (Winter 1972–73).

AKINS, JAMES E. "The Oil Crisis: This Time the Wolf Is Here," *Foreign Affairs*, vol. 51, no. 3, pp. 462–490 (April 1973).

AMERICAN ACADEMY OF ARTS AND SCIENCES. "The Oil Crisis: A Case Study of National, International and Transnational Processes," *Daedelus* (symposium issue, Fall 1975).

AMERICAN ASSOCIATION FOR THE ADVANCEMENT OF SCIENCE. "Energy," *Science*, vol. 184, no. 4134 (symposium issue, Apr. 19, 1974).

BERGSTEN, C. FRED. "The Response to the Third World," *Foreign Policy*, no. 17, pp. 3–34 (Winter 1974–75).

BERGSTEN, C. FRED. "The Threat from the Third World," *Foreign Policy*, no. 11, pp. 102–124 (Summer 1973).

BROOKINGS INSTITUTION. *Cooperative Approaches to World Energy Problems*, tripartite report by fifteen experts from the European community, Japan, and North America. Washington: The Brookings Institution, 1974.

CHENERY, HOLLIS B. "Restructuring the World Economy," *Foreign Affairs*, vol. 53, no. 2, pp. 242–263 (January 1975).

DARMSTADTER, JOEL. "Limiting the Demand for Energy: Possible? Probable?" *Environmental Affairs*, vol. 2, no. 4, pp. 717–731 (1973).

FARMANFARMAIAN, KHODADAD, ARMIN GUTOWSKI, SABURO OKITA, ROBERT V. ROOSA, and CARROLL L. WILSON. "How Can the World Afford OPEC Oil?" *Foreign Affairs*, vol. 53, no. 2, pp. 201–222 (January 1975).

GALL, NORMAN. "The Challenge of Venezuelan Oil," *Foreign Policy*, no. 18, pp. 44–67 (Spring 1975).

INTERNATIONAL INSTITUTE FOR ENVIRONMENTAL AFFAIRS. *World Energy, the Environment & Political Action.* New York: International Institute for Environmental Affairs, 1973.

KRASNER, STEPHEN D. "Oil is the Exception," *Foreign Policy*, no. 14, pp. 68–84 (Spring 1974).

LEVY, WALTER J. "World Oil Cooperation or International Chaos," *Foreign Affairs*, vol. 52, no. 1, pp. 690–713 (July 1974).

LOVINS, AMORY B. "World Energy Strategies: Facts, Issues and Options," *The Bulletin of the Atomic Scientists, Science and Public Affairs*, vol. 30, no. 5, pp. 14–32 (May–June, 1974).

MABRO, ROBERT, and ELIZABETH MONROE. "Arab Wealth from Oil: Problems of Its Investment," *International Affairs*, vol. 50, no. 1, pp. 15–27 (January 1974).

MASSACHUSETTS INSTITUTE OF TECHNOLOGY. "Energy Technology to the Year 2000," *Technology Review* (three-part series), vol. 74, no. 1, pp. 37–48 (October/November 1971); vol. 74, no. 2, pp. 34–60 (December 1971); vol. 74, no. 3, pp. 10–48 (January 1972).

MASSACHUSETTS INSTITUTE OF TECHNOLOGY ENERGY LABORATORY. "Energy Self-Sufficiency: An Economic Evaluation," *Technology Review*, vol. 76, no. 6, pp. 22–58 (May 1974).

MOORSTEEN, RICHARD. "OPEC Can Wait—We Can't," *Foreign Policy*, no. 18, pp. 3–11 (Spring 1975).

MORAN, THEODORE H. "Coups and Costs," *Foreign Policy*, no. 8, pp. 129–137 (Fall 1972).

NORDHAUS, WILLIAM D. "The Allocation of Energy Resources," *Brookings Papers on Economic Activity*, 3:1973, pp. 529–576 (1973).

PACKER, ARNOLD. "Living with Oil at $10 per Barrel," *Challenge*, vol. 17, no. 6, pp. 17–25 (January–February 1975).

POLLACK, GERALD A. "The Economic Consequences of the Energy Crisis," *Foreign Affairs*, vol. 52, no. 3, pp. 452–471 (April 1974).

SCIENTIFIC AMERICAN. "Energy and Power," *Scientific American,* vol. 224, no. 3 (symposium issue, September 1971).

SHIHATA, IBRAHIM F. I. "Destination Embargo of Arab Oil: Its Legality under International Law," *American Journal of International Law,* vol. 68, no. 4, pp. 591–627 (October 1974).

SIMONET, HENRI. "Energy and the Future of Europe," *Foreign Affairs,* vol. 53, no. 3, pp. 450–463 (April 1975).

SOLOW, ROBERT M. "The Economics of Resources or the Resources of Economics," *American Economic Review,* vol. 64, no. 2, pp. 1–14 (May 1974).

SPETH, GUSTAVE J., ARTHUR R. TAMPLIN, and THOMAS B. COCHRAN. "Plutonium Recycle: The Fateful Step," *The Bulletin of the Atomic Scientists,* vol. 30, no. 9, pp. 15–22 (November 1974).

STEVENSON, ADLAI E., III. "Nuclear Reactors: America Must Act," *Foreign Affairs,* vol. 53, no. 1, pp. 64–76 (October 1974).

TURNER, LOUIS. "Politics of the Energy Crisis," *International Affairs,* vol. 50, no. 3, pp. 404–415 (July 1974).

WEINBERG, ALVIN. "Social Institutions and Nuclear Energy," *Science,* vol. 177, no. 4043, pp. 27–34 (July 7, 1972).

WELLS, DONALD A. *Saudi-Arabian Revenues and Expenditures: The Potential for Foreign Exchange Savings.* Washington: Resources for the Future, Inc., 1974.

WILLRICH, MASON, and PHILIP M. MARSTON. "Prospects for a Uranium Cartel." *Orbis,* vol. 19, no. 1, pp. 166–184 (Spring 1975).

WILSON, CARROLL L. "A Plan for Energy Independence," *Foreign Affairs,* vol. 51, no. 4, pp. 657–675 (July 1973).

Official Documents

CABINET TASK FORCE ON OIL IMPORT CONTROL. *The Oil Import Question: A Report on the Relationship of Oil Imports to the National Security.* Washington: Government Printing Office, 1970.

FEDERAL ENERGY ADMINISTRATION. *Project Independence Report.* Washington: Government Printing Office, 1974.

ORGANIZATION FOR ECONOMIC COOPERATION AND DEVELOPMENT. *Energy Policy: Problems and Objectives.* Paris: OECD, 1966.

ORGANIZATION FOR ECONOMIC COOPERATION AND DEVELOPMENT. *Energy Prospects to 1985: An Assessment of Long Term Energy Developments and Related Policies.* 2 vols. Paris: OECD, 1974.

ORGANIZATION FOR ECONOMIC COOPERATION AND DEVELOPMENT. *Energy R & D: Problems and Perspectives.* Paris: OECD, 1975.

ORGANIZATION FOR ECONOMIC COOPERATION AND DEVELOPMENT OIL COMMITTEE. *Oil: The Present Situation and Future Prospects.* Paris: OECD, 1973.

ORGANIZATION FOR ECONOMIC COOPERATION AND DEVELOPMENT, NUCLEAR ENERGY AGENCY, AND INTERNATIONAL ATOMIC ENERGY AGENCY. *Uranium: Resources, Production, and Demand.* Paris: OECD, 1973.

UNITED NATIONS. *Environmental Aspects of Natural Resources Management,* report prepared for the United Nations Conference on the Human Environment. New York: United Nations, A/CONF. 48/7, Jan. 26, 1972.

UNITED NATIONS. *Identification and Control of Pollutants of Broad International Significance,* report prepared for the United Nations Conference on the Human Environment. United Nations, A/CONF. January 7, 1972.

UNITED NATIONS, DEPARTMENT OF ECONOMIC AND SOCIAL AFFAIRS. *World Energy Supplies,* series J. New York: United Nations, issued annually.

U.S. ATOMIC ENERGY COMMISSION. *High-Level Radioactive Waste Management Alternatives.* Springfield, Va.: National Technical Information Service, U.S. Department of Commerce, Wash–1297, 1974.

U.S. DEPARTMENT OF THE INTERIOR. *United States Energy Resources through the Year 2000,* report by Walter G. Dupree and James A. West. Washington: Government Printing Office, 1972.

U.S. HOUSE OF REPRESENTATIVES, COMMITTEE ON FOREIGN AFFAIRS, SUBCOMMITTEE ON NATIONAL SECURITY POLICY AND SCIENTIFIC DEVELOPMENTS. *Commercial Nuclear Power in Europe: The Interaction of American Diplomacy with a New Technology,* report prepared by Warren H. Donnelly (committee print). Washington: Government Printing Office, 1972.

U.S. SENATE, COMMITTEE ON FOREIGN RELATIONS. *Multinational Oil Corporations and U.S. Foreign Policy,* report together with individual views (committee print). Washington: Government Printing Office, 1975.

U.S. SENATE, COMMITTEE ON INTERIOR AND INSULAR AFFAIRS. *Agreement on an International Energy Program* (committee print). Washington: Government Printing Office, 1974.

U.S. SENATE, COMMITTEE ON INTERIOR AND INSULAR AFFAIRS. *Considerations in the Formulation of National Energy Policy,* report prepared by Daniel Beard (committee print). Washington: Government Printing Office, 1971.

U.S. SENATE, COMMITTEE ON INTERIOR AND INSULAR AFFAIRS. *Energy Research and Development: Problems and Prospects,* report prepared by Harry Perry (committee print). Washington: Government Printing Office, 1973.

U.S. SENATE, COMMITTEE ON INTERIOR AND INSULAR AFFAIRS. *U.S. Energy Resources: A Review as of 1972,* report prepared by M. King Hubbert (committee print). Washington: Government Printing Office, 1974.

Index

Index

Abu Dhabi: oil revenues of, 3; "participation" principle of oil production in, 25

Access to markets: for exporting countries, 95–96, 101–102. *See also* Exporting countries

Accidents: effect on environment, 146–147, 152–153. *See also* Environmental risks

Aegean Sea, energy resources in, 90

Africa: independence for, 21; investment of surplus oil revenues in, 138

Air pollution: causes of, 54; global aspects of, 159; impact of transportation on, 161; and nuclear fission, 151; standard setting, 160. *See also* Environmental risks

Alaska oil pipeline, 157

Algeria: Arab nationalism in, 22; conversion of natural gas in, 41 ; nationalization of foreign oil operations in, 25

Anglo-Iranian Oil Company, 18

Antitrust policies in energy industry, 127

Arab nationalism, 22. *See also* Nationalism

Arab oil embargo, 15–16, 66; future possibilities of, 78–79; response of petroleum-importing countries to, 36; supply sources juggled to mitigate damage of, 80. *See also* Embargo

Arab world, economic development plans for, 120. *See also* Middle East

Arctic regions, oil and gas resources of, 112

Argentina, prospects for increase in domestic production of, 91

Armaments for Middle East, 87. *See also* Middle East conflict

Asia, coal resources of, 42

"Assured supply," 184

Atoms for Peace proposals, 33. *See also* Nuclear energy

Australia: as coal exporter, 42; as resource rich, 188; energy security for, 69; prospects for increase domestic production of, 91; uranium reserves of, 46, 84

Bahrain, independence of, 22

Bangladesh, 5; energy security for, 69

Brazil: as resource rich, 188; investment of surplus oil revenues in, 138

Breeder reactors: effect on long-term energy resources of, 49, 60, 61; impact on nuclear power of, 49; and plutonium stockpiling, 75

British Petroleum Company, 29

Canada: and Alaska oil pipeline, 157; coal exports of, 42; energy supplies of, 4, 188; environmental protection in, 144; heavy water reactor developed in, 44; industrialization of, 188; natural gas in McKenzie Delta region of, 41; nuclear power program of, 46; prospects for increase in domestic production of, 91; refining center in, 39; uranium reserves of, 46, 84

Caribbean–Bahamas area, as refining center, 39

Cartel, basis for, 96. *See also* Organization of Petroleum Exporting Countries (OPEC)

Central America, effect of oil prices on commodity exports of, 118

China: coal exports of, 82; energy resources in, 90; energy self-sufficiency of, 4, 89, 91; nuclear arms capability of, 93; as producer of new oil, 80; shift from coal to oil and gas in, 29

China Sea, energy resources in, 90

Climatic change: heat production as cause of, 56, 57; heat discharge limit, 170–173. *See also* Thermal pollution

Coal: effect of, on nuclear power, 154; energy self-sufficiency of U.S. dependent on, 113; effect of oil prices on use of, 31, 59–60; environmental hazards of, 42–43, 57, 82; expanded world market for, 81–82; as imported energy source, 81; as oil substitute, 81; resources, geographic distribution of, 42; stockpiling of, 74; strip mining of, 31, 209; sulphur-oxide emissions from, 150; technological developments in, 31, 43; U.S. use of, 28, 42, 113, 154

Coastal states: jurisdiction on facilities-siting by, 159; jurisdiction on ocean pollution by, 163; management of offshore energy resource extraction, 155; role of, in world political system, 3

Cold War, effect of, on oil resources, 18

Commercial breeder reactor, 35. *See also* Breeder reactors

Common Market, 11

Compagnie Française des Petroles (CFP), 29

Conservation of energy. *See* Energy conservation

Consumer countries, response of, to nationalization of oil reserves, 7. *See also* Importing countries

Continental Shelf: exploitation of, and environmental impact, 55; jurisdiction over, 90; oil and gas resources under, 112

Controlled fusion reactors: as energy resources, 60; feasibility of, 61

Corporations, multinational oil: antitrust policy toward, 127; control over crude oil reserves by, 30; development of, after World War II, 12; evolution of, into energy companies, 125; economic interdependence because of, 13; economic problems, role as scapegoat in, 139–140; economic role of, 14–15, 204–205; freedom of action, restriction of, 7; future role of, 128; government intervention in activities, 126–127; importing countries' governments effect on development as energy companies, 127; importing countries, relationship with,

126–127; industrial countries, management of production rates by, in early 1970s, 29–30; means for energy security, 189; as middlemen in world market, 79; nationalization of oil reserves, 7; oil prices, 111; OPEC, oil price policies of, 24; operation of, 6; as principal actors during cheap energy era, 29; profits, regulation of, 126; role of, in economic development, 124–129; strength of, 13; U.S. import control, effect on, 29; West European countries, taxes on petroleum products, 29; world political system, role in, 2

Cost criteria of energy use, 108

Costs. *See* Energy costs

Crude oil production: monopolization of, 32; refining of, 37

Deficit spending, 133

Demonstration reactors, technological advances in, 61. *See also* Breeder reactors

Denmark, energy resources of, 5

Deuterium, use of, for fusion power, 61

Developing nations. *See* Less-developed nations

Development assistance: and energy security, 85; foreign aid to less-developed nations, 119

Dispute settlement, international institutions role in, 181

Diversification of energy sources, 77–84

East European countries: dependency on Soviet Union for oil and gas, 190; energy resources, development of, 4; natural gas imports for, 81

Economic aspects of energy use, 194–206; access to market, 101–102; cost as criterion of efficiency, 106; efficiency of use, 104–115; oil prices, effect on efficiency of use, 104; petrodollar flows, 129–140 (*see also* Petrodollars); price stability through bargaining with OPEC, 201; private multinational oil companies, role of, 204–205 (*see also* Corporations, multinational oil); surplus oil revenues, investment of, 205

Economic development, less-developed oil importing nations, 115–121. *See also* Development assistance

Economic policies, international, interdependence of nation-states, 11–17

Economic Rights and Duties of States Charter of United Nations, 119

Ecuador, banana production, oil price effect on, 118

Egypt: Arab nationalism in, 22
Electricity, as preferred power source, 36
Embargo: Arab oil embargo of 1973–74, 15–16,
66; Arab OPEC members, possibility of
future, 78–79; destination traced, 79; effect on
importing country, 66; exporter imposed, 66;
preemption of supplies during, by importing
country, 78; U.S. as target of, 79. *See also*
Arab oil embargo
Emission levels, setting of standards of, 149
Energy: economic interdependence and growth
in post World War II period, 13; economies
of scale in industry, 51–53; effect of, on
economy of the world (*see* Economic aspects
of energy use); efficiency as economic use of,
104–115; environmental risks of, 53–58, 141–
179 (*see also* Environmental risks); historical
importance of, 1; security of nations as
factor, 65–102 (*see also* Security, national).
See also Fossil energy
Energy company, multinational oil company as,
125–126
Energy conservation, 176; air pollution as
reason for, 161; economic benefits of, 174;
environmental risks of, 173–179; low oil
prices, effect on, 30; mandatory restrictions,
175
Energy consumption: growth rates in, 30–31;
mandatory restrictions on, 175; per capita,
110
Energy costs, criteria for determining, 106
Energy crisis, international institutions as dispute settlement device, 181; international
political repercussions, 184. *See also* Embargo
Energy economy. *See* Economic aspects of
energy use
Energy efficiency: criteria of, 108–110; energy/
GNP ratio, 108; transportation system and,
109–110; and world oil prices, inefficiency of,
111–115
Energy industry, antitrust policy toward, 127
Energy interdependence, 36–53; coal, 42–43
(*see also* Coal); economies of scale, 51–53;
energy security, 84–88; nuclear power, 43–51
Energy production, efficiency of, 110
Energy resources: "assured supply" of, 184;
consumption of, effect of oil price revolution
on, 59; diversification of, 77–84; efficient
use of, 104–115; exhaustion of, 58–64; extraction of, environmental implications of,
147–148, 154–156; high-cost resources, development of, 114; management of ocean

resources, 164; per capita energy consumption, 110, sufficiency of, as goal of international politics, 184; synthetic fuels from coal
or oil shale, 113–114. *See also* Diversification
Energy security: access to market, 95–96, 101–
102; concepts of, 67–68; development assistance as means for, 85; diversification of, 77–
84; domestic needs as influencing, 80, 90–92;
economic issues involved in, 68, 85;
and exporting countries, 94–102 (*see also*
Exporting countries); financial security for
investments, 95; foreign investments as means
for, 85; importing countries measures to enhance, 68–69, 69–94; and interdependence 84–
88; maintenance of economy at normal level
as goal, 67; and major powers, 188; and
military intervention, 97–101; as national interest, 186–194; offshore energy resources,
jurisdiction over, 90; OPEC, collective security arrangement for, 100; political relations as
affecting, 81; "politically acceptable" situation and, 67; rationing plans, 69 (*see also*
Rationing); and self-sufficiency, 70, 88–94;
and sovereignty, 94–95; and stockpiling, 69,
73–77; and wartime needs, 67
Energy self-sufficiency. *See* Self-sufficiency
Energy supplies: interruption of, 66 (*see also*
Embargo); security of, 66–102. *See also*
Energy security
Energy use. *See* Energy consumption
Environmental risks, 141–179; acceptable consequences as international goal, 185; accidents and, 146–147, 152–153; administration
of, 151; air and water quality standards,
setting of, 148; in air pollution, 54, 159–162;
causation, problem of, 150; climate changes,
56; (*see also* Climatic changes; Thermal pollution); coal burning, 82, 150 (*see also*
Coal); constraints on use, 53–58; detection of,
148; in effects of synergism, 150; emission
levels standards, 149; energy conservation as
goal, 173–179 (*see also* Energy conservation);
and energy policy, 185; facilities siting, 156–
159; fossil energy usage, 55; and heat emission, 57–58, 149, 170–173 (*see also* Thermal
pollution); international management of,
151–152, 207; land use, 154–159; Law of the
Sea negotiations, 165; monitoring and inspection, 151; normal operations causing,
147–151; and nuclear energy, 55 (*see also*
Nuclear energy); offshore energy resources,
extraction of, 155 (*see also* Offshore energy

Environmental risks (*cont.*)
   resources); radioactive waste management,
   166–170; safety standards, 153; Santa Barbara
   Channel blowout, 54; and self-sufficiency, 89;
   social costs of, 106; standard setting of permissible emissions, 150, of strip mining, 154;
   taxation of pollution causes, 150–151, 158;
   and technological advances, 142–145, 158;
   tolerance levels, 148; Torrey Canyon disaster,
   54; "tragedy of the commons," 165; in water
   pollution, 162–165
Ethiopia, energy security for, 69
Europe, oil refineries of, 38
European Atomic Energy Community (Euratom): establishment of, 9; as a force for
   regional cooperation, 20
European Common Market: economic interests
   in, 19; effect of nationalism on, 20; energy
   policy of, 20
European countries, growth rates in, 30
Exporting countries: access to markets, 95–
   96, 101–102; development assistance, 87;
   domestic needs affecting supplies, 80–81;
   energy security of, 94–102; international
   politics to assure interest of, 185; industrial
   diversification in, 123; investment of surplus
   oil revenues, 16, 85, 95, 122, 136–140, 205–
   206; oil price effect on less-developed nations,
   121–124; security against military intervention
   in, 97–101; sovereignty over natural resources,
   94–95
Exxon, 29

Facilities siting, 156–159
Fertilizer production, 123
Fission power, 62
Flag states, regulatory authority of, over ocean
   pollution by tankers, 163
Foreign aid to less-developed nations, 119–121.
   See also Development assistance; Less-
   developed nations
Foreign investments. *See* Exporting countries,
   investment of surplus revenues
Fossil energy, 28–33; economic character of
   drive for, 35; electricity as desirable, 36;
   nuclear fuel in contrast to, 35 (*see also*
   Nuclear energy); use of oceans for, 55
Fossil fuels: carbon dioxide as byproduct of,
   57; climatic changes in, 57 (*see also* Climatic
   change); environmental risks of, 147 (*see
   also* Environmental risks); nuclear energy as
   replacement for, 151 (*see also* Nuclear

energy); stockpiling of, 73 (*see also* Stockpiling)
France: energy security for, 69; national oil
   company of, 128; nuclear power development
   of, 19, 35, 46, 50; oil import costs in 1974,
   130; oil importations of, 13; uranium enrichment in, 47; uranium reserves of, 46
Freedom of the high seas and water pollution,
   164
Fuel supplies. *See* Energy resources
Fusion power, technological advances in, 61–62.
   See also Nuclear energy

Gabon, uranium supply of, 5, 46, 84
Gas station closings, 71
Gasoline for automobiles, 38
General Agreement on Tariffs and Trade
   (GATT), economic interdependence under,
   12
General Electric, nuclear power development by
   34
Geothermal energy, long-term effect of, on
   energy resources, 60
Great Britain: natural gas imports, 41; North
   Sea oil reserves, 4, 91; oil importations of,
   13, 130; uranium enrichment services of, 47;
   use of nuclear energy in, 19, 35, 46, 50
Greece as producer of new oil, 80
"Greenhouse" effect, 57
GNP ratio, relationship with energy consump-
   tion, 108
Gulf, 29

Heat discharge: environmental risks of, 149
   (*see also* Climatic changes; Thermal pollu-
   tion); limits of, 170–173
"Heat islands," 58
Heavy water reactor, 44. *See also* Breeder
   reactors
High-temperature-cooled reactor, 44
Hormuz, Strait of, 66
Hydrocarbons, 113, 114

Importing countries: and Arab oil embargo, 36;
   coal as a substitute energy source, 81;
   deficit spending by, 133; and development
   assistance to exporting countries, 87; diversification of energy supplies by, 78; domestic
   energy resources of, 90–92; economic develop
   ment in, oil price increases affecting, 115–124
   (*see also* Oil prices); effect of embargo on
   energy supplies in, 66 (*see also* Embargo);

energy cutbacks in, effectiveness in, 72; energy industry, investments in, 87; energy security in, measures to enhance, 69–94 (*see also* Energy security); and foreign investment policy, 85, 86; government policy toward private multinational oil companies, 127; import control program in, 132; interdependence for energy sources, 84; international politics to assure interest of, 185; less-developed countries and, 115–121; multinational oil companies, relationship with, 126; national security aspects of energy policy, 66–94; OPEC and, 79, 199; payments for oil, 130–136; preemption of supplies, 78; Project Independence, 36; rationing in (*see* Rationing); resource base of, effect on security, 68–69; self-sufficiency of, 69, 70 (*see also* Self-sufficiency); and stockpiling (*see* Stockpiling); strategic options available to, 68–69; uranium enrichment capacity of, 75; and use of nuclear fuel, 82

ndia: coal reserves of, 42; domestic production, prospects for increase, 91; energy reserves, undeveloped, 4; energy use in, 3; independence of, 21; nuclear energy use in, 50, 91

ndonesia: energy resources of, 5; independence of, 21; as oil exporting country, 97

ndustrial countries: air pollution in, international aspect of problem, 160; and bargaining power with OPEC, 200; political goals of, 183; power shift to resource rich, 189; self-sufficiency of, 188

ndustrialization, oil price control leading to, 30

ntergovernmental Maritime Consultative Organization (IMCO), 152; and environmental controls on ships, 163; minimum safety requirements for oil tankers set by, 153

nternational Atomic Energy Agency (IAEA), 152; establishment of, 9; membership of, 10; and safeguards system, 93

nternational Energy Program: emergency stockpile of oil, 74; nuclear stockpiles, strategic value of, 77; stockpiling of, allocation of, 76

nternational organizations: activity in the energy field, 8; role in world political system, 2

nternational politics: acceptable environmental consequences as goal of, 185; "assured supply" as goal of, 184; energy crisis and, 184; energy economy of, effect on, 194–206; energy goals of, 183–184; energy security as goal of,

186–194; energy situation as transition in, 182–183; environmental consequences in energy use, 206–211 (*see also* Environmental risks); international institutions as means for dispute settlement of, 181; nuclear energy security, impasse on, 191–192; power shift to resource rich countries, 189; trade-offs as approach, 211–212; U.S. dependence on Middle East oil, impact of, 190

Investments: development assistance, 86; in energy industry in importing country, 87; foreign investments by exporter in importing country, 86; long-term aspects of, 107; and oil payment problems, 134–135; of surplus oil revenues, 205. *See also* Exporting countries, investment of surplus oil revenues

Iran: assistance program for India and Pakistan, 120; as importer of nuclear power technology and fuels, 4; military capability of, 32; nationalization of oil operations, 18, 25; as nuclear fuel importer, 77; as oil exporter, 97; oil revenues of, in 1974, 130; as resource rich, 188

Iraq: Arab nationalism in, 22; energy resources of, 5; and nationalization of foreign oil operations, 25; oil embargo, activities during, 79; oil revenues of, in 1974, 130

Israel: establishment of, 22; military intervention in Persian Gulf, effect of, 99

Italy: energy imports of, 13; energy security for, 69; national oil company of, 128; nuclear power program of, 46; oil import costs of, in 1974, 130

Japan: domestic production of, 91; energy imports of, 13; energy resources of, 5; energy security for, 69; energy use of, 3; as industrially developed, 188; investment of OPEC surplus oil revenues in, 138; as liquid natural gas importer, 41; national oil company of, 128; natural gas shipping by, 41; nuclear power industry in, 46, 168; nuclear stockpiles of, strategic value of, 77; oil embargo, effect on, 187; oil import costs of, in 1974, 130; oil stockpiles in, 74; uranium reserves of, 199

Jordan, Arab nationalism in, 22

Kuwait: as financial superpower, 137; oil revenues of, in 1974, 130; and "participation" principles of oil production, 25

Lake Erie, eutrophication of, 143
Land use: environmental risks of, 154–159; and facilities siting, 156–159; and resource extraction, 154–156
Latin America, investment in surplus oil revenues of, 138
Law of the Sea negotiations, 165
Lebanon, Arab nationalism in, 22
Less-developed nations: air pollution in, impact of technology on, 162; attitude toward OPEC, 120–121; economic development in, 115; and Economic Rights and Duties of States Charter of United Nations, 119; effect of economic efficiency criterion on development of, 202; energy cutbacks in, 72; foreign aid in, 119–121; investment of OPEC surplus oil revenues in, 138; and nuclear power, 82, 203; and oil-exporting countries, economic development in, 121, 124; and oil-importing countries, economic development in, 115–121; oil prices in, effect of 115–116; two-tier pricing system for, 203
Liberia: natural gas shipping by, 41; and oil tankers, 37
Libya, Arab nationalism in, 22; and nationalization of foreign oil operations, 25; and natural gas conversion, 41; oil embargo, activities during, 79; oil revenues of, in 1974, 130
Light water reactor, 35, 44. See also Breeder reactors
Liquid metal fast breeder reactor, 44, 60. See also Breeder reactors

Marshall Plan, effect on economic interdependence, 11
McKenzie Delta region, natural gas in, 41
Metals, refined, 123
Mexico, as producer of new oil, 80
Middle East: and Arab oil embargo of 1973–74, 36; armaments, importing of, 87–88; military intervention in, 97; nationalism in, 21–22; as oil consumer, 37; oil reserves of, 37; as refining center, 39; U.S., investment in, 87; U.S. oil imports from, 187
Middle East conflict: Arab oil embargo because of, 79; oil production, effect on, 32; oil supplies, effect on political alignment, 79; U.S. dependence on Middle East oil, impact of, 190–191
Mobil, 29
Morocco, Arab nationalism in, 22

Multinational oil companies. See Corporations, multinational oil
Musaddiq regime in Iran, 18

Nation-states, and role in world political system 2–3
National interests, and energy security, 186–194
National oil companies, development of, 127–128
Nationalism: Arab nationalism, 22; in Eastern Europe, 20; in the Middle East, 21–22; in Western Europe, 19–20; and world politics, 17–26
Nationalization of production phase, 125
Natural gas: and economic interdependence, 40–42; environmental impact of, on the Continental Shelf, 55; importation of, 41; liquefaction of, 112; pipeline networks of, 41 prices of, during 1960's, 107; regulatory polic of, in U.S., 107; reserves, location of, 40; shift from coal to, 28; stockpiling of, 74; as substitute for oil imports, 81; transportation, control of, 40–41; use of, 40
Netherlands: exporting of natural gas from Groningen field, 4; oil stockpiles in, 74
Niger, uranium reserves of, 5, 46, 84
Nigeria: and aid for other African countries, 120; energy resources of, 5; as oil exporting country, 97; oil revenues of, in 1974, 130; U.S. oil imports from, 79
Non-industrial countries, economic interdependence of, 15
Nonproliferation of Nuclear Weapons Treaty, 50; safeguard system of, 93
North Atlantic Treaty Organization (NATO), 17
North Sea oil reserves, 37, 91
North Slope reserves, 3
Norway: development of North Sea oil reserves by, 91; as producer of new oil, 80
Nuclear energy: Atoms for Peace proposals, 33 34; breeder reactor, impact on development, 35, 49 (see also Breeder reactors); coal production, effect on, 154; commercialization of, 7–8; costs of, 76; deuterium, use of for fusion power, 61; development of, 33–36; diversification of nuclear fuels, 83; economic case for, 48–49; and economic efficiency criterion, 201; and energy interdependence, 43–51; environmental hazards of, 55–56, 145 (see also Environmental risks); and Euratom 9; fission power, 62, 148; as fossil fuel re-

placement, 82, 161; fuels, reprocessing of wastes from, 166; fusion power, 61–62; and future postindustrial societies, 1; government control of, 7, 34; and the heavy water reactor, 44; and the high-temperature gas-cooled reactor, 44; importing countries, diversification of sources for, 82; installation of facilities, oil prices effect on, 112; international competition in, 34; less-developed countries, activities of, 203; and the light water reactor, 35, 44; and the liquid metal fast breeder reactor, 44; long-term energy resources, impact on, 60; military weapons program, effect on, 33; multinational approach to development of, 191–194; multinational oil companies activities in, 125; and national self-sufficiency, 92; oil prices effect on, 31; plant, location, and cost of, 46; political motivations for, 35; radioactive waste management of, 166–170; safeguard system in use of, 93; Soviet Union fuel supplies of, to Eastern Europe, 83; stockpiling in, 75, 76; supply interruption as response to diversion, 93; technological developments in, 43–44, 60–62, 202; and the Treaty on the Non-proliferation of Nuclear Weapons, 50; U.S. self-sufficiency in, 198; and U.S. uranium enrichment monopoly, 78, 82–83, 190; and uranium enrichment (*see* Uranium enrichment); weapons use, diversion to, 50, 93; world capacity for, 44

Iuclear weapons, restraints on, 50

)ceans: location of energy facilities, impact on, 158; multiple and conflicting uses of, 165; overfishing of, 165; pollution as result of use of, 55; radioactive waste management, abuse of, 166; and technological management problems, 165; as "tragedy of the commons," 165

)ffshore energy resources: extraction of, 155; jurisdiction over, 90; location of energy facilities for, 158; Santa Barbara oil blowout and, 147; technological development in drilling methods for, 165; U.S. extraction of, 209

)il: development of resources, 29; diversification of supplies of, 78 (*see also* Diversification); economic development of, 115–124; economic interdependence, effect on, 11, 37–40; environmental impact of, on the Continental Shelf, 55; gasoline for automobiles, 38; and nationalization activities, 24; nuclear

energy as substitute for, 49; price of, 104 (*see also* Oil prices); reserves, location of, 37 (*see also* Oil reserves); stockpiling of, 73–74; tar sands and shale, extraction from, 112; transportation of crude oil, 37

Oil companies: national companies, development of, 127–128; U.S., foreign tax credit as incentives for, 29. *See also* Corporations, multinational oil

Oil concessionary system, impact of nationalism on, 24–25

Oil crisis of 1973–74, 15–16. *See also* Embargo

Oil Facility of the International Monetary Fund (IMF), power of, 9

Oil importing countries. *See* Importing countries

Oil payment problems, 130–136; government action in, 135; investments to solve, 134–135

Oil pollution of the oceans, 163

Oil price revolution, effect of on solar energy, 63

Oil prices: and alternative fossil energy resources, 112; and ceiling on imports, 112; commodity exports, prices of, 118; consumption of resources, effect of, 59; cost and price, discrepancy between, 111; declining, impact on growth rate, 30–31; demand, effect of, 112; economic development, effect on, 115–124; effect of, on inflation, 16; "equitable price" as goal, 184–185; GNP, reduction of, 115–118; importing countries, payments for, 130–136; industrialization, effect on, 30; inefficiency of world prices, 111–115; and less-developed nations, 114–115, 118–120, 121–124 (*see also* Less-developed nations); lowering of, means of, 111–112; new discoveries, effect on, 111; nuclear power, effect on, 112; OPEC cartel policy on, 108, 111; OPEC determination of, 24; OPEC quadrupling of, 14; and petrodollar flow, 130; and price revolution of 1973–74, 194–195; and price stability, 201; and two-tier pricing system, 120, 203; U.S. self-sufficiency, impact on, 196–197

Oil production, effect on Middle East conflict, 32

Oil refineries, 37–40

Oil reserves: control of, by multinational companies, 30; development of, slowed because of low prices, 31; location of, 37

Oil resources: Cold War, effect of, 18; development of, by multinational oil companies,

Oil resources (*cont.*)
29; OPEC countries classified according to, 122
Oil revenues: investment of 16, 136; and petrodollar flow, 130; surplus revenues, investment of, 136–140. *See also* Exporting countries
Oil shale: oil price revolution, effect on use of, 59–60; multinational oil companies activities in, 125
Oil spills, 55
Organization for European Cooperation and Development (OECD): composition of, 8
Organization of Petroleum Exporting Countries (OPEC): as a cartel, 8; cheap fossil energy, effect on, 32; collective security arrangement for, 100; crude oil production, takeover by, 124; diversification of energy sources because of, 78; economic development in, 115, 121–124; economic interdependence under, 12; emergency stockpile of oil, 74, 100; formation of, 6–7; indirect attacks on, 111; less-developed nations attitudes toward, 121; and loans from suppliers, 135; negotiations with, over economic development plans, 199; oil-importing less-developed nations, source of help for, 120; oil prices, determination of, 24, 80, 114 (*see also* Oil prices); oil resources, classification according to extent of, 122; and oil supply to importing countries, 79; petrodollar recycling, problems of, 136–140; political relations affecting supply security, 81; revenue from oil in 1973–74, 130; surplus oil revenues for, 136–140; tanker fleets of, 37; two-tier pricing system of, 120
Overfishing, 165

Pakistan, independence of, 21
Panama: natural gas shipping by, 41; and oil tankers, 37
Payment problems, domestic investments as solution to, 134–135
Persian Gulf, military intervention in, 97
Petrochemical industry, 123
Petrodollar flows: oil costs in 1973–74, 130; oil import payments, 130–136; oil revenues in 1973–74, 130; recycling of, 136–140
Petroleum. *See* Oil
Poland, as coal exporter, 42
Plutonium: stockpiling of, 75; value of, 44
Political structure. *See* World political system
Pollution: air pollution (*see* Air pollution);

control of, tax exemptions for, 158; land use, 154–159; taxation of activities, 150–151; water pollution, 162–165 (*see also* Environmental risks; Water pollution)
Port states, regulatory authority over ocean pollution by tankers, 163
Producer countries, nationalization of oil reserves by, 7

Qatar: independence of, 22; "participation" principle of oil production in, 25

Radioactive waste management, 166–170; and global risks, 167; international cooperation in, 168–169; junk disposal methods of, 169; and permanent storage of wastes, 166; and reprocessing of irradiated nuclear fuels, 166; and use of rockets to shoot waste into deep space, 168; and storage of waste by solidification, 168; and temporary storage of wastes, 166–167; time dimension of, 169
Rationing, 70–73; actual energy savings from, 71; controlled use of energy as means of, 71; and gas station closings, 71; by mandatory plan, 72; political acceptance of, 71; restriction of energy consumption by, 72; significance of, 70–71
Refineries, location in producing countries, 124
Resource extraction, 154–156. *See also* Energy resources
Resource rich countries, power shift to, 189
Rotterdam, as refining center, 39
Royal Dutch Shell, 29

Santa Barbara Channel oil blowout, 54, 147
Saudi Arabia: as economic power, 196; and effect of domestic politics on economic fortunes, 6; and fertilizer production, 123; as financial superpower, 137; natural gas, flaring of, 41; oil concessionary system in, 24–25; as oil exporter, 96; oil revenues of, in 1974, 130; "participation" principle of oil production in, 25
Scandinavia, environmental protection in, 144
Security, economic, and relationship to energy security, 68
Security national: economic goals of energy supply, 67; and energy security (*see* Energy security); and Hormuz, Strait of, 66; importing country, energy policies of, 66–94; and "politically acceptable" situation, 67
Self-sufficiency: consumption requirements as

affecting, 89; and economic repercussions, 89; energy security and, 70, 88–94, 186; environmental consequences of, 89; and industrial countries, 188; in less-developed nations, 124; for major powers, 188; means to attain, 89–92; and nuclear power, 92; technological advances and, 90; of U.S., 113

lar energy: energy source outside biosphere, 173; use in future post-industrial societies, 1, 60; technological advances in use of, 62–63

uth Africa: energy security for, 69; uranium reserves of, 46, 84

uth Vietnam, as producer of new oil, 80

vereignty over natural resources, 94–95

viet Union: coal resources of, 42, 84; development of energy resources of, 4; Eastern European communist countries, ties to, 12; as economic power, 196; and energy deals with West, 188; energy security of, 96, 187; environmental choices of, 209; international energy position of, 187–188; natural gas shipping, interest in, 40, 41; nuclear fuel supplies of, 35, 46, 50, 83; and radioactive waste management, 166, 168; and shift from coal to oil and gas, 29; uranium enrichment services of, 47; uranium supplies of, 46

pain: nuclear power program of, 46; uranium reserves of, 46

ri Lanka (Ceylon), independence of, 21

tandard Oil of California, 29

tockpiling, 69; of coal, 74; costs of, 76; desirability of, 73; effectiveness of, 73; emergency use of, during military intervention, 100; of natural gas, 74; of nuclear fuel, 75–77, 175; of oil, 73–74; ownership of, 75; of plutonium, 75; practicality of, 73; rationing of, 76; of uranium, U.S., 198; use of, 76

trikes and supply of coal, 74

trip mining, 31, 154, 209

upertankers, 52

weden: nuclear power program of, 46; uranium reserves of, 46

ynergism, combined effects of, 150

ynthetic fuel industry, 113–114

yria, Arab nationalism in, 22

ankers, oil pollution by, 163

ar sands and shale, 112

echnology: coal conversion, 43; economic interdependence because of, 13; and economies of scale, 51–53; and efficiency of energy use, 105; energy sources, tapping of new, 90; en-

vironmental implications of, 142–145, 158; in the nuclear energy field, 202; in offshore drilling, 165; and oil tankers, 165; thermal efficiency as criterion of, 173

Territorial seas, 164

Texaco, 29

Texas Railroad Commission, 29

Thermal pollution: electric power generation causing, 163; heat discharge limits, 170–173

Thermonuclear energy, use in future post-industrial societies, 1

Third World: industrial development in, 123–124; world political system, role of, 5. *See also* Less-developed nations

Thorium, reserves of, 46–47

Torrey Canyon disaster, 54, 147

"Tragedy of the commons," 165

Transportation, economic interdependence because of, 13

Tunisia, Arab nationalism in, 22

Union of Arab Emirates: formation of, 22; oil revenues of, in 1974, 130

United Nations, Law of the Sea negotiations, 165

United Nations Conference on the Human Environment, 208

United Nations Environment Program, 208

United States: air pollution in, 54, 160; and Alaska oil pipeline, 157; and the Atoms for Peace proposals, 33; and balance-of-payments, 197; coal resources of, 42, 154; domestic politics and energy policy of, 6; and domestic production of energy, 91; as economic power, 195–196; energy imports of, 14, 28; energy security for, 69, 187; energy use of, 3; environmental choices of, 209; European Common Market, attitudes toward, 19; and food exports as means of interdependence, 87; growth rates in, 30; and the Middle East, 87, 98, 190; natural gas in, 28, 40, 41, 107; Nigeria, oil imports from, 79; North Slope reserves of, 3; nuclear power development of, 35, 44, 190, 198, 209; offshore oil and gas drilling by, 209; oil companies, foreign tax credits for, 29; as oil consumer, 37; oil imports of, 3, 130, 187; oil refineries in, 38; oil reserves of, 37; oil stockpiles of, 74; per capita energy consumption of, 110; pollution control, tax exemptions for, 158; post-World War II economic power of, 11; and preemption of energy supplies, 78; private multi-

United States (*cont.*)
national oil companies, future role of, 128; and Project Independence, 36–37; radioactive wastes produced by, 166; rationing in, 72; energy self-sufficiency of, 88, 113, 196–199; surplus oil revenues, investment in, 138; synthetic fuel production, prediction for, 113–114; uranium enrichment monopoly of, 47, 66, 82–83, 96; uranium reserves of, 46, 198; water pollution in, 55

Uranium: as basis for nuclear power reactors, 43–44; exporting countries, 83–84; reserves of, 46, 199; stockpiling of refined uranium, 75; U.S. stockpiles of, 198; world prices of, 198–199

Uranium enrichment, 47–48, 75; IEA activities, 83; multinational ventures in, 83, 192; sources of, 47; technological developments in, 202; U.S. monopoly of, 66, 78, 82–83

Uranium-plutonium fuel cycle, 43–44

Venezuela: and development assistance program in Latin America, 120, 139; economic development in, 121; as oil exporter, 97; oil revenues of, in 1974, 130

Warsaw Pact, 17

Water pollution, 162–165; countries classified as to source of, 162; examples of, 54–55; industrial countries role in, 162; and international regulation of assessment and standard setting, 164; oceans, use of, 55; oil pollution, 55, 163; and the principle of freedom of the high seas, 164; thermal pollution of rivers, 163

West Germany: energy security for, 69; national oil company of, 128; nuclear energy in, 35, 46, 94; oil imports of, 13, 130; surplus oil revenues, investment in, 138; uranium reserves of, 199

Western Europe: coal resources of, 42; domestic production, prospects for increase, 91; energy self-sufficiency of, 89; as "heat island," 172; as industrially developed, 188; Middle East countries investment in, 87; natural gas in, 41; nuclear stockpiles of, 77; oil embargo, effect on, 187; as petroleum consumer, 37

Westinghouse, nuclear power development by, 34

World Bank, economic interdependence under, 12

World economy. *See* Economic aspects of energy use

World political system: coastal states, 3 (*see also* Coastal states); Cold War, effect on, 17; consumer countries (*see* Consumer countries; Importing countries); detente, effect on, 23; division of based on energy consumers and users, 3; free and communist world, 4; domestic political factors, 6; economic interdependence in, 11–17 (*see also* Interdependence) energy politics in, 5; government monetary policies, 14; international organizations, role of, 2; nation-states, 2–3, 10; nationalism, 17–26; nationalization activities of nations, 24; non-industrial countries, economic interdependence, 15; nuclear energy, 7–8; organization of, 2–11; producer countries (*see* Exporting countries); Third World, 5

Yemen, Arab nationalism in, 22

Printed in the United States
By Bookmasters